¡MANTECA!

AN ANTHOLOGY OF
AFRO-LATIN@ POETS

¡MANTECA!

AN ANTHOLOGY OF
AFRO-LATIN@ POETS

EDITED BY
MELISSA CASTILLO-GARSOW

Arte Público Press
Houston, Texas

¡Manteca! An Anthology of Afro-Latin@ Poets is funded in part by grants from the City of Houston through the Houston Arts Alliance and the National Endowment for the Arts. We are grateful for their support.

Recovering the past, creating the future

Arte Público Press
University of Houston
4902 Gulf Fwy, Bldg 19, Rm 100
Houston, Texas 77204-2004

Cover design by Shaggy Flores, Nuyorican Poeta for South of Harlem Multimedia

Photo credits:
Front cover: Syldavia/ iStock / Getty Images
Back cover: Louno_M/ iStock / Getty Images Plus

Names: Castillo-Garsow, Melissa, 1984- editor.
Title: !Manteca!: : an anthology of Afro-Latin@ poets / edited by Melissa Castillo-Garsow.
Description: Houston, TX : Arte Publico Press, 2017. | Includes bibliographical references.
Identifiers: LCCN 2017003703| ISBN 9781558858428 (alk. paper) | ISBN 9781518501241 (kindle) | ISBN 9781518501258 (pdf)
Subjects: LCSH: Latin American poetry—Black authors. | Blacks—Latin America—Poetry.
Classification: LCC PQ7084 .M244 2017 | DDC 861/.708089608—dc23
LC record available at https://lccn.loc.gov/2017003703

♾ The paper used in this publication meets the requirements of the American National Standard for Information Sciences—Permanence of Paper for Printed Library Materials, ANSI Z39.48-1984.

23 24 25   7 6 5 4

DEDICATION

*To all the poets who made this book possible but were not able to see
its completion. They live on in these pages and in future generations
of Afro-Latin@ poets.*

Tato Laviera
(May 9, 1950–November 1, 2013)

Pedro Pietri
(March 21, 1944–March 3, 2004)

Migual Gómez Piñero
(December 19, 1946–June 16, 1988)

Louis Reyes Rivera
(May 19, 1945–March 2, 2012)

Lorenzo Thomas
(August 31, 1944–July 4, 2005)

y

Juan Flores
(September 29, 1943–December 2, 2014), whose life
and scholarship inspired this anthology.

TABLE OF CONTENTS

ACKNOWLEDGEMENTS

First and foremost, I am forever indebted to the generosity of the poets who entrusted me with their work and believed in my ability to put together this anthology. I cannot even express how much it means to be a part of such a rich poetic community. As a poet myself, many of the poets and poems in this anthology have defined my own work and my own sense of Latinidad. I lived and breathed every single one of the poems in this anthology over the years and they help inspire my own poetry every day.

Specifically, I want to give a shout out to two poets in this anthology, Shaggy Flores and Bonafide Rojas who helped guide me through this work. Thank you, Shaggy, for helping me with everything from titles to cover art to contacts y gracias to Bonafide for sending more poets my way than I knew what to do with, helping me with selections and, most importantly, for el apoyo. El apoyo was very much needed.

I still remember that first email I got from Nicolás Kanellos at Arte Público Press. I came to him with a proposal and a list of poets and he just got it, perhaps even more than I did. Most importantly, I am honored that he took a chance on an inexperienced graduate student, saw my abilities and took the time to guide me through this process.

This book would not exist without the work of Juan Flores and Miriam Jiménez Román. From their work on *The Afro-Latin@ Reader* to their leadership of the Afro-Latin@ Forum, they have been pioneers and leaders in the field of Afro-Latin@ Studies, something which I didn't even know existed until graduate school. I am conscious everyday that my work is possible because of the path created by Juan Flores, who has added so much richness to Latin@ studies. You live on in my work and the work of so many.

I also want to thank African American Studies at Yale University. I quickly realized I wasn't in the right place my first semester of doctoral studies. African American Studies welcomed me with open arms and never questioned why I saw my work as part of their department. Gracias especially to my dissertation co-chairs Robert Stepto and Elizabeth Alexander whose teachings and work originally inspired the idea for this anthology.

To my original African American studies professor, lifetime mentor and forever familia, Mark Naison, I look forward to another cerveza and jíbaro to celebrate this book soon.

To my mother, siempre, to my mother. I would be nothing without you.

Introduction
¡Manteca!: An Anthology of Afro-Latin@ Poets

> the internal dance of salsa
> is of course plena
> and permit me to say these words
> in afro-spanish:
> la bomba y la plena puro son
> de Puerto Rico que Ismael es el
> rey y es el juez
> meaning the same as marvin gaye
> singing spiritual social songs
> to black awareness
> *"the salsa of bethesda fountain,"*
> —Tato Laviera

In 1947, Dizzy Gillepse, Chano Pozo and Gil Fuller collaborated on the song "Manteca." "Manteca" would not only become one of Gillespie's most famous recordings but it is one of the foundations of Afro-Cuban jazz. As such, "Manteca" not only represents the significance of African American and Latin@ collaborations, but the beginnings of what can be thought of as a distinct Afro-Latin@ sound in the United States that can be traced through boogaloo to salsa to hip hop. Perhaps, it should not be surprising that many of the first generation of Afro-Latin@ poets within these pages, such as Pedro Pietri, Louis Reyes Rivera, Miguel Algarín,

Sandra María Esteves and Lorenzo Thomas were born within a few years of this song. Although Afro-Latin@s have a much longer history in the United States than just "Manteca," it represents for the first time a period in which Afro-Latin@s had their own recognizable sound and music. And so when, for example, the great Louis Reyes Rivera passed in 2012, that second generation of Afro-Latin@ poets he mentored, such as Tony Medina and Shaggy Flores, honored him with that same *sentido*. As Medina wrote then, and I echo to the other poets who have passed and to whom this volume is dedicated, "I can hear you now shouting out at us from the Spirit World–MANTECA!!!!!!!!!!"[1] Thus this title, like the anthology, represents spirit and history but also an Afro-Latin@ soul that is not really describable. It is felt distinctly and differently by each poet and in each page. For this reason this introduction will not attempt to define what Afro-Latin@ poetry *is*, but instead presents those poets whose words represent the diversity of Latino América.

In their introduction to the *Afro-Latin@ Reader*, the first major academic effort about Latin@s of African descent in the United States, editors Miriam Jiménez Román and Juan Flores struggle to define the term Afro-Latin@[2], asking within a North American context, "What's an Afro-Latin@? Who is an Afro-Latin@? The term befuddles us because we are accustomed to thinking of 'Afro' and 'Latin@' as distinct from each other and mutually exclusive: one is either Black or Latin@" (1). In his poem "the salsa of bethesda fountain," Tato Laviera answers some of these questions. He describes Afro-Latinidad as having its own language, composed both of Puerto Rican and African American musical traditions. For Laviera, being Afro-Latin@ is also a self-proclamation, a self-awareness of cultural and linguistic mixings, that make up every day existence:

a blackness in spanish
a blackness in english
mixture-met on jam sessions in central park
there were no differences in
the sounds emerging from inside
soul-salsa is universal
meaning a rhythm of mixtures
with world-wide bases.

As the poem continues, it becomes clear that this self-identification as Afro-Latin@ is at once a personal statement as well as a commentary that has transnational implications. As Laviera finishes the poem he demands acceptance and recognition not just from those who are visibly Afro-Latin@, or who identify themselves as Afro-Latin@, but as a non-negotiable part of Latinidad both in Puerto Rico and Central Park: "did you want it stronger?" he rhetorically asks? "well, okay, it is a root called Africa in all of us."

Jiménez Román and Flores' questions demonstrate how the term "Afro-Latin@" brings up a complicated series of issues, including race, nationality, ethnicity, heritage and ancestry that manifest themselves distinctly among Latin America's varied countries and cultures and then travel, mix and create new uncertainties for those who find themselves in the United States. Perhaps this is why they find their short answer—"Afro-Latin@s . . . are people of African descent in Mexico, Central and South America, and the Spanish-speaking Caribbean, and by extension those of African descent in the United States whose origins are in Latin America and the Caribbean"—so unsatisfying (1). Still, for Laviera, like the forty other poets in this anthology from diverse backgrounds, an Afro-Latin@ background and identification that complicates an already complicated Latin@ identity in the United States, is also an indisputable part of their poetic expression. Because, as Jane Alberdeston Coralin puts it, "we couldn't shake our skin" ("Rosa's Beauty"),

Laviera demands a space for a poetic language that is "Afro-Spanish," much like a life lived through "a blackness in english/ a blackness in spanish."

Thus, this ¡Manteca!, like Jiménez Román's, Flores' and Laviera's multifaceted definitions of "Afro-Latin@," serves a variety of purposes. It includes selected works from an elite group of renowned poets as well as a talented crop of up-and-comers. Despite the dominance of male poets in the earlier years, this anthology demonstrates the increasing importance of women in Latin@ poetry, presenting twenty female writers (half the contributors). In addition, by focusing on Afro-Latin@ poets, ¡Manteca! strives to highlight an important but often neglected aspect of US poetry: that Afro-Latin@ poets are a key part of poetic expression and innovation that is uniquely (North) American. As such, an important contribution of this anthology is to break the often rigid boundaries between Latin@ and African American poetry, to simultaneously center blackness as an important aspect of Latin@ poetry and Latinidad as crucial to African American poetry. In doing so, I hope to highlight how the work of diverse poets, such as John Murillo, Jane Alberdeston Coralin, Willie Perdomo, Aracelis Grimay, Adrián Castro, Peggy Robles-Alvarado, Natalie Caro, Bonafide Rojas and otras crush existing notions of what it means to be an African American, Latin@ or American poet. It is, I hope, a gathering of exciting work that pushes for an inclusive (but not unselective) definition of US poetry that includes Latin@s of all backgrounds who live and breathe varying conceptions of blackness.

Anthologizing Blackness in Latin America

Although an anthology of this sort, that brings together Afro-Latin@ writers, exists neither in poetry nor prose, antecedents in the past century can be found in the work of anthologizers throughout Latin America who assembled work both by black and white poets and about black life, including writings by African American poets since the 1930s. In "The Emergence of Afro-Hispanic Poetry: Some Notes on Canon Formation," Edward Mullen surveys the first Latin American anthologies of black poetry to demonstrate how an interest in black poetry influenced canon formation in Latin America, resulting in a consideration of black culture as critical to conceiving of a Latin American literary tradition that was separate from a European one (449-450). Significantly, however, the Latin American understanding of what is meant by black poetry in the 1930s and 1940s, particularly that emerging in the Caribbean, demonstrates a very different conception than that outlined by James Weldon Johnson's *The Book of American Negro Poetry* in 1922. As Chilean professor and critic Arturo Torres Rioseco announced in 1942:

> Without assuming the role of an augur, it is permissible to point out a new movement which is encouraging for the future of Spanish American poetry. This is the emergence in the last few years of a highly original genre: Negro verse. That is to say, poetry on Negro themes, using Negro rhythms, and composed by members of both the African and the European races. (127)

Throughout the next three decades, Torres Rioseco's pronouncement was to be repeated in the pages of major anthologies, scholarly journals and textbooks. As the Spanish American literary canon underwent a gradual reevaluation, Torres Rioseco's terminology was to be modified; "negro" was replaced by a series of overlapping labels—negroid, negrista, Afro-Cuban, mulato—culminating in the late seventies with the choice of the term "Afro-Hispanic" to refer broadly to that literature "by, about and written to but not just for people of African descent in the Spanish speaking world" (Lewis 3).

Nevertheless, at its inception, "Afro-Hispanic poetry"[3] or *poesía negra*, was a genre written by blacks, whites and those in between.[4] In fact, the movement to anthologize Afro-Latin American poetry was marked by the participation of white intellectuals, such as Luis Palés Matos and José Zacarías Tallet, who produced a highly picturesque but external view of black culture signalled by a predominance of sensuous images and onomatopoetic rhythms. Moreover, in these early anthologies the majority of the writers included were white.[5] While a study of these early anthologies demonstrates an important development from an Afro-Cuban or Caribbeanist perspective to a more universal (including African American)[6] perspective, as well as one which included more writers of African descent, the most important contribution was the argument made by the early anthologizers, Ballagas and Guirao that the only valid literary expression in Cuba must be black-based, for it was the only form which could be used as an authentic alternative to American and European cultural imperialism (Guirao xix).

Despite the importance of this development in the Cuban and emerging Latin American canon, the interest in black culture has often masked either a folkloric view or fetishization of blackness alongside a discourse of *mestizaje* in Latin American studies that turns a blind eye to the persistence of rampant racism in the academy, and whose influence can also be seen in Latin@ Studies today. Books such as José Sanz y Díaz's *Lira negra* (1945), Emilio Ballagas' *Mapa de la poesía negra americana* (1946), Juan Felipe Toruño's *Poesía negra: Ensayo y antología* (1953) and Simón Latin@'s *La poesía negra* (1956) all anthologized poets from throughout the Americas, yet tended to view black poetry as a folkloric expression or one of social interest. For example, in Toruño's introduction, he prepares the reader for a lack of art and modern innovation in black poetry:

En la poesía dominada negra, hay un problema-arte. Esta es la manifestación de vida resquebrajada y estentórea, ahíta de aspiraciones y deseos. . . . En el arte poético negro no están la estructuras que presentan otras tendencias modernas o ultramodernas en las que se nota la preocupación por pulir, depurar, sutilizar, perfeccionar o aglomerar duples, triples o cuádruples figuras en metáforas que fusionan contenido y continente, como en el Ultraísmo; ni por usar términos u otros recursos estructurales. En la poesía negra compruébese lo contrario. Esta presenta ambientes, sentimientos, ideas, acciones, sucesos, problemas y acontecimientos en corrientes directas y sin oscuranas expresivas. Es un arte poético en que se tipifican estruendo, arrebato, turbulencia, padecimiento, fiebre, escándalo, fiereza y el achatamiento psíquico del negro. . . . En lo negro, con las articulaciones estallantes, están las intenciones al mostrar la existencia sometida a la injusticia, enseñando el tenebroso y tajado panorama de vidas a través de las expresiones que en tal poesía se usan: ausencia de todo refinamiento en la poemática leal a una consigna.[7] (46)

According to Toruño and others, black poetry, especially that actually written by blacks, is a poetry that feels passionately about and expresses the unjust life of blacks in Latin America, but does not do so in thoughtful, complex verses. In spite of this racialized view of black poetry, virtually all the editors dealt with the issue of authenticity—whether whites could write black poetry—concluding that the American experience of cultural *mestizaje* provided the answer: "no se trata aquí de poesía negra en toda su pureza, mitología y originalidad africana, sino de poesía de contraste y asimilación de culturas" (Ballagas, *Mapa de la poesía americana* 8).[8] Although the introduction of poets who were black, such as Candelario Obeso and Jorge Artel, as well as the rare publication of Adalberto Ortiz's *Tierra, son y tambor: Cantares negros y mulatos*

(1945), an anthology edited by an Ecuadorian black writer, would lead to a somewhat more varied and less folkloric depiction of the black experience (especially with the prominence of writers such as Nicolás Guillén and Reginio Pedroso), the existence of racialized distinctions and hierarchies in the world of Latin American poetry was often glossed over in favor of a celebration of a shared mixed heritage.

This literary standpoint was especially influenced by the Afro-Cubanism movement, which from its inception was conceptualized as a reflection of the fusion or union of black and white Cubans. Nicolás Guillén's introduction to the 1931 edition of his Afro-Cuban poetry, *Sóngoro cosongo*, is one of the clearest examples of this interpretation:

> Diré firmamente que éstos son unos versos mulatos. Participan acaso de los mismos elementos que entran en la composición étnica de Cuba . . . Y las dos razas que en la Isla salen a flor de agua, distantes en lo que se ve, se tienden un garfio submarino, como esos puentes hondos que unen en secreto dos continentes. Por lo pronto, el espíritu de Cuba es mestizo. Y del espíritu hacia la piel nos vendrá el color definitivo. Algún día se dirá: "color cubano." Estos poemas quieren adelantar ese día.[9] (240)

The dominance of this idealized *mestizaje* of races is clear from anthologies published in Latin America more recently. For example, in her 1992 *Poesia Negra Brasileira*, Brazilian Zilá Bernd questions the utility of talking about a "black literature" in "um país multiétnico e pluricultural como o Brasil."[10] According to Bernd:

> Que tipo de textos entrariam na classificação de literatura negra? Aqueles que propusessem uma temática negra, não importando a cor da pele do autor, aqueles produzidos por autores negros? Mas como saber, em um país mestiço como o

Brasil quem é negro, ou mulato e quem não é? Contudo, reconhecer a mestiçagem étnica e cultural não apenas no Brasil, mas em toda a América Latina, não deve nos impeder de reconheer igualmente a construção paulatina de uma identidade negra na literatura Latino-americana, onde o Brasil não seria uma exceção, revelando a emegência de um processo de consciência do que significa *ser negro na América*. Torna-se, então imprescindível, ao iniciarmos uma reflexão sobre a literatura negra no Brasil, definer seu conceito. Para nós, o único conceito aceitável de literatura negra é o que se alicerça nas constantes discursivas das obras. Logo, em nossa perspectiva, não sera apenas a ultilização de uma temática negra (o negra como objeto), nem a cor de pele do escritor (critério epidérmico) que caracterizariam a existência de uma literatura negra, mas a emergência de um *eu-enunciador que se assume como negro* no discurso literário. Nesta medida, o conceito de literatura negra associa-se à existência, no Brasil, de uma articulação entre textos dados por um modo negro de ver e de sentir o mundo, transmitido por um discurso caracterizado, seja no nível da escolha lexical, seja no nível dos símbolos utilizados, pelo desejo de resgatar uma memória negra esquecida.[11] (Bernd 13)

In Bernd's picture then, black literature becomes something based on a black protagonist through which Brazil can celebrate a (now past) history of black struggle in a present-day, happily mixed, racially ambiguous society, where it is impossible to determine racial ancestry anyway. While there is nothing innately wrong with a discourse that celebrates racial and cultural *mestizaje* in Latin America, what is problematic is how these interpretations have made racial discrimination seem like a problem of the past. Moreover, in the case of literature, it has often resulted in the exclusion of Afro-Latin American writers, under the guise of racial ambiguity in a supposedly mixed and thus nondiscriminatory area of the world.

In Latin America, a strong interest in Afro-Hispanic culture seemed to reach a peak in the 1970s and early 1980s, a period which saw the publication of more than a half-dozen anthologies: Rosa E. Valdés-Cruz, *La poesía negroide en América* (1970); Hortensia Ruíz del Vizo, *Poesía negra del Caribe y otras áreas* (1971); Enrique Noble, *Literatura afro-hispanoamericana. Poesía y prosa de ficción* (1973); Jorge Luis Morales, *Poesía afroantillana y negrista* (1976); Mónica Mansour and Jose Luis González, *Poesía negra de América* (1976); and Aurora de Albornoz and Julio Rodríguez Luis, *Sensemayá: La poesía negra en el mundo hispanohablante* (1980). Like their predecessors, however, the majority of these volumes treated the poetic production of black and white Latin American authors as part of the same genre of *poesía negra*, *poesía afroantillana* and *poesía negrista* (Arnedo-Gómez 10).

The emergence of the field of Afro-Latin American studies in the United States in the late 1960s and 1970s led to an important critique of these picturesque views of Latin American literature as inclusive of writers from the entire race spectrum. Largely a result of the frequent exchanges between African American and Latin American scholars stemming from political interaction in the Black Power and Civil Rights Movement and the increasing popularity of the Latin American novel, Afro-Latin American or Afro-Hispanic studies was supported by the founding of the Afro-Hispanic Institute at Howard University in 1981 and the establishment of several Afro-Hispanic journals including *Cuadernos Afro-Americanos* (Caracas, 1975), *Negritud* (Bogotá, 1977), *Studies in Afro-Hispanic Literature* (Purchase, New York, 1977) and the *Afro-Hispanic Review* (Washington, DC, 1982, now located at Vanderbilt in Nashville, Tennessee) (Kutzinski 122).

Ironically, this academic progress came at a time when many Nuyorican writers now featured in this anthology, such as Miguel

Algarín, Louis Reyes Rivera, Miguel Piñero, Sandra María Esteves and Pedro Pietri, along with other poets of Afro-Latin@ descent such as Panamanian Lorenzo Thomas, were commenting on the persistence of racism in US Latin@ communities. While this Latin Americanist attention on writers of African descent, as well as on the different but persistent hierarchal race structures of Latin America, led to important critiques of many of these early anthologies that glossed over racial discrimination while excluding Afro-descended writers (Lewis 2), it did not draw an analogous attention within the emerging field of US Latin@ studies.

Nevertheless, while US studies of Latin American anthologies worked to reveal the problematic praise for Palés Matos,[12] anthologizing choices[13] and essentializing characteristics of much of literary criticism done on Afro-Latin American poetry[14], Latin@ poets in the United States were struggling to make sense of racial attitudes often based in Latin America but persistent (though transformed) in the United States. Nuyorican Poets Café owner Miguel Algarín describes his circumstances this way:

My grandmother was black, but my mother is light-skinned. My grandmother worked all her life and wanted her children to have a better life than hers. She insisted that her daughters not greet her or speak directly to her when they were in public because she did not want them to be associated with her. It might limit their possibilities, she thought. That hurt my mother. She had to cross the street or go on the other side of the plaza if she saw Julia coming around the corner. Puerto Rican racism is something terrible. My grandmother was afraid that if people associated her daughters with her, they would not be able to get married to acceptable men . . . When I think about that now, I find it is extremely painful. (Hernández, C 37)

This lack of attention from the academy, in addition to the clear connection and implications of Latin American treatment of Afro-descendants continues to be an issue, as Tanya K. Hernández and Anani Dzidzienyo point out in their respective articles, "'Too black to be Latina/o': Blackness and Blacks as foreigners in Latin@ studies" (2003) and "With the African connection in Latin@ Studies" (2003).

Afro-Latinidad in a US Context

While Jiménez Román and Flores' seminal volume explores what it means to be an Afro-Latin@, ¡Manteca! presents Afro-Latin@ poets, another context where Afro-Latinidad is often not part of a Latin@ conversation. This collection of poets—all active within the last fifty years or so—also draws attention to the difficulty of working with a relatively "new" category. As Jiménez Román and Flores state, "As straightforward as this definition would seem, the reality is that the term is not universally accepted and there is no consensus about what it means. The difficulties surrounding what we call ourselves reflects the complex histories of Africans and their descendants in the Americas" (1). Although some variant of Afro-Latin@ has been used for over a century to describe people of African descent in Latin America and the Caribbean as a whole, the term has only really been incorporated in a US context since the 1990s (Jiménez Román and Flores 2) and even later in (US) Latin@ Studies (Torres-Saillant 435, Hernandez T. 152, Mills "Chitlins" 1, Dzidzienyo 160).

Nevertheless, the history of Afro-Latin@s in the United States predates not just the nation's founding, but the first English settlements (Jiménez Román and Flores 17). The first Africans who came to the Americas as slave labor in 1502 were brought to Hispaniola (now the island that is composed of Haiti and the Dominican Republic) by the Spaniards (Laó Montes 2). Africans were present in the sixteenth-century Spanish forays into what would later become the United States (Wood 19), and these early Spanish-speaking peoples of African descent (both free and enslaved), were some of the main settlers of the Southwest (Forbes 27), as well as New Orleans and Florida (Gould 28). The Afro-Latin@ Pico Family governed Mexican California in the nineteenth century (Forbes 35). Likewise, while there has been significant recent attention by scholars on Afro-Latinidad, scholars such as Antonio López, Frank Guirdy and Adrián Burgos have continued to push scholarship on Afro-Latin@s back in to the eighteenth, nineteenth and early twentieth centurys during the past ten years.

Afro-Latin@s, not unlike Latin@s in general, are often seen as newcomers and foreigners, which makes it difficult to study what can be described as "a diaspora within a diaspora" (Laó-Montes 1). But this long history is not lost in the work of such poets as Adrían Castro, an Afro-Latin@ from Miami, who regularly incorporates African languages, "the ancestor's mother tongue," into his work. In "Pulling the Muse from the Drum," for example, he traces the history of the Spanish slave trade to "Caribbean jungles . . . through stained walls in Little Havana/ graffiti parks Lower East Side/ frozen lake Wicker Park Chaaiitown." It is a history that, much like Laviera's universalizing gaze of African roots, is simultaneously Castro's inspiration and what unites Latin@s, what he calls "the muse that is we."

According to the 2010 Census, 2.5 percent of the US Latin@ population identified their race as black or African American: however, 6 percent identified themselves as of two or more races, and 36.7 percent selected "some other race." Not only did a majority of the Latin@ population choose not to identify as white (53.0 percent), but also, a comparison to the general population demonstrates a clear difference in the way Latin@s perceive race in the United States. Only 2.3 percent and 0.2 percent of the US population selected "two or more races" or "some other race," respectively (Humes et al 6), indicating that Latin@s make up a large segment of the US population that does not fit into what David Hollinger has called "the ethnoracial pentagon" made up of whites, blacks, Indians, Asian Americans and Hispanics (Hollinger 8). Numerous scholars have commented on the variations in the way Latin@s of different national, class, ethnic and racial backgrounds view race in the United States and the barriers this presents for Latin@ unity.[15] At the same time, Dzidzienyo comments, this recognition of mestizaje does little to disrupt hegemonic racialized models:

> The conventional "model" of race mixture, *mestizaje* as a quasi-panacea for race relations elsewhere in the Americas, that is, minus the United States, did not imply combatting either racial hierarchy or privilege. Thus, *mestizaje* on its own is not a sufficient proof of any recognition of the equality of all the component races. At the end of the mixing process, white hegemony remained unchallenged throughout Latin America. In the absence of any unambiguous challenge to white supremacist models, there does not appear to have emerged any alternate models that are free of rank orders, with whiteness at the apex and blackness and/or indigenousness at the base. Neither has the (rhetorical) honoring of specific cultural expressions of African provenance, such as musical expressions, which have been shifted from the margins to the center of national cultural life in specific Latin American societies, resulted in the transformation of the overall negativity assigned to African origins, in looks, speech patterns, and ontologies. (161)

Racialized thinking follows immigrants to the United States and affects darker-skinned Latin@s.[16] However, what is important in the context of this anthology is how it also affects the study of Latin@ literature. Thus while Dzidzienyo unpacks the "conceptual panacea of mestizaje" to reveal the extent to which the pride Latin@s take in being enlightened about race relations as a mixed people is accompanied by the resilience of White supremacist ideals, he also persuasively argues that many Latin@ Studies scholars have been content to focus on *mestizaje* without thoroughly interrogating the subtext of White supremacy. Indeed, one area that is often overlooked in Latin@ Studies is the treatment of Afro-Latin@s within the Latin@ community. As Tanya Hernández points out in "Too Black to be Latina/o," "if the mestizaje race relations mindset were indeed such an enlightened space, one would expect relations with Afro-Latin@/as and Anglo-Blacks in the United States to embody the fantasy of racial democracy so often touted in Latin American countries. . . . Instead, an examination of the Afro-Latin@ context reveals a racialized treatment of Afro-Latin@ identity as foreign" (152). What is most disturbing about this multi-layered dynamic of Latin@s putting forth as an image of enlightened racial thinking by virtue of their racially mixed heritage while simultaneously negating the existence of Afro-Latin@s, is the way in which the mindset obstructs any ability to effectively work through the complexity of the socioeconomic racial hierarchy that purposely discourages racialized groups from attacking White supremacy as a unified force.

In some small part, then, creating an Afro-Latin@ anthology of poets diminishes a reverence for white or European heritage within the Latin@ arts, encouraging a reevaluation of Latin@ literary and American literary canon formation. As African American anthologizers from James Weldon Johnson to Henry Louis Gates Jr. have pointed out, canon formation has everything to do with politics whereby a "broader access" functions as a sign that—in this case—Afro-Latin@s are full and equal members of American democratic institutions (Gates xxix), and are afforded all the rights and privileges that go along with such membership. Whereas James Weldon Johnson believed that the recognition of an African American literary tradition would end racism in the United States, I believe that the recognition of Afro-Latin@ poetry will bring to light new structures of racism that have emerged and entrenched themselves as this country has become increasingly multi-cultural and multi-ethnic.

In Search of an Afro-Latin@ Literature

¡Manteca!: An Anthology of Afro-Latin@ Poets, presents the work of twenty men and twenty women who self-identify as Afro-Latin@s. As editor, I gave no guidelines or definitions to what I thought Afro-Latin@ "poetry" was. When asked for instruction—I purposefully gave none, as this response to one query demonstrates: "The anthology is an anthology of Afro-Latin@ poetry, but I would never try to categorize that in any particular or limiting way. Just send me your best work, the work that you feel represents you best as a poet, present and/or past, if you're so inclined." As I began to receive work, I realized that the experiences and poetic expression of Afro-Latinidad were so diverse that I wouldn't and couldn't begin to categorize an "Afro-Latin@ Poetry." Not only were these poets diverse in their heritage, location and poetic thematic, choices and influences, some came to Afro-Latinidad via middle passage and/or migration and others through the more recent marriages of their family. In many ways, Bonafide Rojas' "Thirty Ways to Look at a Nuyorican" demonstrates a microcosm of what this anthology represents as he pushes readers beyond common definitions of puertorriqueñidad.

Examining the treatment of Afro-Latin@s is work that begins with us Latin@s and especially those of us in Latin@ literary studies who with rare exceptions do not reflect the experiences of Afro-Latin@ poets in our research. In dealing with questions of race, Latin@ Studies has privileged an indigenous form of *mestizaje* that excludes the reality of millions of slave bodies (as well as Asian bodies) and the increasing occurrence of intermarriage. It has felt comfortable with a poem like "Here" by Sandra María Esteves, in which she describes the wounds of being Puerto Rican in the United States,[17] but not a poem like "Not Neither," where she struggles to reconcile not just the different cultural and linguistic aspects of her identity but the racial components as well:

> Being Puertorriqueña Dominicana, Borinqueña Quisqueyana,
> Taíno Africana
> Born in the Bronx, not really jíbara
> Not really hablando bien
> But yet, not gringa either
> Pero no, portorra. Pero sí, portorra too
> Pero ni qué, what am I? . . . (*Tropical Downpour* 26)

The preference for poems that reflect migration or assimilation experiences, as opposed to those that interrogate questions of race, reflects neither the experiences nor oeuvre of Nuyorican poets, however. From 1983 to 1985 Esteves was a producer and director of the African Caribbean Poetry Theater in New York; while such poets as Victor Hernández Cruz proudly wrote of their Afro-Latin heritage. Yet scholarship on them is often couched as bridging "the Latin@ and mainland cultures of the U.S.," (Maraca) the culture of the country of origin and the country of immigration, and most often Spanish and English. As such, while one might see a struggle for linguistic identity through Esteves' use of Spanish and English or for a way to connect to Puerto Rico through her reference to Puerto Rican independence fighter Lolita Lebrón, I cannot disconnect these themes from her self-definition as "Taíno Africana," where her claim to indigeneity is embedded in her recognition of her blackness. Her struggle for language, like Tato Laviera's, is not just linguistic, cultural or national, but also racial. When Esteves cannot find her voice, "Pero con what voice do my lips move?/ Rhythms of rosa wood feet dancing bomba/ Not even here. But here. Y conga," she turns to African rhythms present in

Puerto Rican music. The "we" then that "defy translation" and are "Nameless," then are not just Nuyoricans. They are Afro-Latin@s.

These leading Latin@ poets, who also identify as Afro-descendants, defy common expectations of Latinidad. In this way, the voices in this anthology build on the work of Jiménez Román and Flores, who write:

Afro-Latin@ is at the personal level a unique and distinctive experience and identity because of its range among and between Latin@, Black, and United States American dimensions of lived reality. In their quest for a full and appropriate sense of social identity Afro-Latin@s are thus typically pulled in three directions at once and share a complex, multidimensional optic on contemporary society. Taking a cue from W.E.B. Du Bois, we might name this three-pronged web of affiliations "triple-consciousness." To paraphrase those unforgettable lines from *The Souls of Black Folk* (1903) in studying the historical and contemporary experience of United States Afro-Latin@, one ever feels his three-ness, -a Latin@, a Negro, an American; three souls, three thoughts, three unreconciled strivings; three warring ideals in one dark body, whose dogged strength alone keeps it from being torn asunder. Du Bois's reference to strength and resilience bears emphasis: the multiple experiences and perspectives—including the contradictions, pain, and outrage—does not necessarily translate into pathological confusion. As many of the contributions to this volume suggest, embracing and celebrating all the dimensions of one's self has not only been possible but has also resulted in significant innovations at the personal and collective level. (15)

For me, Flores and Jiménez Román's final point is what makes *¡Manteca!* so unique and also inspiring. Within the still incipient study of Afro-Latin@ literature, where the Afro-Latin@ is somewhat known in prose through insightful accounts such as *Black Cuban, Black American* (Evelio Grillo 2000) and *Down These Mean Streets* (Piri Thomas 1967), as well as through the figure of Arturo Schomburg, the creativity and diversity that results from the multiple dimensions of the Afro-Latin@ poet can only be found in the present *¡Manteca!*

Inspired by Grillo, Thomas and Schomburg, then, at the foundation of this anthology is also a recognition of the close relationships between African Americans and Afro-Latin@s (who are also African Americans); these relationships have been significant for both groups from collaborating in politics to working together in the arts for the past one hundred years. This relationship is what was "¡Manteca!" in the 1940s and continues to be ¡Manteca! in the poetry of this anthology. Latin@s have been at the center of African American verse since its inception, as evidenced by Weldon Johnson's discussion of and admiration for black poets in Latin America. Likewise, connections between Harlem Renaissance poets and Afro-Latin American poets are numerous. [18] This is an artistic connection that has grown within the United States, as the poets of this collection powerfully testify.

Since the 1960s, for instance, the poetry of Miguel Algarín, Lorenzo Thomas and Victor Hernández Cruz has exemplified the overlapping and intersecting expressions of an Afro-Latin@ consciousness. Hernández Cruz and Thomas participated in diverse arts movements, organizations, anthologies and recordings, including the Black Arts Movement and the Umbra Writers' Workshop, infusing the content of their poetry with the specificity of their Latin@ identity, while still incorporating characteristics that defined the new black poetry of the times. Hernández Cruz appears in a host of collections affiliated with the Black Arts Movement, such as *Black Fire: An Anthology of Afro-American Writing* (1968), edited by Amiri Baraka and Larry Neal, and *The New Black Poetry*

(1969), edited by Clarence Major, as well as numerous black poetry journals and anthologies of black writing, including *New Black Voices: An Anthology of Afro-American Literature* (1972) *Dices or Black Bones: Black Voices of the Seventies* (1970) and *3000 Years of Black Poetry* (1970). Similarly, Nuyorican poet Felipe Luciano was a member of the predominantly African American performance-oriented poetry troupe, The Last Poets, and was co-founder of the Young Lords Party in New York, a Puerto Rican revolutionary nationalist organization modeled after the Black Panther Party. Likewise, more recent collections such as *Bum Rush the Page: A Def Poetry Jam* (2001) and *Black Gold: An Anthology of Black Poetry* (2014) also bridge the gap between African American and Latin@ by incorporating numerous Afro-Latin@ poets. Still, I find that the richness of the three generations of Afro-Latin@ poets presented in *¡Manteca!* and the "triple consciousness" that Flores and Jiménez-Román so aptly described demonstrate the necessity for a volume of its own.

¡MANTECA!

As the epigraph to this introduction demonstrates, Tato Laviera's Afro-Latinidad clearly emerges in the influence of Caribbean and African American music, orality and rhythms in his poetry. In a similar fashion, Miguel Algarín dedicated poems to Ray Barreto as well as to salsa's African roots, using a mixture of Spanish and English, as well as the orality and rhythms of both Caribbean and African American music and speech to reflect the intercultural activity of the period's Black and Latin@ musicians. What Algarín's music-inflected poems or Laviera's more political "commonwealth" or "Lady Liberty" indicate are not just the interstices of Black and Puerto Rican experiences, but a particular focus that honors Puerto Rican blackness as distinct from that of an African American or a person of African descent from another part of the world. As Tato Laviera describes it, his poetic connection to African Americans comes from the necessity of a language that cannot be white in either the United States or Latin America:

> Fifty percent of my poetry, of my recitals, are for the black constituency of the United States for three reasons: they are very interested in my sense of Caribbean blackness, and of urban blackness, and they are interested in the rhythmic quality of my poetry. Whether or not you like it, if you're a Caribbean writer, in the United States you don't write in white verse, you write in black verse. You write with the attitudes of blacks which are very important to the Puerto Rican community. (Hernández C. 81)

On the one hand, such figures as Arturo Schomburg, who intentionally integrate themselves into Africa-America, point to the intellectual possibilities as well as conversations among Latin@s and African Americans. On the other hand, the example of Schomburg also highlights the complexities of such allegiances within the context of New York City's African-American and Puerto Rican communities (Dzidzienyo 164). Schomburg would not give up his Afro-Latin@ identity, even though his blackness was often contested because of his Puerto Rican origin and light skin color. His project of black cosmopolitanism, then, was based on a recognition of diversity and complexity in the multiple racial regimes and cultural practices that composed the global African diaspora. He was a "transamerican intellectual" who promoted a diasporic project in which identity and community were conceived through and across difference (Laós-Montes 8). As such, it is not without thought that ¡Manteca! ends with a collaboration between Afro-Mexican poet Joaquín Zihuatanejo and Antwaun "Twain" Davis, who attribute the oppressions of people of color to larger histories and structures of violence.

Without negating the importance of these African American and Latin@ connections, ¡Manteca! is not about collaborations but about people, those Latin@s who "couldn't shake their skin" or their Latinidad. Here, "Afro-Latin@ literature" celebrates those whose very existence is a product of relationships (forced or voluntary) within the African diaspora. In "Living 'In Between': The Identification of Afro-Latino/a Literature," Fiona Mills relates her experience trying to broach the subject of Afro-Latin@ literature by proposing "a new way to read, understand and interpret African American and Latino/a literature under the rubric of 'Afro-Latino/a Literature' through the examination of the complicated exchanges between these two literary traditions" (Mills 113). While I agree that it is important to break down resistance between "those within and without the academy to keep the disciplines of African American and Latin@ literature separate, whether consciously or unconsciously," unfortunately, her argument also works to obscure an Afro-Latin@ tradition that is written by Afro-Latin@s (112).

In the end, I hope that reading ¡Manteca! will quash the assumptions that "authentic black literature" is marked by a series of concrete themes and concepts (Arnedo Gómez 15). What I have found in sifting through the rich work of Afro-Latin@ poets is that an "essentialist conception of black culture" does not exist among this group that makes its homes across the country and traces its ancestries to places around the world. While some poems, such as Shaggy Flores' "Negritude," Anthony Morales' "Afro-Latinidad" and Peggy Robles-Alvarado's "Negrito Lindo" directly take up the topic of the Afro-Latin@ experience and history, others explore varying topics, from family to religion to love to poetry itself. Likewise, while Afro-Latinidad is often thought of in an Afro-Caribbean context, I found a growing generation of young Afro-Mexicana poets, such as Ariana Brown and Natasha Carrizosa, who proudly explore their identities and experiences.

¡Manteca! supports the view of Countee Cullen that "the poet writes out his experience, whether it be personal or vicarious, and as these experiences differ among other poets, so do they differ among Negro poets; for the double obligation of being Negro and American is not so unified as we are often led to believe. A survey of the work of Negro poets will show that the individual diversifying ego transcends the synthesizing hue" (Cullen xii). Not surprisingly, a wide range of poems make up *¡Manteca!*, written by such diverse poets as Aracelis Girmay (winner of the 2011 Isabella Gardner Award for a poet in midcareer with a new book of exceptional merit); she was born and raised in Southern California, with roots in Puerto Rico, Eritrea and African America. Both a Cave Canem Fellow and an Acentos board member, Grimay writes poetry deeply rooted in a temporally close African heritage. Her poem "Teeth," subtitled *for cousin Gedion, who drove us to Massawa*, begins:

Two sisters ride down with us.
It is liberation day in Massawa.

The older sister is the color of injera; her teeth are big
& stuck-out.
The younger sister is a cinnamon stick.

Their almond eyes are the same.
Ink black hair falls beautiful down both their backs.

Others poets take on the Latin@ celebration of *mestizaje*, pushing it to include both indigenous and African heritages, as does Jane Alberdeston Coralin, whose collection *The AfroTaina Dreams* is simultaneously black, Latina, Puerto Rican, Womanist, spiritual, academic and personal (Alvarado "A Flower"). In "Rosa's Beauty," for example, she struggles to make sense of her "un-Puerto Rican" hair:

it was a ritual
one Saturday a month
storm or shine, broke or not
Mami would drive us to Rosa's Beauty
near la 17 in Santurce
where a barrio's history is the mad work of knives and men
but there we were on our way to get our hair done,
to be called *chinitas*
straighten out kinks we couldn't correct in our everyday
couldn't make family better, bring fathers back home
but we could look real nice
like real Puerto Rican girls should [. . .]
five hours amid smoke and ash
lotions and dyes tinting the air
scissors and mouths moving
to any Mambo radio tune
and by then my head was burning alive
with the power of the relaxer
unable to wash it out
for fear of staying black
and we all knew that's what we didn't want
we wanted to shake our hair
(since we couldn't shake our skin)

Coralin, like all the poets in this anthology, writes about a wide variety of topics, ranging from Puerto Rican identity, ruminations on Amiri Baraka, and her father's depression, but through all of this she is still searching for a Afro-Latin@ expression, what Laviera calls an "Afro-Spanish," what for others is an "Afro-Spanglish," or that at times has nothing to do with Spanish at all. For Miami poet Adrián Castro, this search for a language that expresses his experience takes him back to call-and-response rhythms and African languages, while in "My Father Is a Brown Scar," Tony

Medina captures the heartbreak of seeing his diminished father in the hospital:

> His mouth wrenched open
> to received holy communion
> from the world of medicine
> and science, the world
> of mechanical breathing
> and silence.

In one of the poems making up *My Old Man Was Always on the Lam*, Medina writes a blues memoir in verse, echoing the voices of Harlem Renaissance poets. Other poets in ¡*Manteca!* incorporate music differently, updating the Nuyrican poets' incorporation of salsa, funk and boogalu for hip hop's linguistic possibilities, strongly present in the work of Río Cortez and Afro-Chicano poet John Murillo. Murillo bridges blues, funk and hip hop in "Renegades of Funk":

> The art of spitting fire? How to smoke
> a fool without a gun? We learned that too.
> We studied master poets—Kane, not Keats;
> Rakim, not Rilke. "Raw," "I Ain't No Joke,"
> our Nightingales and Orpheus. And few
> there were among us couldn't ride a beat
> in strict tetrameter. Impromptu odes
> and elegies—instead of slanting rhymes
> we *gangster* learned them, kicking seventeen
> entendre couplets just to fuck with old
> Miss Jefferson, the Newton freak.

Murillo's work demonstrates, as does that of the other poets in this volume, the richness of Afro-Latin@ literary traditions. From

Murillo's sonnet sequences to Gustavo Adolfo Aybar's knowledge of baseball history, Afro-Latin@ poets draw on Anglo, African American, Latin@ and Latin American canons with great proficiency. And they draw on each other—in these three generations of Afro-Latin@ poetry there is a clear sense of mentorship both physical and through the literary.

James Weldon Johnson's project to collect poems and songs by various authors written at different times under the rubric "Negro American" brings a distinctly racial element to the anthology form, resulting in the study and broader availability of African American poets. As Tess Chakkalakal reflects, "By collecting works by 'Aframerican poets' to form a Negro anthology, Johnson hoped to show that African Americans were vital to making America . . . different" (537). Like Johnson's, in the end, ¡Manteca! is not just a collection of "black poems" or "Afro-Latin@ poems" but inventive, envelope-pushing American poems, many of which have nothing overtly in their content about issues of race. These poets both demonstrate the richness of the Afro-Latin@ experience and artistic expression and defy expectations of what "black" or "Latin@" poetry should sound like. This anthology is by no means conclusive, suffering from the lack of representation by important but non-Spanish-speaking populations such as Brazilian and Haitian-Americans, yet it is offered with the hope of initiating a study of a literature that has too long gone unrecognized. In this way, an important segment of America, in the most transnational sense, will soon be able to stop defending, apologizing and explaining skin colors that do not fit within a "Latin@ mold." Because the poets in this collection can't just not "shake their skin." They don't want to.

Melissa Castillo-Garsow
Spanish Harlem, NY
Aug. 1, 2015

1. Medina, Tony. "On the Passing of a Major Revolutionary Poet: Louis Reyes Rivera." *Nuyorican Negritude: The Official Website.* 3 March 2012. < http://www.shaggyflores.com/louis-reyes-rivera-in-memoriam/>

2. Like Jiménez Román and Flores, I opt to use "@" for "Afro-Latin@" and "Latin@" to indicate gender inclusion, something which is politically important in both Latin@ poetry and the anthologizing tradition that has often been male dominant. I also choose to use Latin@ over Hispanic, in order to include those countries in Latin America that are not Hispanophone. Nevertheless, in many of the works referenced Latin@ and Hispanic are used interchangeably.

3. Here I am using "Afro-Hispanic" because it is the predominant terminology in the academy, but I prefer to use "Afro-Latin American" poetry, because the term Afro-Hispanic as defined by Mervin Lewis in 1983, does not include Afro-Brazilian poets—who are both widely recognized and who represent the largest population of Afro-descendent people in the Americas—as well as other non-Spanish speaking populations in Latin America. According to Lewis, "The idea that this literature is about, for, and by blacks, with black sensitivity and sensibility, is essential in any discussion of Afro-Hispanic poetry. Afro-Hispanic poets interpret their experiences from within rather than by merely describing a set of circumstances with which they are familiar. They tend to stress positive human qualities and values from a culturalist perspective. In Spanish America the term *poesía negra* has some of the same problems of application as *poesía mulata* due to both ethnic and ideological reasons. . . . The writers include *negros, mulatos* and *zambos.* Of course none of the authors in this study concentrates entirely upon black topics, but a significant portion of their literary production interprets the experience of blacks in the Americas based upon first-hand experiences and knowledge. Afro-Hispanic is therefore intended to suggest both ethnic categories and a type of literary output. Since black (*negro*) in Spanish America also carries negative connotations, my discussion centers on poets who acknowledge their black African heritage as being important in their artistic and personal lives but who do not necessarily write from a racist perspective" (3).

4. This can vary greatly by country. For example, in 1976, the Brazilian Institute of Geography and Statistics (IBGE) conducted a study to ask people to identify their own skin color, which resulted in 134 different terms (Grillo, C.).

5. The three fundamental works are responsible for the foundations of Afro-Hispanic poetry in the 1930s were Emilio Ballagas' *Antología de la poesía negra hispano-americana* (1935), Ildefonso Pereda Valdés', *Antología de la poesía negra americana* (1936) and Ramón Guirao's, *Órbita de la poesía afrocubana 1928–1937* (1938). All three anthologizers were white middle-class individuals also engaged in writing verse about the black experience, and these books were published and distributed by very well-known publishing houses (Aguilar, Ercilla, Ucar y García) that enjoyed considerable prestige throughout the Hispanic world (Mullin 443). In Ballagas' *Antología de la poesía negra hispano-americana*, in spite of the suggestive title, the vast majority of the poets (thirteen) were from Cuba and only three of the poets were black (Mullin 443). Ramón Guirao's *Órbita de la poesía afrocubana 1928–1937* is the longest of the three and represents the most ambitious effort, presenting seventy-nine poems drawn from the work of fourteen Cuban poets (Mullin 445).

6. For example, Ildefonso Pereda Valdés expanded on Ballagas' anthology demonstrating the influence of books such as James Weldon Johnson's *The Book of the American Negro Poetry* (1922) and Countee Cullen's *Caroling Dusk* (1927). His book anthologizes some twenty-nine poets from six countries including the United States, Haiti, Argentina, Brazil, Cuba and Uruguay. According to Mullen, "In short, by rejecting the literary nationalism which informed Ballagas' work, Pereda Valdés created the prototype for later anthologies, which were clearly to become more universalist in orientation. The move from Afro-Cuban to Afro-Hispanic had already begun" (Mullen 445).

7. My translation: "In the poetry called black, there is a problem—art. It is the manifestation of cracked and stentorian life, filled with aspirations and desires. . . . In the black poetic arts, there are not the structures present in other modern or ultramodern tendencies where, it is noted, the concern to polish, purify, subtilize, perfect or cluster double, triple or quadruple figures in metaphors that fuse content and continent as in the Ultraist movement, nor the concern to use terms or other structural recourses. In black poetry, you find the opposite. It presents environments, feelings, ideas, actions, events, problems and occurences in direct currents and without obscure expressions. It is a poetic art characterized by noise, rage, turmoil, illness, fever, scandal, ferocity and the psychic annihilation of blacks. In the black,

within the bursting articulations you find the intention to demonstrate an existence subjected to injustice, sharing the dark and severed panorama of lives through expressions used in that poetry: a lack of all refinement in a poetry faithful to a motto."

8. "This is not black poetry in all of its purity, mythology and poetry, but poetry of contrast and assimilation of cultures" (my translation).

9. "These poems are mulatto. They are made of the same elements that make up the Cuban ethnicity . . . And the two races on this island that rise up to the surface of the water extend an underwater hook to each other, like those deep bridges that unbeknown to anyone, join together two different continents. For the moment, it is clear that the Cuban soul is mulatto. Our definitive color will come to our skin from our soul. One day, people will say 'Cuban color.' These poems want to make that day come sooner" (Translation from Arnedo Gomez 6).

10. "a country as multiethnic and pluricultural as Brazil" (my translation).

11. My translation: "What kind of texts would go into the classification of black literature? Those that propose a black theme, no matter the skin color of the author; those produced by black authors? But how do you know, in a mixed country like Brazil, who is black, or mulatto and who is not? However, recognizing the ethnic and cultural mixing not only in Brazil but throughout Latin America, should equally not prevent the recognition of a gradual construction of a black identity in Latin American literature, where Brazil is no exception, revealing the emergence of a process of awareness of what it means to be black in America. It is then essential, as we begin a reflection on black literature in Brazil, to define the concept. For us, the only acceptable concept of black literature is one grounded in the discursive constants of the works. Thus, from our perspective, it is not just the use of a black theme (black as the object), or the color of the writer's skin (epidermal criteria) that characterize the existence of a black literature, but the emergence of an I-speaker who is assumed to be black in literary discourse... This way the concept of black literature is associated with the existence, in Brazil, of an articulation within texts given by a black way of seeing and feeling the world, characterized be it on the level of lexical choice, be it at the level of symbols used, for the desire to rescue a forgotten black memory."

12. The central figure in Puerto Rican "negrismo," Luis Palés Matos continues to be a literary icon in Latin American literature, despite the heavy criticism some of his work has received for his portrayal of black subjects, which echoes the racist discourses European writers used as they "rediscovered" Africa in their literature and art. Ruíz del Vizo, for example while accepting his place in Caribbean poetry, writes, " . . . la 'negrería' de Palés es tan soñada, tan fantasmal, está 'mas allá de las órbitas del tiempo'" (115).

13. By this, I mean the previously discussed tendency to define black poetry thematically, resulting in the overrepresentation of white poets or non-identified poets writing on "black" topics. To this criticism, I would add the almost total exclusion of female poets. As such, for much of the history of Afro-Latin American poetry, blackness has been defined by white men for white men (see also Feal).

14. By essentializing, I mean the view that there is such a thing as a definable black poetry distinguished by certain characteristics. For example the 1971 anthology, *Poesía negra del Caribe y otras áreas*, almost wholly limits its selection to poems on "black themes", as can be seen by titles such as "El buque negrero," "La guitarra de los negros," "Angelitos negros," "Viejo negro del Puerto," and many others (Ruíz del Vizo 165-167). Moreover as Jean Muteba Rahier notes in his work on Afro-Ecuadorian poet Décimas, "Ironically, with the multicultural turn came about a discursive tendency for ethnic absolutism wherein both political activists and their partners in academia embrace essentialist narratives about indigenous and Afrodescendents' cultures" (33). Against these scholarly traditions, more recent critics in Latin America and the USA ask, how do these supposedly characteristic elements of blackness reinforce traditional racial stereotypes? (Andrews, Dzidzienyo, Mills, Hernández T., Jiménez Román and Flores, Torres-Saillant) This is also a central question of this anthology.

15. As Torres-Saillant explains, "Comparing the plight of a Latina whose ancestors came to New Mexico four centuries ago as part of the entourage of Juan de Oñate with that of a New York City Latina born in 1970 to recent Dominican immigrant parents or a Chicana whose indigenous roots in the Texan soil stretch back 25,000 years might require a somersault of the imagination" (128). Christina Bel-

trán further explores this issue in *The Trouble With Unity: Latin@ Politics and the Creation of Identity.* (Oxford: Oxford UP, 2010).

16. For example, that the preference for a White racial identity continues to hold currency with many Latin@s was illustrated by the fact that the Association of White Hispanics was the largest of 33 groups petitioning to add "White Hispanic" to the census form (Hernández T. 156). Also see Negrón-Muntaner (2002) for the commercial implications of the privileging of whiteness in the Puerto Rican community.

17. I am two parts/a person
boricua/spic
past and present
alive and oppressed
given a cultural beauty
. . . and robbed of a cultural identity (*Yerba Buena* 20).

18. According to Mills, "Artists such as Hurston, Hughes, and Sanchez have spent time in Latin American countries and Mexico and have linked their struggles against oppression as African Americans to that of Latin@/as. For example, Lorde not only spent time in Mexico (about which she writes in her 1982 biomythography *Zami. A New Spelling of My Name*), but also wrote a short unpublished prose piece, entitled 'La Llorona'. . . . Sanchez, like Lorde, also has visited various Latin American countries, including Cuba and Central America, and has incorporated the concerns and culture of the Latin@/a community in her work. Notably, she acknowledges the influence of Latin American poets Pablo Neruda and Nicolás Guillén on her work. Sanchez has also spoken openly about her interest in the relief of racial and political oppression on an international level, and this commitment is reflected in poems such as 'M.I.A.', in which she makes references to 'disappeared' villages of El Salvador's repressive government. Poet Rita Dove has also demonstrated a similar commitment to representing the struggles of oppressed peoples of Latin American descent. Still other African American writers, such as Ntozake Shange and Barbara Smith, have collaborated with Latina authors—most notably in works such as anthologies from the Woman of Color Press and the Kitchen Table Press, including the well-known volume *This Bridge Called My Back. Writing by Radial Women of Color*" ("Living" 120-121).

BIBLIOGRAPHY

Algarín, Miguel, and Miguel Piñero. *Nuyorican Poetry: An Anthology of Puerto Rican Words and Feelings*. NY: William Morrow and Company, Inc., 1975.

Albornoz, Aurora de, and Julio Rodríguez-Luis. *Sensemayá: La poésia negra en el mundo hispanohablante (Antología)*. Madrid: Editorial Orígenes, 1980.

Alberdeston Coralin, Jane. "Rosa's Beauty." *Poetry Quarterly*. 2.3 (Summer 2001). Web. 21 Dec. 2011. <http://washingtonart.com/ beltway/alberdeston.html>.

—. *AfroTaina Dreams: Poems*. Chicago: Tell Me Somethin Books, 1999.

Alvarado, Lisa. "A Flower in her Heart: Jane Alberdeston Coralin." *La Bloga*. 28 June 2007. Web. 18 Dec. 2011. <http://labloga. blogspot.com/2007/06/flower-in-her-heart-jane-alberdeston.html>

Andrews, George Reid. *Afro-Latin America, 1800-2000*. Oxford: Oxford UP, 2004.

Anzaldúa, Gloria. *Borderlands/La Frontera: The New Mestiza*, 2nd ed. San Francisco: Aunt Lute Books, 1999.

Arnedo-Gómez, Miguel. *Writing Rumba: The Afrocubanista Movement in Poetry*. Charlottesville: University of Virginia Press, 2006.

Ballagas, Emilio, ed. *Antología de poesía negra hispanoamericana*. Madrid: Aguilar, 1935.

—. *Cuaderno de poesía negra*. Habana and Santa Clara: Editorial La Nueva, 1934.

—. *Mapa de la poesía negra americana*. Buenos Aires: Pleamar, 1946.

Baraka, Amiri, and Larry Neal, eds. *Black Fire: An Anthology of Afro-American Writing*. Baltimore: Black Classic Press, 2007.

Beltrán, Christina. *The Trouble With Unity: Latin@ Politics and the Creation of Identity*. Oxford, UK: Oxford UP, 2010.

Bernd, Zilá ed. *Poesia Negra Brasileira. Antologia*. Porto Alegre, Brazil: Editora AGE, 1992.

Burgos, Adrián. *Playing America's Game: Baseball, Latin@s, and the Color Line*. Oakland, CA: University of California Press, 2007.

Captain, Ivone. "Writing for the Future: Afro-Hispanism in a Global, Critical Context." *Afro-Hispanic Review* 13.1 (1994): 3-9.

Chakkalakal, Tess. "'Making a Collection': James Weldon Johnson and the Mission of African American Literature." *South Atlantic Quarterly* 104.3 (Summer 2005): 521–541.

Chapman, Abraham, ed. *New Black Voices: An Anthology of Afro-American Literature*. NY: Signet Classic, 1972.

Cortez, Río. "Structural Damage." jdbrecords. 19 April 2010. Web. 21 Dec. 2011. <http://jdbrecords.blogspot.com/ 2010/ 04/structural-damage.html>.

Cullen, Countee. *Caroling Dusk: An Anthology of Verse by Negro Poets*. NY: Harper & Brothers Publishers, 1927.

Dzidzienyo, Anani. "Coming to Terms with the African Connection in Latin@ Studies." *Latin@ Studies* 1.1 (Mar. 2003): 160–67.

Espada, Martín, ed. *El Coro: A Chorus of Latin@ and Latina Poetry*. Amherst: University of Massachusettes Press, 1997.

Esteves, Sandra María. *Yerba Buena* [*The Good Herb*]. Greenfield, NY: Greenfield Review Press, 1981.

—. *Tropical Rains: A Bilingual Downpour*. NY: African Caribbean Poetry Theater, 1984.

Feal, Rosemary. "Bordering Feminism in Afro-Hispanic Studies: Cross-roads in the Field." *Latin American Literary Review*. 20.40 (Jul.–Dec., 1992): 41–45.

Fernandez, María Teresa. "Poem for My Grifa-Rican Sistah, Or Broken Ends Broken Promises." *Centro Voices*. 10 April 2015. Web. 25 Dec. 2016. < https://centropr.hunter.cuny.edu/centrovoices/letras/poem-my-grifa-rican-sistah-or-broken-ends-broken-promises >.

Forbes, Jack D. "Black Pioneers: The Spanish-Speaking Afro-Americans of the Southwest." In Jiménez Román and Flores. 27–37.

Gates Jr, Henry Louis, and Nellie McKay, eds. *The Norton Anthology of African-American Literature*. 2nd ed. NY: W.W. Norton, 2004.

Goldberg, David Theo. *Racial Subjects: Writing on Race in America*. NY: Routledge, 1997.

González, José Luis, and Mónica Mansour. *Poesía negra de América*. México: Ediciones Era, 1976.

Gould, Virginia Meacham. "Slave and Free Women of Color in the Spanish Ports of the New Orleans, Mobile, and Pensacola." In Jiménez Román and Flores. 39–50.

Grillo, Christina. "Brasil quer ser chamado de moreno e só 39% se autodefinem como brancos." *Folha de São Paulo*. 25 June 1995. Web. 2 Jan. 2012. < http://almanaque.folha.uol.com.br/ racismo05.pdf>.

Grillo, Evelio. *Black Cuban, Black American*, Houston, TX: Arte Público Press, 2000.

Grimay, Aracelis. *Teeth*. Evanston, IL: Curbstone Press, 2007.

Guillén, Nicolás. *Songoro consongo*. Madrid: Grupo Anaya Comercial, 1981.

Guirao, Ramón, ed. *Órbita de la poesía afrocubana 1928–1937 (Antología)*. La Habana: Ucar y García, 1938.

Guridy, Frank. *Forging Diaspora: Afro-Cubans and African Americans in a World of Empire and Jim Crow*. Chapel Hill, NC: University of North Carolina Press, 2010.

Hernández, Carmen Dolores. *Puerto Rican Voices in English: Interviews with Writers*. Westport, CN: Praeger, 1997.

Hernández, Tanya K. "'Too Black to Be Latina/o': Blackness and Blacks as Foreigners in Latin@ Studies." *Latin@ Studies* 1.1 (Mar. 2003): 152–159.

Hernández Cruz, Víctor. *Snaps: Poems*. NY: Random House, 1969.

—. *Maraca. New and Selected Poems: 1965–2000*. Saint Paul, MN: Coffee House Press, 2001.

Hollinger, David A. *Postethnic America: Beyond Multiculturalism*. NY: Basic Books, 1995.

Hughes, Alan, and Milca Esdaille. "The Afro-Latin@ Connection: Can This Group Be the Bridge To a Broad Based Black-Hispanic Alliance?" In Jiménez Román and Flores. 364–370.

Humes, Karen R., Nicholas A. Jones, and Roberto R. Ramírez. "Overview of Race and Hispanic Origin: 2010." *2010 Census Briefs*. March 2011. Web. 23 Nov. 2011. <http://www.census. gov/prod/ cen2010/briefs/c2010br-02.pdf>.

Jahannes, Ja A. *Black Gold: An Anthology of Black Poetry*. Savannah, GA: Turner Mayfield, 2014.

Jiménez Román, Miriam, and Juan Flores, eds. *The Afro-Latin@ Reader: History and Culture in the United States*. Durham, NC: Duke UP, 2010.

Johnson, James Weldon, ed. *The Book of American Negro Poetry.* Revised Edition. Orlando, FL: Harcourt, Inc. 1983.

Kutzinski, Vera. "Afro-Hispanic American Literature." *The Cambridge History of Latin American Literature: The Twentieth Century.* Ed. Roberto González Echevarría. Cambridge, UK: Cambridge UP, 1996. 164–194.

Latin@, Simón, ed. *Antologia de la poesía negra.* Buenos Aires: Nuestra América, 1956.

Laó-Montes, Agustín. "Afro-Latin@s." *Origins: Schomburg Studies on the Black Experience.* Eds. Dodson, Howard, and Colin Palmer. East Lansing: Michigan State UP, 2008. 137–168.

Lewis, Marvin A. *Afro-Hispanic Poetry 1940–1980: From Slavery to "Negritude" in South American Verse.* Columbia, MO: University of Missouri Press, 1983.

Lomax, Alan, and Raoul Abdul, eds. *3000 Years of Black Poetry: An Anthology.* NY: Dodd & Mead, 1970.

López, Antonio. *Unbecoming Blackness: The Diaspora Cultures of Afro-Cuban America.* NY: NYU Press, 2010.

Luciano, Felipe. "You're Nothing but a Spanish Colored Kid." *The Poetry of Black America: Anthology of the 20ᵗʰ Century.* Ed. Arnold Adoff. NY: Harper Collins, 1973, 501.

—. "Jíbaro/My Pretty Nigger." In Jiménez Román and Flores. 244.

Major, Clarence, ed. *The New Black Poetry.* NY: International Publishers, 1969.

Medina, Tony. *My Old Man Was Always on the Lam.* NY: New York Quarterly Foundation, Incorporated, 2011.

Medina, Tony. *Bum Rush the Page: A Def Poetry Jam.* NY: Broadway Books, 2001.

Mills, Fiona. "Living 'In Between': The Identification of Afro-Latin@/a Literature." *Bloom's Modern Critical Views: Hispanic-American Writers.*Ed. Harold Bloom. NY: Infobase Publishing, 2009. 111-132.

—. *"Chitlins con carne": Cross-Cultural Connections in Afro-Latin@/a Literature.* Dissertation, University of North Carolina. Chapel Hill: ProQuest/UMI, 2003. (Publication No. AAT 3086583).

Miller, Adam David, ed. *Dices or Black Bones; Black Voices of the Seventies.* NY: Houghton Mifflin Co. 1970.

Morales, Jorge Luis. *Poesía afroantillana y negrista.* Río Piedras, PR: Editorial Universitaria, 1981.

Mullen. Edward. "The Emergence of Afro-Hispanic Poetry: Some Notes on Canon Formation." *Hispanic Review* 56.4 (Autumn, 1988): 435–453.

Negrón-Muntaner, Frances. "Barbie's Hair: Selling Out Puerto Rican Identity in the Global Market." *Latin@/a Popular Culture*. Eds. Michelle Habell-Pallan and Mary Romero. NY: NYU Press, 2002. 38–60.

Noble, Enrique. *Literatura afro-hispanoamericana: Poesía y prosa de ficción*. Lexington, MA: Xerox, 1973.

Ortiz, Adalberto. *Tierra, son y tambor*. Quito, Ecuador: Casa de la Cultura Ecuatoriana, 1953.

Pereda Valdés, Ildefonso, ed. *Antología de la poesía negra americana*. Santiago, Chile: Ercilla, 1936.

Rahier, Jean Muteba. *Blackness in the Andes: Ethnographic Vignettes of Cultural Politics in the Time of Multiculturalism*. New York: Palgrave McMillan, 2014.

Rodríguez, Clara E. *Changing Race: Latin@s, the Census and the History of Ethnicity in the United States*. NY: New York UP, 2000.

Ruíz del Vizo, Hortensa. *Poesía negra del Caribe y otras áreas*. Miami: Ediciones Universal, 1972.

Sanz y Díaz, José. *Lira negra*. Madrid: Aguilar, 1945.

"Sandra María Esteves." *Puerto Rican Poetry*. PBS.org. Web. 29 Nov. 2011. <http://www.pbs.org/wgbh/masterpiece/americancollection/woman/ei_poetry_esteves.html>.

Thomas, Piri. *Down These Mean Streets*, NY: Vintage Books, 1967.

Torres-Rioseco, Arturo. *The Epic of Latin American Literature*. NY: Oxford UP, 1942.

Torres-Saillant, Silvio. "Problematic Paradigms: Racial Diversity and Corporate Identity in the Latin@ Community." *Latin@s: Remaking America*. Eds. M.M. Suárez-Orozoco and M. M. Paez. Berkeley: University of California Press, 2002. 435–455.

—. "Inventing the Race: Latin@s and the Ethnoracial Pentagon." *Latin@ Studies* 1.1 (Mar. 2003): 123–151.

Toruño, Juan Felipe. *Poesía negra: Ensayo y antología*. México, DF: Coleccion Obsidiana, 1953.

Valdés-Cruz, Rosa E. *La poesía negroide en América.* Long Island City, NY: Las Américas Publising Co., 1970.

Vasconcelos, José. *The Cosmic Race/La Raza Cósmica.* Ed. And trans. D.T. Jaén. Baltimore and London: The Johns Hopkins University Press, 1997.

Wood, Peter H. "The Earliest Africans in North America." In Jiménez Román and Flores. 19-26.

ELIZABETH ACEVEDO

FEBRUARY 10, 2015

for a man nicknamed Tulile in Santiago, Dominican Republic

it never begins when the body hangs from a silk tree.

it always begins when the body hangs heavy and knotted
to the silk tree, and the tongue slips out of the mouth
—like a swollen maggot?—no, simply like tongue.

this began when the body hung heavy from rope,
knotted to the silk tree and the tongue, swollen with creole,
slipped out of the mouth, a simple tongue.

it didn't begin with the tongue, swollen with creole,
slipping out between blue lips; hands bound as if praying
couldn't push the tongue back into the mouth.

did it begin with the tongue, swollen with creole?
the shoeshine polish on the long fingers clutching a winning
lotto ticket, a stolen lamp, the tongue bragging with glee?

it will begin again by forgetting the tongue, the black shoeshine polish
on the long fingers, winning or stealing, the dirt caked on bare feet,
the tree bowing low in the park plaza in this city of caballeros.

begin here: black polish, skin, dirt. a city named after gentlemen.
the shoeshine boy, not yet twenty, known by no real name,

known for no real reason, strung up the way only a black bruised
    body takes flight.

it never ends here—does it, ti cheri? The bodies hanging from silk
    trees.

REGULARIZATION PLAN FOR FOREIGNERS, 1937

Trujillo says: *I will fix this.*
                    And so the man digs the ditches.
The dirt packs beneath his nails and when his wife kisses
his fingers at night she tells him they smell of graves.

He holds her close, his bella negra of accented Spanish,
who does not think how a single word pronounced wilted
            could force him to dig a ditch for her.

Some nights, he dreams of yellowed eyes. Of sweat-drenched
dark brows. Bodies stacked like bricks
                building a wall that slices through the sky.

Borders are not as messy as people think.

They are clear, marked by ditches, by people face down,
head-to-ankle skin-linked fences: Do Not Cross.

¿Puedes ser nada disfrazado en piel y pelo?

He's learned to turn his ears down like a donkey
when the children of Haitians plead, *Yo soy dominicano.*

At best they're mules,
                    El Jefe tells the ditch digger, who is glad
he was born on this side of the flag. *This remedy will continue,*
El Jefe *says.* And so the ditch digger repeats the instructions
        like a refrain for cutting cane:

aim low, strike wide, look away as the open earth swallows them.

JUAN DOLIO BEACH

The white man holds the girl's breast to the sunshine.
Rubs a thumb across the nylon fabric covering her nipple.
Squeezes. To test firmness? Ripeness. Her body
a highway-side fruit stand, she is chosen the same way
Momma taught me to pick avocados.

Don't stare, my cousin says. *It's just a part of the tourism.*
The girl bats at his hands, playfully. Not so playfully.
I can't tell, too far in this area of beach
where I toe the sand and sip Presidente.

The man's accent isn't English, the bills Euros and wet
as he pulls them out of his swim shorts' pocket.
She steps away. He pinches her ass. Playfully. Not so playfully.

I try to think of sex worker's rights as I watch her,
skin colored like a bruise, thick patch of sun-lightened hair.
Barely older than the last time I was here when I was fourteen.

The white man says something into her ear and laughs loud;
her smile is like the edge of a butter knife,

and my breath catches, can't tell if the sweat on my palm is mine
or the beer's. My throat becomes a tostonera
that presses the words flat
                              —Auxilio! Auxilio!—
the cries from a crowd near the water splits open the moment
and the girl runs towards the drowning.
The white man doesn't look at her as she runs
and I will his eyes my way, to see all I've been wanting to say,

but I am not really a woman from here: I own nothing he wants.

WALLFLOWER MAMBO

You ain't Dominican she says
—envious eyes admiring the shorter

gradually balding man a car's length away,
whose arms move like a tropical storm,

twirling his partner at sixty miles per hour.
Pulsing with wild abandon, fingers touching slightly,

spirits dancing swiftly; exchanging alluring glances
and inviting smiles.

Los Dominicanos they're born dancing,
and oye nene, you've already stepped on me twice.

Gaze drifting back to the balding man
wishing to charm him with her enchantress eyes—

believing that executing a fancy dip or an elegant twist
is indicative of a people's essence or a nation's pride.

I stepped on her twice. Like twice the American government
intervened and occupied the country with its military might

during the 20th century. Like twice, the number of times
we fought to gain our independence against French Haiti,

and 2/27 is the day we celebrate our liberation.
Like too many cultures are entwined in our geneology

to ever simply say
—*I am Dominican.*

Because our sultry Spanish accents stem
from conquistadors, explorers and religious zealots

with an unquenchable thirst for gold and land used to destroy
a jungle of souls which sprung from indigenous fruit.

Because our Taíno culture dates back to around 800 A.D.
and one interpretation of the island's name, Quisqueya,

means mother of the earth.Because our descendants endured
the Middle Passage, sugar cane and rice plantations,

plus the percussive beating of our hearts resemble African
    drumbeats
like Tito's congas and timbales and their steps live in the clave.

So this is my Yoruba song chanted to a Catholic saint,
meant for the thunder god, Changó.

This is my flamenco scream, plucked from inebriated guitars
—clinging to a lover's memory in brokenhearted bachata laments.

This is my flamenco stomp echoed in ballet folclórico footfalls.

This is my Dominican hue. This is my Dominican kink.
This is my Dominican twang. This is my Salsa twirl.

This is my Merengue swing. This is my Dominican dance.
This is my Dominican dance. This is my Dominican dance.

AN ABSOLUTE NECESSITY

i be
   working
   11-7

she be
   2-11

we be
   weekends together
   eating late
   sleeping late

& we be
   eating
   Haagen Daaz
   Dulce de leche
   with bananas

& we be
   watching
   new releases
   or WB
   at 2
   in the morning

or we be
   love jonesin'
   i be darius
   she be nina

i be

     say baby
     can I be your slave

she be

     uh huh

then
it gets
started

     this game
     we play
     where
     my lips

kiss

     parted hips
     thighs
     crescent moon
     birthmarks
toes too
     because
     she likes that shit

& i be

     take that
     take that
     take that

she be

     don't stop
& i be

yellow
traffic
signals
or
yield
signs
cause
were not on
any schedule
so there's
no need
to rush this love

& she be
        like
        quit
        teasing
        me

& i be
        like
        hssssh

delivering
        warm
        sensations
        to exposed back
        to tense shoulders

relishing
        strong
        loving
        masculine
        hands

constantly separated
by an
excess
of obligations

she be
tonight's
obligation
sensitive to
desperate
for my
touch

she be
daisies or
forget-me-nots
submissive
to my wind

she be
this this
little piggy
straw house

i be
big bad wolf
blowing her
house down

we be
lionel and flashdance
dancing on the ceiling
and *oh oh oh*
what a feeling

we be

    amnesic

i be

    what's my name
    what's my name
    what's my name

she be

    do you
    love it baby
    is it good
    to you
    baby

we be

    muffled screams
    through
    sweaty palms

we be

    thump thump
    thumping
    pound pound
    pounding
    sleeping walls

we be

    back scratching
    biting
    breathing heavy
    & sweating
    & sweating
    & sweating
    & com

    pletely
    soiling
    clean sheets

we be

       ohhhh god

we be

       legs cramping
       toes curling
       & bruised

we be

       hmmm

we be

       ummmm

we be

       weekends together

BASEBALL'S TRAVELIN' MEN: IN PRAISE OF THE LATIN AND NEGRO LEAGUES

After Martín Espada's "Alabanza"

Alabanza. Praise the ballplayers with their call and response
and scars on their bodies that said Oye,
black athletes with ties to the Negro Leagues,
the sole option for play decades ago.
Praise the talent in the Negro Leagues: men
black as the bottom of the sea, to a honey gold.
Alabanza. Praise the Kansas City-Paseo YMCA
where Rube Foster and others birthed the teams,
plucked dirt from the gutter, refined it to cleanliness.
Alabanza. Shall we praise Gus Greenle, his numbers racket and
   Pittsburgh,

for providing a place where only the ball was white,
so that every action meant a hurling, a casting out,
a slamming away and dismantling the institution, sanctifying
blackness. Praise the blackness. *Alabanza.*

Praise Quisqueya's shine from across the Atlantic ocean,
like gold glimpsed through the eyes of ancient conquistadors.
Praise the conquistadors, the island's Taínos, its fruit, its soil.
Alabanza. Praise the brutality of Rafael Leonidas Trujillo Molina
    (Chapitas)
taking Greenle's ballclub and putting it in Santo Domingo.
Praise the breaking of contracts, luggage filled with cash, Satchel
    Paige
and Cool Papa, Josh Gibson and Sammy Bankhead, Cy Perkins
    and the others arriving on
biplanes landing on the Río Higuamo,
right in front of the main church.
Alabanza. Praise Trujillo's friends, enforcers of the national image
and their leader's prestige: murdering civilians
who opposed him—inserting politics into a sport developing its
    purity.

Alabanza. Praise the scout under Trujillo's orders who conspired
    to defraud the
Crawfords of Satchel Paige and got arrested twice during his
    pursuit. *Alabanza.*

After the applause wilder than applause,
after Satchel and the team understood
that anything bearing Trujillo's name will not lose,
after unveiling the secrets of a thousand pitches: the trouble ball,
the triple curve, the whipsy-dipsy-do, a swing, a miss,

after military forces clobbered those against Ciudad Trujillo,
after the near loss of three games to none,
and the winning of the pennant by Ciudad Trujillo,
for a time the Latin and Negro Leagues shined
with the greatest players to ever play,
like the conquistadors' gold. Gold I say, even if the fans cannot
    tell us
about the gray in Trujillo's mustache, shaved at the edges,
except the three to five centimeter above the centre of the lip.
Because he had no lips.
Gold I say, to name the fastballs flung in revolutions
across the mound of this stadium and stadiums to come.
Alabanza, I say, even if Trujillo had no lips.

Alabanza. When the leagues began, from America, Latin
    America,
México and the Caribbean Basin,
revolutions of fastballs rose and drifted towards each other,
lightening-crowned, and one said with a Spanish tongue:
Let me play. We have no field here.
And the other said with an African tongue:
I will let you play. Baseball is all we have.

BREAKING STRENGTH

Maybe she knows.
Maybe she averts my gaze

so as not to reveal the feeling is mutual;
maybe she wants her razor-thin lips

to slice fragments of her smile
into my tongue

—like I do; like I thought
minutes after meeting her.

Maybe this talk of poetry & art
will lead her fingers

to graze the qualities
& intersections of my hands,

to detect the Mount of Luna and of Venus,
and how we hold words differently.

I have despised this part of my body,
this vestige of molecules

that bind my father to me:
his other women, neglect,

his scent of whiskey, Menthol Lights.
A poacher's knot, properly dressed & set

tightening its hold
for a smile wide enough

to hold my family's future;
teeth white enough

to purify the abandonment
of home.

MORIR SOÑANDO*

The art is in the squeeze:
in the pushing & pressing
of palm & tabletop;
in the rolling & pounding

of lemon on floor or wall.
Tío Eliezer said this
to all us children. We watched
as tío mixed milk & sugar—

introduced spoon to mouth,
tongue to drink. Nostrils clenching,
lips pursing. Repeating the process
until raising the corners of his lips

into a neat grin. We waited
seasons for moments of beverage
& bonding. We mimicked man
while vaguely aware of the meaning.

Sometimes, I turned the crank,
sharp wheel cutting into metal lids.
Tío adding evaporated milk,
2 cups of lemon juice & vanilla extract,

then serving it
over crushed ice.

---

*Morir Soñando, literally means "To Die Dreaming," is a delicious drink from the Dominican Republic very similar to an Orange Julius. My uncle prepared it with lemons.

Now,
as a father,

I know the secret lies
in a relaxed & stable grip—
keeping the thumb powerful
& the hand soft, wrapping fingers

around the handle
—as if a bow—
& in the continuous stirring
of sour with sweet.

SURVIVAL

the struggle is really simple
i was born
i was taught how to behave
i was shown how to accommodate—
i resist being humanized
into feelings not my own—
the struggle is really simple
i will be born
i will not be taught how to behave
i will not make my muscles vestigial
i will not digest myself

A MONGO AFFAIR

On the corner by the plaza
in front of
the entrance to González-Padín
in old San Juan,
a black Puerto Rican talks
about "the race"
he talks of Boricuas
who are in New York on welfare
and on lines waiting for food stamps,
"yes, it's true, they've been taken out
and sent abroad, and those that
went over tell me that they're
doing better over there than here;
they tell me they get money

and medical aid
that their rent is paid
that their clothes get bought
that their teeth get fixed,
is that true?"
on the corner by the entrance to González-Padín
I have to admit that he has been
lied to, misled,
that I know that all the goodies
he named humiliate the receiver,
that a man is demoralized
when his woman and children
beg for weekly checks,
that even the fucking a man does
on a government-bought mattress
draws the blood from his cock
cockless, sin espina dorsal
mongo—that's it!
a welfare fuck is a mongo affair!
mongo means flojo
mongo means bloodless
mongo means soft
mongo cannot penetrate
mongo can only tease
but it can't tickle
the juice of the earth-vagina
mongo es el bicho Taíno
porque murió
mongo es el borinqueño
who's been moved
to the inner-city jungles
of north american cities
mongo is the Rican who survives

in the tar jungle of Chicago
who cleans, weeps, crawls
gets ripped off,
sucks the eighty dollars a week
from the syphilitic
down deep frustrated
northern man—
viejo negro africano
Africa Puerto Rico
sitting on department store entrances
don't believe the deadly game
of northern cities paved with gold and plenty
don't believe the fetching dream
of life improvement in New York
the only thing you find in Boston
is a soft leather shoe up your ass,
viejo, anciano africano, Washington
will send you in your old age
to clean the battlefields
in Korea and Vietnam;
you'll be carrying a sack
and into that canvas
you'll pitch
las uñas
los intestinos
las piernas
los bichos mongos
of Puerto Rican soldiers
put at the front to face
¡sí!
to face the bullets, bombs, missiles
¡sí!
The artillery

¡sí!
to face the violent hatred of Nazi Germany
to confront the hungry anger of the world
viejo negro
viejo puertorriqueño
the north offers us pain
and everlasting humiliation
IT DOES NOT COUGH UP
THE EASY LIFE: THAT IS A LIFE
viejo que has visto la isla
perder sus hijos
are there guns to deal with
genocide, expatriation?
are there arms to hold
the exodus of borinqueños
from Borinquen?
we have been moved
we have been shipped
we have been parcel posted
first by water, then by air
el correo has special prices
from the "low island element" to be
removed, then dumped
into the inner-city ghettos
viejo, viejo, viejo
we are the minority
here in Borinquen
we, the Puerto Rican,
the original man of this island
is in the minority
I writhe with pain
I jump with anger
I know

I see
I am "la minoría de la isla"
viejo, viejo anciano,
do you hear me?
there are no more Puerto Ricans
in Borinquen
I am the minority everywhere
I am among the few in all societies
I belong to a tribe of nomads
that roam the world without
a place to call a home,
there is no place that is ALL MINE
there is no place that I can
call mi casa,
I, yo, Miguel ¡Me oyes, viejo!
I, yo, Miguel
el hijo de María Socorro y Miguel
is homeless, has been homeless
will be homeless
in the to be
and the come
Miguelito, Lucky, Bimbo
you like me have lost
your home,
and to the first idealist
I meet I'll say
don't lie to me
don't fill me full of vain
disturbing love for an island
filled with Burger Kings
for I know
there are no cuchifritos
in Borinquen

I remember last night
viejito lindo
when your eyes fired me
with trust,
do you hear that?
with trust
and when you said
that you would stand by me
should any danger threaten
I halfway threw myself
into your arms to weep
mis gracias
I loved you
viejo negro
I would have slept
in your arms
I would have caressed
your curly gray hair
I wanted to touch
your wrinkled face
when your eyes fired me
with trust
viejo corazón puertorriqueño
your feelings cocinan
en mi sangre
el poder de realizarme
and when you whispered
your anger into my ears
when you spoke of
"nosotros los que estamos
preparados con las armas"
it was talk of future
happiness

my ears had not till
that moment heard such
words of promise and of guts
in all of Puerto Rico,
old man with the golden chain
and the medallion with an indian
on your chest
I love you
I see in you
what has been
what is coming
and will be
and over your grave
I will write
HERE SLEEPS
A MAN
WHO SEES ALL OF
WHAT EXISTS
AND THAT WHICH WILL EXIST.

A SALSA BALLET: ANGELITOS NEGROS

Willie Colón, Composer
Marty Sheller, Conductor

2 trumpets
1 trombone
2 saxophone / alto and baritone
1 bass
1 piano
1 guitar
1 trap drum
1 bongo

1 conga
1 timbalero
6 violins
1 flute and piccolo

Prologue
Good Vibrations Sound Studio,
the date is for three
but we arrived at 2:30 p.m.,
the occasion: the first recording
of Willie Colón's score of "A Salsa Ballet":
the studio is refrigerator cool,
the vibes are mellow,
the rhythm is sleepy slow,
the set is slowly pulling together,
musicians arrive, slapping hands
talking through months of absence
into hugs and tightly held hands,
they are coming together
to invent
the sound that Willie
has in his head,
musicians are Willie's brush,
musicians are Willie's sound partners,
today's the day for an orgy of sounds,
today is the day for the birth
of a new Latin perception
of sound,
Willie walks around,
four months into his pregnancy,
I see prenatal rhythmic juices pour
out of his pores as notes shoot
pitches of sounds high into the atmosphere,

musicians come together in a holy
trust, the bond of marriage for
a trumpet and a saxophone
is in the listening
that they do to one another,
there in the listening,
there is hope.

Take One
Jon Fausty engineers
the recording machine,
his hands control the sound
that is recorded,
what people hear
is the selection and balances
that he invents at his electronic
keyboard,
the heat is rising,
the ears are hot,
attention is total,
the blend is on and as
everybody listens
the salsa melts individuality,
the flow is clear sound,
every instrument can be distinguished,
the Latin beat is on electronic
tape.

Take Two
"Hey Marty, let's put one
on from the top,
I haven't done one yet,"
Marty shakes his head

"OK."
Take two: trap drummer
is added,
Marty beats out
basic rhythms,
the drummer riffs as he
plays into recording track.

Take Three
The piccolo player argues
that the ear cans are too loud,
"lower the ear phones,"
the take starts but Mauricio
stops it,
"still too loud,"
Jon,
"still too loud?"
Mauricio,
"Yes."
Jon,
"I'll turn them down."
Willie,
"wait, wait, wait,
he's got to do the bomba."
Marty,
"yes, wait."
The take is played,
Marty asks Mauricio
if he wants to hear
the solo—he nods yes.
Jon asks the drummer,
"is there anything you need in your ear?"
drummer,

"yeah, a little more bell."
Alfonso listens to the tape,
feels the rhythms,
lets loose
and moves deep into
the salsa, till he releases
his rhythms and drum talks
his soul to the tape.
Mauricio takes up the flute,
listens for another count,
then plays into the tape what Willie has
in his head—and it is
clear that the other
mind here is the electronic
composer that Jon is engineering.

Take Four
Four violins
two cellos
have been prepared
for electronic digestion
and integration onto
master-minded
Master Tape
"phones on the way, Martin,"
Jon puffs his Kool,
jumps out of his chair,
runs out to fix the phones
comes back, looks around,
spins his chair, checks the
temperature, pushes start,
Marty motions,
"I want to run it through
once before we take,"

Jon understands,
the take begins but Marty's
running fast,
Willie stops the take,
"Marty, it's really half of that."
Jon plays with the quality
of the sound as he searches
for a brassy violin tone,
Jon's balance is a treble
pitched violin that's almost
square dance Nuyorican salsa
electronically conceived.
Jon,
"Marty don't count aloud,"
the string players are excited,
one of them looks up astonished,
"hey, you've got a lot of heavy stuff
on that tape,"
Willie smiles and suggests,
"Marty, why don't you direct,"
"that's what I'm doing," Marty says,
he directs a take,
looks up, face full of sweat,
"let's take a break,"
string players reject the break,
"let's do it again," they say,
Marty comes into the control booth,
Mauricio suggests that the horns
be taken out of the can,
it's done and the string players feel
it's easier so the take is final
and the string players leave
joyous,

Marty comes into the control booth,
Jon starts from the top and as the
tape plays Marty shakes Jon
on the shoulders and says,
"Pisces produce,"
Jon smiles as George, the young blood
that works for them, slaps
Jon five because he's Pisces too.

Take Five
Yomo Toro comes next,
here comes el cuatrito
de los Nuyoricans,
aquí viene Yomo Toro
Puerto Rico,
Yomo's next but first he
makes a call,
he's watched it all
and now comes Yomo,
he records the prelude
of the ballet,
Willie asks him for something
"más ajibarao."
Yomo grounds the chords
in Nuyorican salsa as
Willie calls out,
"algo bien cabrón"
Yomo says,
"no me jodas, Willie
manda un violín."
Yomo is master cuatrista
showing his pleasure
in calling his

performance, "un concierto,"
Willie agrees to the last take
and the tape is moved to the
bomba and Yomo listens
before doing a take,
the rhythm moves in as Willie
sings it and Yomo tries,
Yomo says to Willie
"Oye, vente tú aquí
y cántame el totín totín ese,"
Willie leaves the electronic capsule
and begins
"totín, totín
totín, totín."
Yomo shifts chords transforming
el cuatro into a classical rap
and today a salsa ballet
has just been put on
the face of the planet
Earth.

RELISH/SABROSURA

I'm frightened by so much heat,
sweating so much desire, sliding,
greased by tenderness,
enduring the sensual whirlpool
of your lips moistened by mutual saliva,
your hands caressing
my juices, transforming them into flesh,
made of blood and sperm,
the only actual possibility
for desire become the gelatin

of you and me
writhing in the sea.
Me da miedo sentir tanto calor,
sudar tanto deseo, resbalar,
engrasado por la ternura,
que perdura en el remolino sensual
de tus labios mojados con saliva mutua,
tus manos acariciando
mi sabrosura, convirtiéndola en carne,
construida de sangre y leche,
la única posibilidad actual,
del deseo hecho el tembleque
de tú y yo
estrujándonos en el mar.

RAY BARRETO: DECEMBER 4, 1976

Eddie Conde, congas
Edwina, congas
Richie Cruz, timbales & congas,
trio of intense rhythmic improvisation,
mobilizing muscle energy to pleasure,
as Barretto articulates
the pain of being artit in need of fair recognition,
he looks out and delivers medicine
to ears that follow the rhythmic clear talk
he gives out with the prac-ca-ta of his voice,
Barretto maestro,
Barretto, maestro to futuristic people
who have wakeful dreams for breakfast
and soured-up imagination for supper,
daylight is a long Star Trek episode
that matures to ripe old age by day's end,

Eddie, Edwina, Richie
mystical musicians inventing
patterns tailored to desire,
breaking through the present tension precision
into salsa root sinceridad,
Barretto maestro,
listening to Eddie, Edwina, Richie,
paying respect with your ears,
just like they learned your manhood through their ears,
Barretto, Doctor of Body Motion,
you release the monster that chews
the working man from inside out,
la gente se menea con tu ritmo,
sus músculos sudan cansancio,
sobre el piso que los zapatos limpian
según bailan tu música,
Barretto, yo he visto un baile entero,
un baile de 20,000 personas
en Madison Square Garden,
respirar como si fueran una sola persona,
no miles, pero un solo corazón boricua,
Barretto, maestro del working class,
when you arrived at the Nuyorican Poets' Café
our hearts swung open for you as we made way
for your centered presence,
qué limpio tú estás,
no static in your pure intent of love.

PROEM II

Infirmities take over the body without warning or proclamation.
The potential for infection is endless and the capacity for the body
to restrain and combat the armies of trillions of cells that would

destroy the biological balance and health of the body is, at best, limited. Very often, the body's defenses are helpless.

We have known the power of plagues from the beginning of time. It is not new to die by the hundreds of thousands. It is often hunger that claims whole populations. However, in the late twentieth century, it is not hunger alone that is responsible for mass death, but viruses. These viruses have a capacity for mutating so rapidly that medication is rendered useless before it can successfully treat the symptoms or help the body retrieve its innate fighting capacity. In the face of this biological warfare, we must devise a moral field that defines our behavior towards each other. There are plagues carried by the air—in those cases, we quarantine the bearer. There are, on the other hand, plagues that can be controlled if we use personal restraint and care in how we meet to share love with each other.

HIV

I.
Revelation
To tell in strength. "The telling," when to tell, leads to a discovery between the teller and the listener. Acquiring knowledge; the teller holds his/her information as a tool for health, movement towards truth.

II.
Salvation
To converse as an attempt to recuperate, a holding on not to die.

III.
Speech
To acquire "language" for talking about a plague in the self.

IV

Sharing Secrets

Who to tell? Is there someone? The search for what to tell.

V.

Mature Masculinity

Welcome the responsibility to do the work of building verbs, adjectives and nouns for mortality and its subsequent eternal breaking of concrete.

I. Revelation

Revel at ion,
rebel at I on a course
to regret erections,
to whip the cream in my scrotum
till it hardens into unsweetened,
unsafe revved elations
of milk turned sour
by the human body,
of propagation of destruction.
The epiphany: I am unsafe,
you who want me
know that I who want you,
harbor the bitter balm of defeat.

II. Salvation

If I were to show you
how to continue holding on,
I would not kiss you,
I would not mix my fluids with yours,
　　　　for your salvation
　　　　cannot bear the live weight
　　　　of your sharing liquids with me.

III. Language

To tell,

to talk,

to tongue into sounds

how I would cleanse you with urine,

how my tasting tongue would wash your body,

how my saliva and sperm would bloat you,

to touch you in our lovemaking

and not tell you

would amount to murder,

to talk about how to language this

so that you would still languish

in my unsafe arms and die,

seems beyond me,

I would almost rather lie

but my tongue muscle moves involuntarily

to tell of the danger in me.

IV. Of Health

To use my full and willing

body to reveal and speak

the strength that I impart

without fear,

without killing,

without taking away what I would give,

to use my man's tongue

to share,

to give,

to lend,

to exact nothing,

to receive all things,

to expand my macho

and let the whole world

into the safety of my mature masculinity.

V. Quarantine
Sometimes I fear touching your plump ear lobes,
I might contaminate you.
Sometimes I refuse odors that would
drive my hands to open your thick thighs.
Sometimes closing my ears to your voice
wrenches my stomach and I vomit to calm wanting.
Can it be that I am the bearer of plagues?
Am I poison to desire?
Do I have to deny yearning for firm full flesh
so that I'll not kill what I love?
No juices can flow 'tween you and me.
Quicksand will suck me in.

NUYORICAN ANGEL VOICE

Little Jimmy Scott speaks music,
stringing his lyrics together,
never has any angel heard him sing a melody,
"All of me,
why not take all of me."
Jimmy talks his passion by hitting the syllables
the joy of sweat on limbs becoming one blood flow
"That's deeper than the deep blue sea is,"
you see
"that's how deep it goes if it's real
but if you let me love you
it's for sure I'm gonna love you
all the way."
Never just a melody,
always hitting the feeling,

androgyny never existed except in someone's body,
if it's a question of "*all the way,*
only a fool can say,"
without being loved all the way,
yes! "*all the way,*"
'til "*day by day*" we make it deeper by far
than any ocean,
I am wider than your hold can take,
but I'm yours to stay
through the years
"*day by day*"
you're making all my dreams come true,
all the way to where I am yours alone
yes, I am yours to stay,
'til you understand how much I love you
and those mourning roses
I've sprinkled with tears,
how I've traveled to be where you are,
how long is the journey from here to your star
and if I ever lose you
how much would I cry
"*just how deep is the ocean*
how high is the sky,"
just how long is the suffering
yes, "*how deep is the ocean,*
how high is the sky,"
before seeing you gets hazy
and a gentle touch turns hard.

NUYORICAN ANGEL PAPO

(The Bi-Sexual Super Macho)

I.
The Fourth of July fireworks
went unseen by me.
If you could not see them
then I would not see
the New York skyline
ablaze in colored fire.
The red, white and blue
would climb to the moon
without my Fourth of July
Coney Island, Bushwick, Brooklyn
churchgoing,
newfound friend,
we parted in the name of fear,
the not falling into the black hole
of speedy passions
and underdeveloped love.
I drove you home,
shook your hand as we opened the trunk
to get your pack,
but you know, really,
I almost pushed you back
into the car, the hearth,
the fireplace of warmth,
the wheels that would have,
could have crossed the Williamsburg Bridge,
into Loisaida,
driven us into a nest of dreams
and corruption,
and purity and cleanliness

entwined in next to perfect lust,
yet, no, instead,
I didn't see the fireworks.
Instead, I sat thinking about
how nice it was to have left you
without our rushed desires fueling
the blazing Fourth of July skyline of New York.

II.
I tried
to separate
where we should start to touch.
I tried postponing, first with "Straight out of Brooklyn,"
then food,
but you were on an impulse
to burn fire, to scorch passions,
I should've left you in Bushwick,
without numbers exchanged,
I could have lied about my name,
yet could have and would have
live in conditional tenements,
where on the third floor
we committed unconditional love,
knee-to-knee
nude from the waist down,
lust-fueled hands full
of belly buttons, buttocks and meat.

TAÍNA DREAMS

(let's hear it for Cristobal Colón)

>The children give themselves to the ground
>their chests whistling like the wind
>
>We did nothing
>to stop their singing
>Fed their dreams
>the white meat of the *batata,*
>manipulate their mouths
>open
>watch them eat the pulp
>the color of our nightmare's skin
>
>the worn prepare the soil
>for graves
>our throats rattling like gourds
>with the names of our fallen forebearers
>the organs of their language
>held within our molars
>like flecks of gold

ROSA'S BEAUTY

>it was a ritual
>one Saturday a month
>storm or shine, broke or not
>Mami would drive us to Rosa's Beauty
>near la 17 in Santurce

where a barrio's history is the mad work of knives and men
but there we were on our way to get our hair done,
to be called *chinitas*
straighten out kinks we couldn't correct in our everyday
couldn't make family better, bring fathers back home
but we could look real nice
like real Puerto Rican girls should
it was like walking into your girlfriend's house,
Rosa's, with its lime green tile floor,
slippery with black hair clippings
under a forest of high-heeled, flip-flopped women
spitting fire in Dominican Spanish,
frying pan hot, *ají* in each word
room aflame with their lipstick
all talking the same *bochinche*
about who was doing who
and who got deported off the island
and what *puta* cut what *cabrón*
five hours amid smoke and ash
lotions and dyes tinting the air
scissors and mouths moving
to any Mambo radio tune
and by then my head was burning alive
with the power of the relaxer
unable to wash it out
for fear of staying black
and we all knew that's what we didn't want
we wanted to shake our hair
(since we couldn't shake our skin)
loosen wool into Chinese silk
smooth flat and fit for feathering
on Antillen days under salt and sun
ruining a girl's reputation for looking right and good

now I'm thirty and a box of Dark and Lovely is a stinging
memory of a young girl's addiction
dishonoring the women born of the coastline
mother, grandmother, before even them
women swimming seas, bearing storms, fighting misery
with hair stronger than the ropes that held them

FOR BLACK GIRLS WHO DON'T KNOW

Amiri Baraka at HR-57, Washington DC, 1995

I was a girl who knew nothing
of jazz. Just another girl in line, waiting for you to read
the rest of a twenty-volume suicide note.
What did I know of your coming music,
your blue-banded heart, slit-gong tongue,
hepcat in all your bones. I was a girl
who knew nothing of love supreme, still stuck
in her papi's lounge-singer record scratches.
How you would leave me shook, body
a gourd in the hands of egun-eguns, dug up
for song, rolled under my skins,
tripping me up, rocks in my soles,
forgetting me how to heel-toe.
You walk in hot,
hot with flu, 103 degrees of hot
and climbing mountains
in your strut, hands fast and flailing,
flinging words with sweat, cool,
but not yet hot like cool.
You step up in that right knee strut,
heathens!
Stage-stride in a broken line,
your body stamping out a long-lost morse code.

Freedom Jazz, you call it and
throw your shoulders back,
back against the band's yielding riffs,
bent back, as if your poem were a sax against your lips,
reaching towards the ceiling for legroom.
What shaman in your staccato, hand-smacking leg,
as if all of you were made of word,
tapping the air, our ears, the wall with bop,
backbeat, timbale, crisp lettuce sound.
You start the long Whoooooo towards eeee
and I think of the dizzy ways we mourn.
Blood confetti storms, scattering.
Right there In that moment, I loved you.
You with your eyes closed against the room,
as if you could make that horn just be.

PORTORICAN ANTHEM

El esterio-típico

I am a puertorriqueña
spic in foreign tongue
I brought the cockroaches to new york
and ruined chicago slums

the caribbean's footless black oyster
sucking on neighboring juice
I drink ron all day and
lace these veins with poppy tea

aye, Papi
I prostitute for rice and beans
yeah—I eat government cheese

a true patriot to my red white and blue?
I broke my inglés long ago
and blew america up

and like a conch-shelled demon
I fell
my legs parted
one foot in the gringolandia sand
the other
in the wet crotch
of my old
San
Juan

PULL

Sec. Barranca, Km. .08, Arecibo, PR

By the roadside a colt just shy of revelation yanks back at the
reins of his master's hands. They are a boy's hands, nervous, new
in the art of command. To passerby, it is a *plena* of sneakers and
hooves, *jíbaro* and colt, youth bareback and leaning against the
sunset shade of a cowboy western, their neighing broken and
high, only the street certain of their divide widening.

Between them the brink, the everyday, the gossiping backroad,
the lazy eyes of houses, loom of telephone wire, cigarette talk, the
envelope of their bony breath. Between boy and horse, the
avenue's constant caulk and rail. What will it do, after everyone's
been called home?

And who says the boy has learned anything about the grit of a horse's gait. And what could he know about the machine of a sky bent on storm. Who knows what tooth sensed rain. What fly buzzed against cheeks flushed with the work of being man.

And who will hold them back, boy and boy, two legs and four, the spike of a field waiting, the leather snapping strap watching their stop, rush and tug, the dust road devouring a sting of asphalt and mistake. It takes only a strike and the rider sways, clockwork, they both are towed, eyes peeled back, somewhere in them the momentum of a herd, their manes a gust of what it means to go.

MAKE-BELIEVE

33 Chestnut Street, Binghamton

I have grown tired of skunk. His smell pervades everything, weaving though window screens, sewing itself to bath towels. It speaks to me from radio speakers. I confuse it with the news.

The first time its funk found haven in my nostrils, I woke with a start, rushed around the house, checking furnaces and burners for dead pilots. Could not help but inhale the odor of borderlines,

country to city, trail to alley, trespass and trolls, bedtime stories coming in on a wolf's wet fur. Dawn and I catch the scent of all things I've ever run from: sulfur, exhaust, armpit, the body's slow

uneven push towards the end of the road. Winter helps the skunk forage into Leroy trash cans, nuzzle twiggy hydrangeas, rove into backyard piss and corner oil slicks. 5:10 and an errant townie skunk nudges me listless, reminds me to change sheets, empty ice cube trays, move the Hoover from its post in the hall. Those days, I beg to collect the remnants of a Puerto Rican make-believe,

the wonder in a graveyard of guavas, cracked and leaking on a hill. On those early mornings, all the generalizations of what is island are brought back to life: breath in yucca and orchid skin,

overtures of rue and bay leaf, the dark beer aura of cabbage escaping out a kitchen door. I squint and am tangy with cliche, close to the fragrant part of a grandmother's hair, nutmeg and salt, a hint of geranium

dirt. I dive, inhale two hundred kilometers deep, nostrils flared like the entrances to sweaty caves.

BOCA GRANDE

I was always been called *Boca Grande.*
My imagination too loud for our small two-bed room apartment.
My singing solos into the hairbrush too intense.
Roared high-pitched monologues on make-believe stages in the
  living room.
until the stern looks of adult eyes drowned my speech—

¡Cállate! ¡Baja la voz, niña!

Silence has never been in my nature.
Roared in my mother's belly;
conceived from her desire, released in speech
I was her wish, her prayer,
her first spoken word.
Born to the sound of thunder;
to whisper with the dead,
to shout with the living,
I was born to make noise
to rattle shells, to beat drums, to chant, to dance
to dream in free verse, to bless and to curse—

¡Porque mami dijo que así es que se reza!

I may be too boisterous for church pillars and Corinthians,
but I got the perfect pitch for areytos, pow-wows and bembés
and God reassured me she speaks my language.

Boca Grande.
Wear that title proudly.
Use it to juxtapose the mantra fed to me by inferior boys
who feared my sassy wit
and pitchfork sense of humor.
Hoping I would buy into the belief
que esta boca es buena pa' mamar y más na'.

As my tone grew a little deeper,
framing itself to fit my womanhood
I realized I was gifted this voice, these lips,
to combat my height,
to challenge the limitations placed on my sex,
to reclaim the forbidden sounds attached to joy,
to moan and stretch in satisfaction, cry in awakening,
sing pleasure in staccato, give its rightful name,
scream it aloud through the night—

¡Boca grande pero con gusto!

Many have tried to impose silence on what was born of light,
of blare, of uproar. To silence the years of ancestral voices that
    surge through my fingers,
that form petroglyphs on my fingerprints, that possess my feet.
To re-enslave the spirits of *la madama, la morena, la doncella y la
    gitana,*
that have walked with me since conception,
whip them back into submission at the hand of your disapproval.

Do you know the sound of freedom?

It is in each syllable that escapes
the throats of little girls who play loud games
of pretend and splatter paint on satin dresses.

Freedom:
It is in young ladies who are called *desobediente y malcria'*
for daring to talk themselves into a new form of existence.

Freedom:
It is in the descendants of Boricua women whose wombs were
made barren too soon by government doctors cutting fallopian
tubes in the hopes our vocal cords would follow.

Freedom:
It is in the butterflies that grew wings despite Trujillo's attempts
at making insubordinate Dominican beauties extinct, ignoring
the power of the collective female voice to do more than just
soothe babies.

Freedom:
It is in the hands of clandestine teachers that patiently instructed
illiterate *campesinos* how to curl their soil-stained fingers around a
pencil for the first time

Freedom:
It is in the mysteries whispered by Yoruba priestesses that guard
sacred songs and rituals of ceremonies until we are ready to
receive them.

Yes, I am *Boca Grande!*

Presenta',

Hija de Yemayá, there is no taming this ocean

This voice will continue to ripen in tune with my body,
continue to command airwaves until I can no longer retain a
    single breath,
and even then
my spirit will rattle trees and ring bells,
and although you may want to dismiss it as just the wind,
I will remind you that even she has a name,
and you will say it.

Bringing forth the memory of all the women throughout history
who have fought to break sound barriers,
who have mended their broken tongues,
who will no longer bite their lips,
who will be feared by the same social norms
and proper etiquette that tried to restrain them,
warning them
of their delicate *re-PUTA-ción*.
Esas malditas de Bocas Grandes who
refuse to keep still and be quiet.

NEGRITO LINDO

Aquí to be called Negrito means to be called love —Pedro Pietri

¡Negrito lindo, tú eres la Bomba de barrio!

He is brown sugar, *melao encorbatao*.
Fights against the black man's burden,
the Boricua blues, all with a swagger *ensazonao*.
Un hombre cordial con el tumbao de la calle.

Made of East HHHhhhharlem street concrete.
Flavored with Brooklyn cement sentiments,
entered the belly of the beast,
emerged a transformed man.

Through academia he redeemed
his once blood-stained hands.
His empowerment was self-taught.

Went from Young Lord fitted berets,
to Caribbean fedora hats,
expensive suits, wing-tip shoes,
his *jibarito* smile completes that suit and tie.
A once hot-headed street thug, now a classy cool cat,
he believes education helps develop tolerance.

¡Negrito lindo!

Proclaiming our people have the genes of geniuses,
so we must refuse to be mules.
Still releasing the trauma of conquest.
Trying to shed the overseer's side effects.
Pain slowly released over centuries,
he demands more of our youth,
the next generation, *la juventud–*

> *"Párate firme, que*
> *tú no naciste para sentarte,*
> *tienes que ser fuerte fuerte,*
> *pa' lante pa' siempre"*

He advises them to
read, speak and write well.
Encourages them to find role models within themselves.
Some say the big fish die by the mouth,
but not this one, no sir!
Él tiene la clave en la boca,
que entona con el pra-ca-ta y el gua-guan-có del corazón.
Cadence of his voice resurrects the kings of the past,
calls on caciques to rise.

The tempo of his speech steady,
with the strength of an old Negro spiritual,
the heat of a *rumbero*, the grace of *el flamenco*.
He is the descendant of *los pioneros.*

Refuses to be intimidated by any crowd,
never to be placed in just any one category,
never to be boxed in.
The census needs a new form for this kind of man.
He is more than simple set of words.
No one definition, ever-evolving
life-long learner, international traveler—

¡Negrito lindo!

Orgulloso de todo que es de color.
No set of parenthesis can define,
contain or restrain this blood line,
that holds the beauty of the world
it each of its DNA strands.
A genetic rainbow
set in the soil of many distant lands
that stretch to Africa, Asia, Europe, Ponce, San Juan,
Cuba, Nueva York, el Bronx, *de aquí, hasta el monte.*

He took our dark-skin *abuelas* out of the kitchen
and invited them to dance;
celebrated their hereditary *sancocho,*
savored their racially mixed *mofongo,*
relished in their *café con poquita leche* without shame.
Found beauty in the mahogany *tabaco y ron* hues
of our people.

Made it safe to say: ¡Yo soy negro!

He took
Black, Kinky, Nappy, *Prieto, Moreno*

He took
Boricua, Jíbaro, Jabao, Mulatto, Mestizo, Mesclao

He took
Ex-con, *Boca grande, Malcriao, Desobediente, Presentao*

He took
Calle, Tíguere-intranquilo, Rebusero-reformao

And made it
           all so beautiful

            ¡Negrito lindo, tú eres la bomba del barrio!

¡BOMBA!

No nací en Puerto Rico
        pero nací con este ritmo
                encarnado a mi ser
                        es el llamado del antiguo africano
                            que al palenque fue a caer

Cimarrona en el alma que descarga
cuando oigo ese ritmo seduciéndome
es el sentido de la bomba
heredado, encarnado
en las plantas de mis pies

No tomé clases, ni escuché al profesor de baile
                porque puede que me dañe lo que surge
                naturalmente

no se escucha con oído, es un sentido distinto,
        que hace que yo tome pasos de hace muchos años
           antes de yo nacer
              porque la bomba y yo nos
                conocemos
                  desde el momento que mi
                    alma entró en este ser

Hay los que me critican,
me dicen:
"Pero tú no eres negra, nena,
ni si quiera tienes piel canela,
y mira esa melena, muy buena"

Y yo le digo:
        ¡Bomba!
Vuelvo y le repito:
        ¡Bomba!

Porque por vía de mi abuelito
        la bomba me trajo ese sentido
           y por eso te digo
              vuelvo y repito
                que aunque no nací en
                Puerto Rico
                  la bomba y su ritmo
              está encarnado a mi ser

WHEN THEY CALL MY NAME

for Pedro Robles Miranda

Papá
I search for you

in dusty census records, immigrations logs, voter lists,
call your name in empty libraries,
and I am regularly disappointed by your absence on ancestry.com

I call for you and hear lies

They tell me you are gone, eclipsed your Taíno spoken word with
European written records and call you illiterate, question the
purity of your blood, claim your nation vanished in the 1500s,
told me our people perished in a sea of canons and Christianity,
bounced and buried our babies in blankets of small pox, broke
our maracas, drums and caciques until we forget our songs, and
mocked our accents when we finally learned to speak again

Papá
they lied

Told me they burned all your wooden cemis, encased the Gods
in glass and sold them to the Smithsonian, outlawed farming of
yucca and yautia so you'd starve, obscured our yucayeques and
ball courts so we would forget the feeling of community, called
our bohikes senile, snorted the last cohoba at a presidential
celebration, uprooted our family trees to hold ornaments and
tinsel, plucked the feathers of the last guacamayos for quills,
used our war paint to try and write us *desaparecidos o esclavos,*

made the word *campesino* a cast system curse, shamed us into
believing the worst insult was to be called *indígena o jíbaro*

Papá
you are not
of half histories poorly quoted by disparaging foreigners,
not of artifacts mislabeled *primitive,*
not of extinction or elapsed time,
not of documents and forms,
not of casket and faded headstone,

you are of infinite memory
of words in a hand written letter addressed to a three-year-old
granddaughter
you named *palomita y víbora* because you understood the balance
between water and fire

You are of cells
caught on a cotton swab rubbed on the inside of my cheek to
prove that your tribe persists in the deepest part of my marrow
and my red blood cells bear witness to
your resurrection in the birth of each of my sons

You are of dreams
that led this New York City dweller to find your boarded-up, one-
room, mountainside home in Jaguas, Ciales, without using a
map or GPS because I got all the direction I need
with you as my guide

Papá
I now call your name where only the divine like you can be found

I call you cacique in limestone caves filled with the heartbeat
of hundreds of Cimarrones

I call you Baba when divining at an altar of 9 glasses of water
where your picture sits as center
I call you Tata when walking in the woods asking trees for
permission to cut a piece of their bark
I call you Pedro Robles Miranda

Abuelo paterno de Peggy Robles-Alvarado
when I correct false documents, write elegies, broken sonnets
and narratives
to challenge the lies of
who they say you were

to document
who you really are

Papá
I write these poems
so when my children's children call my name
in dusty census records and immigrations logs,
when they find me in Bronx voter lists or defunct libraries
they can also

find you

IF ONLY THEY KNEW

"The one who knows the truth does not die like the one who does not know"
—Proverb of Obara Meji when divining with diloggún

If only they knew they were descendants of displaced kings
then maybe they wouldn't bow down to these streets

Young men loving the concrete more than self, welcoming the mischief that a charged street corner can invite, tongues tied submissive to street lingo cause all you need to know is how to sell that yeyo, doo rags replace your *pañuelos* but still have the persistent desire to protect your head, your knives no longer require ceremony, elders seen as meddling fools; displaced walking legends, your poorly strung beads no longer blessed; just another accessory—proudly displayed like loose nooses linked to colors you are quick to claim

Young man, you have an innate inclination towards being part of a crew, twisted memories of a missing sense of community where aggressive nature was natural; warfare was tied to discipline and not genocide, the dead try to speak advice as you pour rum— unsure as to why but you think it's cool before you take a swig, seek solace in corners you guard so diligently, decades of displacement, modern-day gentrification has you claiming rights to blocks, and avenues

fists pumping chests in hopes of freeing trapped souls

   —*"You don't know how hard you can really be, son"*

Taught to dismiss your natural instincts, replace intuition with hallucinogens, dreams dispersed on the tips of blunts, as years of shame illuminate under street lamps

   —*"How can you dream if you are constantly breaking night?"*

               If only they knew they were descendants of queens
               then maybe they wouldn't bow down to these streets

Legacy of rape has you giving it away before it's even asked for; no courting necessary, ashamed of skin tone, curves in hips, broken backbone that once stood erect, all the feathers have been plucked out of your headdress my love, as time passed you kept shaking that ass, memory fading misplacing all traditions, rituals no longer in practice are most certainly forgotten, erasing all traces of the royalty you once were, too much make up on what once displayed war paint footprints all over your white skirt, prayers stifled by clenched teeth, void left in space above the pit of your stomach once filled with *Ashé*

Drowning in dark rum and empty promises, your nicknamed lover's moans all sound the same, a risky game of roulette played between your thighs, cracked lips blow pain-filled kisses my love, tongue tracing to many belt buckles silenced your voice, on your knees picking up your pieces like picking cotton, shackled for the pleasure of trespassers

a bowed head cannot properly carry a crown, baby girl

> *—"How many times must your midriff whine on the crotch of acquaintances before you fracture?"*

How will your children know they are descendants of displaced kings and queens if you insist on mimicking paupers? Perpetuating mental poverty, fighting each other for scraps, knowing that retired ganstas get no pensions

> *—"What will you leave your children?"*

fill your wounds with knowledge
fill your wounds with love
fill your wounds with persistence
fill your wounds with motivation

rid yourself of regret
of hate
of blame
of sorrow
of woe is me

learn about yourself just like you know those streets

become better than the elders you once lost, before the sins of
the mothers and fathers follow them, let the children know their
life is full of purpose, deliberate, intentional even if their
conception was not, let the children know they can get lifted
through strengthening their spirit

    Let the children know
              they are descendants of kings and queens

JOSEFINA BÁEZ

"NOSOTROS NO SOMOS COMO USTEDES"

Me dijo la mamá de mi amiga y compañera de volleyball
en un español pronunciado con zetas.
Estaba tomándome un maví hecho en su casa.
Maví con yaniquecas.
Me atorugué.
Me añugué.
Se me fue por el camino viejo.
Se fue por el camino viejo.
El camino viejo.
Pasé, dije. Pasao. Not Sak passé. Vieja pasá.
"De tu país salen los nadie. Todos los nadie.
Todos" siguió la doña, ya indignada, a nivel.
"Del nuestro sale quien puede. Y quien puede siempre tiene
    educación.
E d u c a c i ó n de muy alta calidad, la que nos enseñaron en
    Haití.
Y por eso representamos nuestro país siempre bien, en cualquier
    lugar donde llegamos.
Por eso es difícil ver a uno de nosotros en factoría".
"No, no trabajamos en factoría."
Yo le dije, "Mi hermana también dice siempre eso último que
    usted dice".
Mi amiga me hizo un guiño y ahí entendí todo.
La doña no aceptaba esos amores de ella con el dominicanito de
    la 110 hijo del súper.
Y yo que los presenté a que vivieran su 'Ligia Elena'.
Se casaron.
Tienen tres hijos y dos hijas.
Yo madrina tía muchas veces.

Viven en la frontera en Arizona.

Ella viene cada año en Thanksgiving.

Ella sola.

Todavía su mamá no conoce a sus hijos.

No es problema me dice.

No somos la historia. Esa es la bendición.

Hoy.

En esa casa, en Arizona, se habla español, Creole, inglés y francés.

Los muchachos están aprendiendo Nauált me dice.

En esa casa, en Arizona, su dueña duerme con rolos y un
 pañuelo

de seda, amoldando el pelo dezrizado por su cuñada,

en 'Quisqueya Sonora, el primer salón estilo dominicano en el
 desierto'.

PEDACITO DE MI ALMA

La historia te escribió para que camines sola.

Y en el camino nutras a muchos más.

I never wrote this letter.

Instead, I planted in your lerí, tu cabeza, your altar, your head,
 brown kernels.

I planted a seed of life for life.

Yours. Many.

I planted a seed of life, even knowing that your journey thru life
 redefines life itself.

Life as we knew it has changed in the midst of the ever.

What could I give you to take to uncertainty but life itself?

What could I give you to take from Africa to the new land?

If new? If land?

I never wrote this letter.

Instead, I sent rice to a land that will be yours.

If land? If yours?

Share our rice and our know-how. And we will be there with you.
   Always.
In the sharing. Always.
We will be there in every grain planted.
In every pregnant rice tree.
In every harvest celebrated.
In every song sang in the field.
I never wrote this letter.
This letter is a fact.
Already sealed in its forever. Before and after.
A poetic act.
Yes. Rice first came to America from Africa in the braids of my
   child Amina.
Yes.
See you always in nurturing, dear,
pedacito de mi alma.
Love,
siempre.

"COM'ON EVERYBODY CLAP YOUR HANDS, OOOOH YOU'RE LOOKING GOOD"

My brother Luis could twist
He taught me, his little sis'
Chubby Checker limbo rocked la Santa Rosa 58 while outside
our old wooden-frame painted for Christmas sky blue
white rim the sun was dimmed
predicting a toque-de-queda.
Doña María Cordero bought a tree branch
painted snow white
the Caribbean 'tis the season tree
soon to be decorated with very very very fragile red balls
Balls balls he had balls

Even if the only gesture seen was his frown forehead
while three skinny policemen
dressed in the panic color of the times grey
color that lingers on today grey
Took him down forced by culatasos
to fit in La Perrera
Defiant firm
Sins expressed just by his red socks
He smiled to me
Julito, Julito, manito come back quick
Mamá viene mañana en Pan Am.
Rafa arrived from Elisa
Realized matured skinnier
involved in a more thinking silence
and reviewed with me the multiplication litany
9 X 9 7 X 7 8 X 6
No matter what we will always be 10
Distance death distance 10 no matter what Los 10 Morenos
    Negros Prietos.
Gogui tried to knit the basic cadeneta that Doña Josefa taught me
huge immense hands ashy dry awkwardly turned up and down
    and around la agujeta
juguetona
Cholo called from la acera thru the half-door opened
Cito, standing up behind him, blew his extremely fine black hair.
Caribito was there too. I could not see him but I heard BORDA —
    in his laughing-talking tone
I knew my game was over. Gogui left for La Bomba
two points. Two points. Back then there was no distance worth
    three.
Basketball under an almond tree. Now is poetry
Back then it was afternoon's rhythm
paving the way for el Toro con el Santo de Jobo Bonito

el equipito Ebaheba y plus
"Let's twist again like we did that summer . . . "
Mis Cinco Prietos Báez.

MY NAME IS PURE HISTORY

Seat. Seat and listen:
My name is Quisqueya Amada Taína Anaisa Altagracia Indiga.
You can call me Kay. El cocolo, mi Timacle calls me chula and
    his derriengue.
And the rest Gorda.
They call me La Gorda . . .
—Yo. Yo soy afro-dominicana.
*¿ah, afro que?
—Afro-dominicana. Afro-África . . . get it?
*¿Te vas a buscar una moneda con los morenos de aquí?
Si no es así, debes de saber que no es necesario el nombrecito.
Eso se lo inventaron aquí en una universidad, para una cogioca,
    engañadera, una política.
Mil a mi que hay un profesor-licenciado-busca vida con flu, un
    sabe
mucho dirigiendo la cogioca.
Pero recuérdate que aquí hay negros como nosotros,
pero son A me ri canos.
Yo no he visto a ningún moreno llamandose African American.
They are black. Y punto.
Con que tú seas una prieta que diga lo que piense y hagas lo que
digas, ya con eso le hiciste los mejores honores a Afro-África. Get
    it?
—Sister Kay, you are wrong. You are wrong to think like that my
sister.
*I might, my sister. In Fact, I am almost always
wrong, my sister. Were we looking for the right thang?

You might be right. I might be wrong but I ain't carrying
    nobody's
freaking right flag.
If you ain't blind you know that I am black. Prieta.
Morena. Negra.
I will not call myself black Dominican.
Go for it, if you need to.
I do not need it.
Búscatela.
Pero you know that I know.
I do not need to put más azúcar a lo dulce.
But I respect
you sis, even if you don't respect me.
Power to you sis.

REMEMBRANCE

Part 1

Babalú Aché
Orishas
Bembete
Ay, dénme la porción
Orischas
Swirl Aché
Asfalto bembeando
candomblé candombeando
Sirenas
dance ando
Los sueños
penetrando
Dance ando
Enchanted souls
embrújenme
Ay con el son
Come
swirl Aché
Orischas swirl Aché
Orischas swirl Aché
Aché
Aché
Aché

Part 2

To understand

You need to taste
      memories of salt and water
    blood
    chains
D
  R
    O
      W
        N
       I
        N
         G
In the middle of the ocean
    A Christian boat
foreign tongues
memories
sounds
    Despair swallows souls
    Yemayá
    Yemayá
    llévame
    Yemayá

Parte 3

Llena de cadenas
soledades muertas
el silencio de mil años
aumenta

El vaivén de las olas
acarician los calientes sueños
de un mundo lejano
El vaivén
Va y viene
El vaivén
Va
Va y ven
Va y ven
Viene
encrespado en amapolas
solas
amapolas solas
escuchando las olas.

Part 4

I cry
No más
silences
in the tumultuous morning of desires
dreaming
castañuelas
noche eterna

SEÑORA

Tun   Tun
pasa y grifería
Tun ca tun tun
in the city
Babel
Extasieria

Run ca tun tun
Negra, ven
cobíjame del hierro
Negra
     rumbanbéame
    del dream
    Tun tun
    no tengo sueño
    Run ca tun
Pasiones
Runcatuntun
Tus eyes
Tun ca tun pa
Tus ojos
    eterna
    melancholia
     hundreds of tuns
     masked my pain
        Negra
      Run ta

Tun tun ca pa
Your eyes
eternal
melancholia
Hundreds of tuns
masked my pain
Negra
Run ta
Tantanea
In your dreams
despiértame del sueño
My tears
Tun tun ca

Make love to my canto
Tun tun ca ta
Yemayá
Runcatunta
Báñame ya
Yemayá
Ahora
ya
ahhhhhhhhh
báñame toda
Rumbanbéame
Cancanéame
Tunantéame
Yemayéame
Remenéame
Ven
y
tómame
Señora

OYE, MIGUEL

To Miguel Algarín

¿Qué pasa, papá?
Celebrating your cumpleaños
Your birth
birth
day
as in giving birth
Nacimiento
movimiento of voices
cadencias de mambo y conga

rumba y timbales
songo
y Bemba
Ayyyyyyy
menéamelo bien
Mixing the language of the Bard
Rutgers
professor emeritus
Canon
nixing
a new lexicon
Española
English
Spanglish
NuYorican
Spanish
coloreado con
working-class English language
en el Lower East Side
Loísa
Loísa . . . ida
Lower east side
se convirtió en
Loisaida
porque
aquí estamos
con las credenciales of
one hundred years of coloniaje
1898
1917
Our language is written in blood
El chef del language atribulado
creative sounds

of us
for us
by us
Cooking mofongo of the Puerto Rican soul
Puerto Rican
Nuyorican
sancocho y salsa
Creating a sacred place
to celebrate our cultures
embracing the universal
Ay, bendito
Miguelito
tú visión acurrucó
mi imaginación
Tú me distes tu bendición
Your cooking partners
Pedro, Sandra, Papoleto, Piñero y Nancy
enriched the legacy of
Chaucer
Cervantes
Palés y Lorca
y tú

Miguel
con tu permiso y bendición
quiero celebrarte
como padre de un movimiento
You show us el soneo universal
rumbeando palabras
soneando
nuestra esencia en la virtud del poema.

EL BRONX

Songo
Songo
　Dreaming in the

asphalt　　　　jungle
conga
rhythms
in the midst of the
urban LULLABY

　　El Bronx
　THE BRONX
Sonéame en dos
two for two
Love me NOW
timbales
touching ME
UP AND D
　　　　O
　　　　　W
　　　　　　N
Hmmmmmmmmmm
sonéame
congonéame
Así, así
bamboléame
muslos y piernas
remenéame
Tito
me toca
caliente

y Baretto
me hace sudar la frente

En PS. 52
los músicos gozaron
creating sounds
que Obatalá y Shangó bailaron
Ay salseros del ayer
sáquenme
los sounds
y el ay bendito
en la ciudad de Babel

El Cross County Express
nos dividió
while the Caribbean
nos bautizó
y sé que estoy aquí en Nuyol
but
is not Nuyol
is The Bronx
da' Bronx
el south Bronx
el south Bronx of the Yankee Stadium of '73
of the mambo
of the streets
of the dreams left behind
in a suitcase
Guardados
en el clóset
hasta el próximo viaje
Yes,
the next trip

because, tú sabes
Puerto Ricans are here
and there
But no
we are here
da' Bronx
songoneando
in da' Bronx
guaracheando
in da' Bronx
sandungueando
in da' Bronx
salseando
congoneando
soneando
We are here
You hear me, World!!!!!!!!!!!!!
We are here to stay

RICAN ISSUES

Say **What?**
Could you please, Pleaseeeeeeeeeee repeat
Did you said: "Molleta?
Prieta?
Morena?
Ohh African!"
Hmmmmm, **Soy Puertorriqueña.**

Yes, **Puerto Rican.**

That I don't look **What?**
Oh, I guess I don't look café con leche

mancha de plátano
mulata,
high yellow
grifa
By the way

I did not know that there was a Puerto Rican look.
And, what exactly is that?
That I just look more what?
Well
¿y tu abuela dónde está?
I should said abuela, tío, tía y todo el barrio
Let me tell you something
for your information
most Ricans are a mixed of Africans, Spaniards and Native
      Americans called Taínos
By the way no one has seen a Taíno in the last 500 years.
So exactly . . . You know what that means

My **English** is covered with spices
spices from the Caribbean
Spices that you might find **Strange**
because you were born in this cold fast-food mall of a country
where Spanish is a foreign word
that you are ashamed to learn
and when you try
is not there
only mumbles of a murmur
susurrando el olvido
a regañadientes
pretendiendo
escondiendo la vergüenza.

You remember Puerto Rico on the 2nd Sunday of every June
when everybody is suddenly proud to be Puerto Rican.

No the word is Boricua
Boricuas here, **Boricuas** there, **Boricuas** everywhere
And everyone waves the flags
the flags that they don't even understand
and no one knows why they are here.

Yes HERE Now
Do you Know?
Why your parents or grandparents, vinieron aquí?
¿De   qué   Pueblo?
¿Cuándo te bañastes en las aguas calientes del Caribe?
Better yet
do you really know that . . .
we all came from the motherland
Africa?

Even the Spanish people that came with **Colón, Columbus**
however you want to say it
lived 700 hundred years under the **Moors.**
You heard that right.
The moors as in Arabs as in black Arabs
SO . . . in other words
not only I
but **we**
have over 500 years of African mestizaje
The so called "white people that everyone is so proud of"
as in "my grandparents are from Spain"
well, if they are . . .
they
too   have **negrITOs** in them.

Remember the **gitanos**
but that is another story . . .
Getting back to the **Boricua's issue**
what history do you know?

Ever heard of
Agueybana
Albizu Campos
Palés Matos
Rafael Betances
Arturo Shomburg
Francisco Oller
Julia De Burgos
Rafael Hernández
Segundo Ruiz Belvis
Enrique Laguerre
Mariana Bracetti
Pedro Pietri

Still havING problems figuring me out?
Or is it that you just don't know
who you are?

◦ **ARIANA BROWN** ◦

RECOVER

After Martín Espada's "Imagine the Angels of Bread"

Key

It begins with a white man
I have killed
& the country wrapping around his legs;
& me,
eyeing the country, asking
how to stop
the sound of a dying empire.

& the country says,
"open it."

What I Found Inside the Scream

Cortés & Columbus were small men, terrified
of anything they hadn't yet named. Now, they scurry
to the corners of the sound, terrified of my fingers,
of the hands that return for the master's gold. I yell,
"Kneel" & they transform;
the order barked & tapping along their bones. I yell,
"Search" & the world opens to its hot fist. I yell,
"Pry" & the two boys with men's names throw themselves to
the flame.

Before burning, they sing. & it is a first for them,
to sing & pray at the same time.
Did you know when white men sing
they also die?

& let a black girl open wide for a music. Let someone dark
hold everyone's sorrow so it don't infect the work. I can't
listen to "Wade in the Water" without shedding
something I can't get back. On second thought, I say "Return"
& the two fools clutch at their lives. I ain't givin'
'em permission to speak, but I want what they got. I tell
'em, open their pockets & cover their eyes. Here,
a hundred languages to plant, children of the earth.
Maps written for me. How it feels to gather up the world
& be still starving. I say "Weep" & the men are undone.
Their bellies fill with salt, near to bursting. I say "Release"
& the men's demons issue from their throats:
their reflections in the water, the fevered Atlantic,
women glittering at the mouth. I say "Purge"
& I have been reckless. I have not prepared. So the slew of bodies
pouring from their frames. Seaweed & earthworms.
Coral for crowns, black as the oldest kingdom,
brown as the first world, brilliant forms waking.
I glance at the men, left panting as the ancestors take back
their wind. & don't we know the value of white men's breath?
Haven't we wished them well aloud but dead inside?
Wind as weapon, bodies ripe with the anger of silenced gods,
my kin shake the men inside out. Recover pyramids,
the temples Cortés burned, the city center, the way it looked
before it was ruined, and the names of all my ascendants
come trickling out like smoke.

AHUACATL*

My mother
knows the art
of filling a bottomless
pot. Fideo, frijoles, some
two-ingredient Depression dish
handed *tiny green* down like an
heirloom *song/quiet fruit* to collect
dust in *with a mouth/thick* our bellies.
Only when *hearted/black body soft-* there is extra
money, ella *ening with age/lil inside out* me compra
un aguacate *tree/slick lung in a black* to cool the
tongue. She *sling/sweet dewy* knows chalupas
are my nemesis *meat/stubborn* since I learned
they mean we *pit in the* are poor. Enter
ahuacatl**: brown *chest* hearted guitarra,
a salvar mis chalupas tristes
from my foul american
taste.

---

*Mexico is the world's largest exporter of ahuacatl/aguacates/avocados. Mexica people are known for mashing avocado into huaca-milli, or guacamole. Other Mesoamerican people, such as the Maya, were known to slice the fruit and eat it in corn tortillas as early as 8000-7000 B.C.

**Because avocados did not remain fresh on long ocean voyages, they remained an oddity to Europeans for many years. They, unlike other parts of nature, did not assist Europeans in the conquest of Mexico.

COATL: AN OLD MYTH & A FEW NEW ONES, IN THREE PARTS

after ntozake shange

i. capital

when it was finished,
the city
was so beautiful
it nearly blinded its
makers. a ripe
gold, their Tenochtitlán
was, glossy splinter
in the eye.
each man
lifted an arm
for shield;
upon seeing this,
the snakes, feeling
generous, wound
themselves
into the temples,
crawled into the mouths
of their gods
as to soften the beauty.
the people,
twice saved by
the serpent,
listened
for the beating
of the city's heart,
& finding
it, rejoiced,

& Tenochtitlán, bristling
with the creatures,
rose.

ii. cholula

how many gods/do you know/that can fly/Quetzalcoatl*
& his feathers/polished teeth/& scales
flew to Cholula/insisting on something jeweled/& grand
got/the largest pyramid in the world/to show
gathered himself
& let everyone kiss/his wing
every mouth/wanting
a piece/of the god of/
the morning star/everyone's
god-father

iii. coatl, in which a white man becomes a snake

Cortés was never a god/a lesser animal/perhaps but/if even the
serpents are/holy/a white man/must be so guilty/to not deserve/
power/& men like Cortés/desire power if it means/legacy/which
led him to/Malintzin/who said too much/remembered a native
tongue/took him to/Cholula/where Mexica warriors/thought to
surprise him/only the snakes/did not help them then/for Cortés/
had been speaking to them/laying/low among the slithering/a
hunter/learning his prey/got a twitch/in his cheek/a sweet
tooth/para sangre/& there in Cholula/there was a massacre/
Cortés' tongue/licking hot remains/tasting gold flecks/in his
speech/& he wrote or told someone/to write about him/to say he
was Quetzalcoatl/in human form/come to claim/his belongings/

---

*Aztec feathered serpent god whose name derives from the bird quetzal & the Náhuatl
word "coatl," meaning "serpent". One of the creators of mankind.

who knew/this would become the oldest legend of all/a white
man/invoking the heavens/upon the world/Tonatiuh*/ tired from
another journey around the earth/felt a change/in supply/&
exhausted/bellowed a call/to Tenochtitlán/said/he had been
counting/the days/said/he could not live/on the blood of the
defenseless/that if they wanted their sky lit/they would have to
fight/& the people of the sun/listened again/to their anxious
city/quickening its pace/& vowed/to never shed/skin or blood/for
anyone other than/a god/that there should be no man/equal to/a
serpent/not even/in his most wild/& thirsty greed

A QUICK STORY

*"The evidence is heavy that Anglos perceived the physical contrasts of Mex-
icans as indicating mental and temperamental weaknesses."*
                              —Arnoldo De León, *They Called Them Greasers*

I. My Mother

met my father in Wichita Falls,
Texas. Choctaw land.
Her 4'11" frame bursting
with *run*, his big laugh
saying *catch*.

II. La Tierra

in 1886,
a flood destroyed
the falls in Wichita
the same year
20 blacks were

---

*Aztec sun god & principal deity as depicted in La Piedra del Sol; born each morning,
   journeys about the earth, and dies each night; requires human blood for fuel.

killed in Mississippi,
where the Choctaw
are originally from.

III. My Father

was raised by his grandmother,
Ella Mae Tucker; daughter of
a sharecropper from
Hurst, Texas. Granny's boys
got themselves into
the military or
college. Wilbert Tyrone
Brown III wound up
next to my mama
in Air Force basic training.
Said he was "from an island".
Nobody's fool, my mama
rolled her eyes and said,
"Galveston ain't no island."

II. La Tierra

Galveston's own Karankawa and Akokisa
watched Cabeza de Vaca wash up on their beaches,
shipwrecked, & call it his. Now, there's a Michoacana
on the corner. Paved roads sinking to the sea. You could
live thousands of years swaying by the water.

IV. My Parents

My mother says
"Your dad & I
were best friends."
My father, dead,
sits by the sea,
conjured up by Otis
Redding & my mother's
voice.

I. My Mother

"Do you know why
it never bothered me
that we were poor?

Because I loved
your father. & that
meant I already had
the best I was ever
going to get."

III. My Father

Galveston & Wichita
seen natural disasters.
The plane crash in '92,
I suppose you could
call that one, too. I'm
this tall 'cause of all this
love in me, sproutin' up
like a song. Thicker than

any sea. Don't you know
I knew your mama didn't
need me? She told me
plenty of times
it was so. I'm 6'2"
and black; never been
scared of anything, 'cept
your mama. That little lady
could raise a country, raise hell,
raise me right out the ground
if she could. A world all by herself,
she was. Your mother didn't ever need
fixing. Just a place to fall in love. I made that.
She made you. & named you Ariana Mae. After
Granny. We wasn't wed but she gave you a piece'a
me anyway. Brown. The color of you. A good color. An
anchor to keep you near me: that's why you can't help but
sway when you hear an old song. That's my love, girl. Risin'
in you. Why you fell in love with a woman who loves the ocean.
I seen it all. That's why I knew my passin' wouldn't destroy nothin'.
Your mama might be small, but she kept you both alive. Where a white
woman would cry, your mama would grow a new life & throw her feet
    to the
ground to make her way forward. You were born as I lay dying. Women
    like your
mother survive all disasters—especially the ones they never saw coming.

CRUZ

We all bore the curse.

My brothers bore theirs
like the cross in their last
name.
My curse was red and came from
Eve,
their curse was brown and came
from my stepfather

(the real reason my grandmother
hated him).

Bronze had burned her,
and it would light through them
like flames along an El Dorado
skyline.

The white wooden house we came from
did little to save them when
their eager bodies moved
            from space to   space

their boredom and frustration
becoming frenetic   energy.

The white coats, later, only added letters
to teachers notes and signed

prescriptions to be filled;
      something to keep them   still.

Their curse was a cloak of visibility
Brown bodies   in a white world.

DEAR WHITE PEOPLE

     we stopped slamming
     like that   in 1992;

     you should look towards
     your own past too   sometime.

     We'd look at our own,
     except we don't have one.

     dear white people
     you came to save us,

     from ourselves
     and the dimness
     in our marrow.

     dear white people
     thank you
     for giving us   Christ

and the one drop
that redeemed
some of us.

dearest of white people
please teach us how
to speak more loudly,

like you do,
when we talk
about   where we are from.

PENNIES IN MY BLOOD

there are pennies in my blood

i could lie
and tell you i do not know
where they came from
or how they made their way
down my throat and into my belly

but the truth is
i swallowed them as a child

once playing a game
in the dark with maria elena
waiting on our mothers
to finish casting spells on strange men

the men were always there
drunk on budweiser
and the spanish that spilled
from my black mother's tongue
like honey

i grew with honey
and peacock feathers in my hair
i am child of oshún

there are pennies in my blood
i could close my eyes
and pretend i never saw the altar
in mimi's apartment
the one she shared with marlena
i was mesmerized
by this cuban woman soldier
who dawned an afro like halo
mimi loved marlena
like she worshipped ogún

mi mamá made sure i knew
the hands of sacrifice
the eyes of truth

when i was young
i reached out
to the iron in my blood
the popcorn and copper
on mimi's altar
laid out like birthright
my mother told me
not to play with
she must know
i was born with a machete in my mouth
i witnessed her cut men
split them in two
like fire wood
ogún is not like man
he is not to be toyed with

i was born
with pennies in my mouth

i cannot explain
how i knew
to call the name of elleguá
when the chains came
to call the name of mi hermana—giselle
i cannot explain
how i knew
to take the egg
and roll it down
from our faces to legs
from our heads to feet
and break the yolk
at the foot of a tree

i cannot decipher the copper song
that ran from my tongue
like flame
it shook steel from drum
calling the name of ancestors
one by one
out of shadows
and back into my bones

oh oh oh
yemayá
yemayá

there are pennies in my mouth
my head and neck are on fire
bring the coco y arroz
boil the eggs
build a tower
for obatalá

to restore peace
i cannot explain
how pennies made their way
into my blood

i was fire
before man knew flesh
i was shangó chant
before slaveships came

i counted pennies with God
before i knew my name

MEJIAFRICANA

born with two tongues
i speak of—hablo de
i write of—escribo de
mi vida cultura colorada
pintada—painted a picture
para que puedan ver
that i am
mejiafricana

that's half and half
but whole—as in
an entire empire of aztec warriors
breathed orange red fire into my lungs
that's half and half
but whole—as in
an entire tribe from the congo
rained blue black blood into my soul

i am that red brown black sista
thinking and breathing them poetic thoughts
that prolific prophetic poet
with them red brown twisted locks
i see and record the world in black ink
like the skin of my people
i am fierce like panthers
militant with pen as they be
hot water cornbread oxtails and collard greens
chanting down babylon with
jah! rastafari beats
i am ghetto soliloquies of haitian refugees
spoken underneath harlem's balconies
i represent the black freedom
of which the negro spiritual speaks
i am all things black
and all black things I be

yo soy la morena
la poema
que despierta su mente
que enciende su alma
con papel y pluma
i can make the sun and moon rise
at the same time
i am el viento que viene de méxico

el este y el oeste
esta es la verdad
i am the song on pancho's lips
as he sits and eats un burrito de chorizo con huevo
praying for a job to feed his niños
salsa picosa

como willie colón frankie ruiz y celia
una mariposa en may
and may i say that brown and proud
is what I will remain
staining this life with my mark
because you see
my sico is just as bad as my bark
because porque
i am una niña del yucatán
chichenizta
quezacoatl kissed my mother
and here i am
landed on this land with pen in hand
to tell the tales of mi gente
mayans aztecs and incans
roofers day laborers carpenters
lo que sea
es la misma cosa
sangre
i am una niña de mi país
una de una raza tan fuerte
una niña de méxico y así me quedo

born with two tongues
i speak of—hablo de
i write of—escribo de
mi vida
cultura colorada
pintada
painted a picture para que puedan ver
that i am
mejiafricana

CATCH A FIRE

catch a fire
balance in the wind
like bird on a wire
up roots like words
with my mouth
take the reigns
from the God ground
and build a birdhouse
speak truth
live Most Higher
take spirit from sound
burn them from the inside out
take embers from the flame
build an empire
admonish the wicked
and dem babylonian tower
put on the full armor of God
polish my peace
every minute
every hour
time waits for no man
time come now
to take a stand
hands up
black power fists balled up
man down
freedom fighter
buffalo soldier up
beat chest with both hands
until your heartbeat rings out

don't eat dem devil handouts
stand your ground
from the ghetto
to the prison yard
from the projects
to the white house
from the southside
to the north star
no more black face
song and dance
this is mama africa's black hands
freedom ringing
the necks of the oppressors
this is haitian slave rebellion
cane field burning
no more weeping and wailing
no more black bodies in the streets
this is nail in the cross
gnashing of teeth
a blood sacrifice for the ancestors
this is bigger thomas
this is black wall street
this is nat turner uprising
this is us realizing
they are not bigger than us
this is for the whites of their eyes
this is for the white lies
this is for the bloodshed
this is momma said
if you let them whip you
when you get home
i'mma whip you

this is whips and chains
this change ain't gone come
til we do

this is blood on the ground
bird on a wire
this is get together
to get higher
this is catch hell
for every one of us they caught
this is take back
for every one of us
they sold and bought
this is cry blood
for every one of us they killed

this is truths and rights
this is we were born free
burn them slavedriver
this is them catch a fire
for every time they touch we

MOKONGO Y TO' ESA GENTE

Eyibaríba eyibaríba enkamá
Wá [chorus]
Eyibaríba eyibaríba enkamá
Wá [chorus]
Sounds that spread through past wombs
those before Mokongo y toda esa gente
sound too much like thumps
like the procession of feet from Abakuá
on that day carrying casket y bailando la caja
teetering on bounce of 6/8 rhythm
like an incomplete thought between bone & spirit—
we were born on such a day
on such a day we kneeled before certain clouds
& chose our calabash full of destiny
The hardest thing to remember
is sounds from those wombs before Mokongo—
Eyibaríba eyibaríba enkamá
Wá [chorus]

4 years he wandered streets in Regla
lingering like delicate webs of tabaco smoke
or inside vacant bottle de aguardiente
(That's why bottles should be layed to rest while empty)
Even two miscarriages our mother had
so they clipped a bit of ear from the stillborn
to identify him indelibly upon return
y to assure he did not leave again
fastened small chain around left ankle

[*Abakuá: Secret society of men in Cuba. Formed by descendents of slaves from the Calabar.*]

After 4 years Mokongo y toda esa gente
decided to help
On such a day
we sealed the pact with death/ikú
ikú would have to filter through thick curtains of mariwó
though the sounds thumped like a procession of feet
against the ear missing a snap—
Eyibaríba eyibaríba enkamá
Wá [*chorus*]

What about Feyo, Frank, Emilio, Luis y Mongo
their hair their platinum teeth
How they were men y mostly fathers
One young guerillero leaning on steel bars
shot in Santo Domingo
They keep waving flags of rainbow
asking for glass of water
flores y perfume
claiming they're still here—
though de vez en cuando
some café spills prior to being served
or a plate with morsels of plátanos, arroz y pollo asado
cracks in approval like an offered eucharist

And how can we forget Alfonsa—
placed like a dune of stone on the shore
smiling like someone whose known you for a while
dress of blue gingham/guinga flapping
like waves of laughter

In an isolated house
a father remains alone wearing
milky silky slacks y guayabera
watching the mediterranean stucco & tile

[*mariwó: Palm fronds.*]

asking certain stones & ceiba
wind & streams who animate things through the other world
to deliver this message to his son
We need the skull of a ram carnero o sheep—
just like bone is past memorized
just like blood is life actualized
so is spirit time humanized

Eyibaríba eyibaríba enkamá
Wá [*chorus*]
Eyibaríba eyibaríba enkamá
Wá [*chorus*]
Tó Egúngún!

INCANTATION FOR THE WORD

Shi-shi shah-shah shi she-eeh
is the music of divination powder
Takatakatakataka
is the music of palm nuts conversing/(ikin)
Ikin can
speak of a certain matter burrowed in sand
Odù is the music of
Omolú is the music of
that speech

And we arrived with these pronouncements
circling a wooden tray
circling those signatures (who summon the true name of things)
like coded messages from birds soaked
with the dew of universe
archetypes & all
past present & therefore
future
many languages with rhythm & all
even tonal
circling a wooden tray
tray who circular implies
WORLD
And it is word who causes this dance
And there are rhythmic leaps into
the sweetness of abundance into
the iron crest of creativity
And there are herbs who cause the invisible to manifest
And it is word who causes this dance
Takatakatakataka
is the music of palm nuts conversing/(ikin)
Yes we can initiate a dialogue between known &
unknown
between those who flow round jagged stones of ignorance
river-like
like wise fish
we can bring messages regarding history
the ineffable speech of music
the music of verse
vibration from spirits through ripples
rhythm residing deep among the lushness
An old beaded crown invokes the power of poem
—in an incantation we can

Odù is the music of
Omolú is the music of
that speech
Shi-shi shah-shah shi she-eeh
shshsh!

MISA CARIBEÑA

Verde de ver green was her eyes
where the story began
hidden among almendras
dates, twigs of olive dripping oil

The sting of salt pooling
around ambitious brows
la misa begun by 3 boats
(rickety in their raucous bouts with breeze)

    *

     How to proceed
     when your script has been writ by others
     declared to be in your best interest
     without finding your best interest
        . . . history
           with all its difficulties
           rises from incantation
           like musk deep
           in the earth . . .
     —retelling

There's a bundle of bridle memories
                wrapped in white, deep red, then
                                black cloth
strewn like an old photo
                                we turn away from
—retelling
                La liturgia can be bilingual
Latín con Yoruba
Spanish y Spanish
English con Spanish
Spanish con Latin
Cubano con Yoruba
someone
                has to orchestrate this—

El Proceso:
Burn a collection of twigs (Amansa
                Guapo, No-me-olvides, Vencedor, Paramí, Quita
                Maldición, etc. . . .)
Filter to fine dust
Add dried quimbombó
Gather witnesses
Hang the white, red & black cloth flag-like
Prepare herbal solution for bathing afterwards
Spread ash circular on the ground
Begin writing symbols to span the column from earth to other
        world
Symbols born from word

There are delicate songs
                that web these worlds
A gourd with salted water
                is waiting their arrival

When drops pool around fingers
          sliding like rain
               mist of spirits
arrive in chronological death
the sting of salt pooling
          inside our gaping memory
For the future—
we place a table blanketed with pools of cups
fistful of flowers
          candles
here they
          los muertos
can swim
          frolic
After this ash has been etched
we understand how the dead has been received

               *

This is goodbye—
la gran despedida
circled by candles infinite
it can be a signature of sorts
una caja de muerto
the difference is we live
& we continue an odd embrace
               rhythmic

It has been established that
life begins in the ocean
Indeed she who floats on a mantle of blue
sequined with stars & moonlight
is motherhood en persona

& the one chained at the depths who
no one has really seen
collects fragments of bone from
sand
the sound of water choca con hueso
welds the primal bond deep
in the unconscious
Here is where life begins
Here is where
        we
            began
with words on sand
        (close to the tide)
you accepted
I accepted—

A kissed history has dug into the sand
trying to erase the echo of what was writ
You alone gnawing at the mystery
manifested seed-like in my hands
challenging all my efforts
They now have slid off unto
            otra

I thought though in sand
impermanence would not victimize us
the crystals in your eyes
        my eyes
sharp & crackling with hope
I thought my feet could shuffle scissor-like slide
         side to side on sand
printing mysterious messages to you
     (of love, of future, of promise)

I thought the bay pooling around our oath
the reflection of words crystalized there
floating
sinking
delivered with 3 drums bàtá to the origins
I thought they would become sand, then bone
I thought then maybe a child
now I realize
you thought
you thought . . .

                    *

            How to proceed
            when your home itself
            simple & predictable
            is an abiku—
                        . . . born transient
                        with scars from previous lives not
                        really indefinite
                        but transient
                        clenching fists of young frustration not
                            yet established alive . . .
                "comb the language"
    with the dorsal from wise fish
    encrusted with coral
            filter the rhythm
                    music of
    accents
    "or else"
    end up at the bottom of the sea
    grinding bone con bone
    busy trying to get born

again
in another place—

drops pool from salt
from fingers sliding like rain
unto the green
verde de ver green was her eyes
where the story begins again
hidden among almendras

un llanto gitano se oye
un llanto gitano dice
"Que no me lloren
que no me lloren
que tengan azucenas
una gitarra cajón y compás de bulerías
pañuelos verde y blanco
que me lloren así"

This is no secret:
we are children of death
bundled bulky in history
one white
deep red
                one black
        textured hymns
ruffled by boats in their raucous breeze
fingering our skin
only a sense
that pools from salt
sand
water
from fingers sliding like rain down skin

unto green verde de ver
       again
       again
       green was her eyes

Misa because there's sand
Misa because there's memory
Misa because there's transformation
Misa because there's fish
because there's ritual
because there's tragedy
Misa because there's music
because there's love
because we mix we survive reborn
Misa porque tú con yo yo con tú
todos mezclados—
Misa caribeña

I'M FORCED TO IMAGINE THERE ARE TWO OF ME HERE

To fit in   we practice not dancing   I pull her hair
   against our head & burn
the water out   she sucks-in the lip of our belly

I call her Rio   say Rio   remind them of our white
   grandmother
Do what it takes   to make them think   we are like
   them

But it is a risk to want us   we close the bedroom door
   she reaches under
the blanket   It's just   me Rio   &   The Dark
does she part my legs   or The Dark's   I spit into
   our hand   & touch her

Sometimes she bites our lips   to make them smaller
   we refuse
to dance   we do what it takes

I let her drive Little Cottonwood Canyon   It is night
   we hit a deer   breath
from its nostrils cloud the windshield   It feels like
   there could be more
of us somewhere   she opens the car doors   we show
   each other mercy

take the same bite of cracked rib   I move to kiss the
   animal   blood from her mouth

HAVANA GHAZAL

Moths fly in the open window during the night while it rains.
Piles of letters addressed to my mother, not one will I send to her.

Mold spreads under the floorboards, dust my lungs in the night.
The neighbor prays to a Black San Lázaro to comfort her.

Vultures circle Hotel Habana Libre in broad daylight.
Cira wants to know how to say "I love you" in English, so I tell
her.

Coconut ice cream for sale on every corner at December.
Havana surrounds herself with walls, but so many come inside her.

Bats stuck in the palm leaves outside the terrace ledge.
A Santero falls into the trance of Ochún, after all, he belongs to
her.

Some say the patroness of the island isn't really a white virgin, but
a woman so dark, after sunset, not even Good notices her.

TRIP FOR A WHILE, AFTER CURTIS MAYFIELD

I'm your halflight/I'm your dark earthy thing
High priestess of rap videos/Proof you dig black music

Two people on the lip of a broken glass
fucking the other for comeuppance

I'm your mother's locked dresser drawer/a half-drawn bedroom
curtain

I'm your boredom-breaking machine/I'm your breakdancing
     fetish

Foaming up at the mouth
an exploded can of cream soda
at first unseen, and then it starts to drip
onto your blue jeans, this sticky thing
almost embarrassing

I'm your last drop/I'm your lone fountainhead
Splitting light from the ground up

TO THESE POETS

for Tato Laviera

These poets, these messengers,
these teachers who come into our lives
from places beyond with lessons to be learned,
crafting similes and metaphors,
comparing and contrasting,
full of dramatic alliterations, dynamic allusions,
flying rhythms and syncopated beats in harmonic fusion.

What is this gift that opens itself to see?
What is their cause and reason?
What is this message, and why?

These masters, these word warriors
who give voice to highways in the cosmos of thought,
who stand up, who rise up from their sprouting seeds
to be counted, to declare,
to claim their place in the circle of life,
who are *¡presente!* to confront injustice
and reach out to another,
to show, to give, to nurture,
who are mountains and thunderstorms,
lakes and gardens,
who are songs of humanity,
sad songs and fast songs,
holy songs,
songs that embrace and celebrate,
songs that shine light into darkness,

songs that are rooted in the real,
full of passion, songs that heal.

These teachers,
this symphony of voices and meaning,
this mothership of community,
these spirit guides who call our names,
this circle that pulses, burns and unravels,
who hide in their internal silence
then burst into us like fire and sunlight,
who paved the road long before we were born,
who endured profound sacrifice we cannot even imagine
in our comfortable and spoiled lives,
who marched through neighborhoods
armed with history and knowledge
to knock down indifferent doors,
who lived in subsidized housing,
who stood on pantry lines to feed their families,
who forced open the gates of biased universities
so that we could be educated,
who dismantled the hypocrisy of apartheid,
who brandished nation-building tools
with visionary minds,
who read books about art and revolution
and wrote the book of struggle and freedom,
who descended from indigenous peoples
who were slaves in factories and warehouses,
who moved from tenement to tenement
and from island to island,
who lit candles with offerings to honor our ancestors,
who raised the children and did not abandon them,
who changed diapers, scrubbed floors, washed dishes,
cooked delicious feasts every day

and did all that was necessary,
who buried brothers and mothers
and still found ways to console each other,
who never gave up when they were expected to fail,
who made magic in music and danced mean mambos,
who kicked butterflies and backstrokes
in the oceans of survival,
who farmed the land and harvested its bounty,
who transformed the limitations of ordinary existence
into extraordinary creativity.

To these mothers and fathers,
sisters and brothers, daughters and sons
who embrace each other's differences,
who search for knowledge in obscure locations
because they need to know
and leave the stories and records of their poems
long after they are gone
with imagination that penetrates beyond thick walls
transcending the boundaries of space
with strength and elegance,
whose fresh water circulates in the river of our being,
who carry us to the shores of creation
with words that are swords,
that fulfill and liberate,
that caress and adore,
that are tools to sculpt and shape paradigms,
that mark a path into the cinemascope of tomorrow
to reach and teach all of us who will follow
how to be fearless, to dare and to dream.

To each of these urban griots,
for each syllable of sound sent to seek us,

for each verse that lifts us from the abyss,
that comes to bless us,
for each door that opens to welcome us,
for each bridge in the crossing,
for each soul saved . . . .

we celebrate your being and say
thank you, merci, arigato,
danke, shukran, grazie,
asante sana, gracias y más—
con bendiciones recibidos
en muchísimo aché.

WHERE I'M FROM

We come from the America of are and be, of soy y somos.
It is an America that does not belong to one race or one tribe.
It is even more than Black and White.
Our America is made up of mountain flutes and ancient step
    pyramids;
of bright color woven fabrics
and tobacco fields worked like black gold by dark hands;
of Asian blood and sweat operas
on railroad tracks and concentration camps;
of Mexicans who still live on the land of their ancestors,
even though its name was changed to
California, Arizona, Texas, Nevada, Utah—NEW Mexico;
of many diasporas trapped in urban landscapes;
of motherless children whose daddy is at war;
of crowded streets, long lines, empty pockets
and unjust verdicts for police who destroy;
of massacred ancestors, English-only rules, sterilized wombs
and an island tethered to unexploded target-practice bombs;

of the cupboard is bare, no one cares,
while children in limbo are searching for the sun.

Our America speaks Choctaw, Crow, Nez Perce and Zapotec,
Ojibwe, Patois, Pidgin and Portuguese,
Mandarin, Mayan, Korean and Quechua,
Creole, Danish, French and Dakota,
Punjabi, Hindi, Nagual and Sign,
Arabic, Congo, Swahili
and too many dialects of Spanish to count.

In this America you can sit anywhere on the bus,
talk however you must, receive self-knowledge you can trust.
This America is a Nuyorican-Diasporican-Afrorican state of mind,
that celebrates difference, educated in defiance,
peace-loving, stands up for justice,
that knows when to walk away and let go,
and does not seek to be something other than itself.

Where I'm from thoughts rise up from creation stories
passed on through grandmothers
and God is also a woman whose spirit is as evolved as any man's.

Where I'm from, no matter what color your skin,
you can dance and worship at the same time
and God will descend from heaven to speak with you face to face.

Where I'm from there are no free rides,
only hard work and short nights
in a world full of stars, and poets, and artists, and teachers,
and healers, and thinkers, and seers and dreamers;
where everyone has a place to be,
can go deep within and learn to be free,

expect respect and claim our voice,
pursue our form of happiness and our right of choice.

In this America our capacity to love is what defines us, unites us;
and what we give with our heart is the essence of our true value.

Where I'm from, love is real, and it starts by giving
into the circle in and out of ourselves.

PHILOSOPHY OF COOL

for Craig Harris

There is a love poem here
searching to say more
than can be said on any page.

It is a love song
wanting to sing,
waiting to be heard,
hoping to be found,
yearning to be closer
than skin to skin,
than air to breath,
than mind to soul.

It is a heartfelt,
         . . . heart   felt,
heart—
              felt
                         poem;
flies through the atmosphere
invisible and sincere,
a drumbeat and mountain flute,

sweet sweet music in your ear,
the quintessential kiss. . . .

It was always here.
It will never leave you.
It is much more than these words can describe.

In the long list of important worldly things
there is a great giving,
soul lifting,
tender caring poem
that is here right now.

This is all that matters.

All you need to know is
you are the poem.
You are this great love poem here.

PUERTO RICAN DISCOVERY NUMBER ONE, IN THE BEGINNING

In the beginning was the word
and the word became light
and the light became sound
like the universe exploding;
it came, took form, gave life
and was called Conga.

And Conga said:
Let there be night and day
and was born el Quinto y el Bajo.

And Quinto said: *Give me female*
and there came Campana.

And Bajo said: *Give me son*
and there came Bongoses.

They merged, produced force,
Maracas y Claves,
Chequere y Timbales.

¡Qué viva la música!
So it was written
on the skin of the drum.

¡Qué viva la gente!
So it was written
in the hearts of the people.

¡Qué viva Raza!
So it is written.

AMOR NEGRO

in our wagon oysters are treasured
their hard shells clacking against each other
words that crash into our ears
we cushion them
cup them gently in our hands
we kiss and suck the delicate juice
and sculpture flowers from the stone skin
we wash them in the river by moonlight
with offerings of songs
and after the meal we wear them in our hair
and in our eyes

FOR TITO

You, macho machete
are all the fine conga rhythms
played on the street, in parties, in spring;
all the beautiful vibes of la playa sextet
washing up against the palms in the hairs of my back,
turning my blood into salsa
and filling me up inside to swell
with who I am.

You, macho paciencia,
are the star of my aqua sea;
and when there are no more sunsets
and I become alone and lost,
it is your brown hands holding me steady
around my waist
to move and sway with.

You, macho soledad,
are a unique language,
the one filling my eyes with heat for you,
growing
with all the desire of your drum,
pounding with my womb,
planting seeds in the night.

Together
we reap mystical sugarcane in the ghetto,
where all the palm trees grow ripe
and rich with coconut milk.

FROM FANON

We are a multitude of contradictions
reflecting our history,
oppressed,
controlled,
once free folk,
remnants of that time interacting in our souls.
Our kindred was the earth,
polarity with the land,
respected it,
called it mother,
were sustained and strengthened by it.
The European, thru power and fear, became our master;
his greed welcomed by our ignorance,
tyranny persisting,
our screams passing unfulfilled.
As slaves we lost identity,
assimilating our master's values,
overwhelming us to become integrated shadows,
undefined and dependent.
We flee escaping, becoming clowns in an alien circus,
performing predictably,
mimicking strange values,
reflecting what was inflicted.
Now the oppressor has an international program
and we sit precariously within the monster's mechanism,
internalizing anguish from comrades,
planning and preparing a course of action.

HERE

I am two parts/a person
Boricua/spic
past and present
alive and oppressed
given a cultural beauty
. . . and robbed of a cultural identity.

I speak the alien tongue
in sweet Borinqueño thoughts,
know love mixed with pain,
have tasted spit on ghetto stairways,
. . . here, it must be changed—
we must change it.

I may never overcome
the theft of my isla heritage,
dulce palmas de coco on Luquillo
sway in windy recesses I can only imagine
and remember how it was,

but that reality, now a dream,
teaches me to see and will
bring me back to me.

PUERTO RICAN DISCOVERY NUMBER THREE, NOT NEITHER

Being Puertorriqueña-Dominicana,
Borinqueña-Quisqueyana, Taíno-Africana
Born in the Bronx.
Not really jíbara.
Not really hablando bien.
But yet, not gringa either.
Pero ni portorra.
Pero sí, portorra too.
Pero ni qué what am I? Y qué soy?
Pero con what voice do my lips move?
Rhythms of rosa wood feet dancing bomba.
Not even here, but here, y conga.
Yet not being. Pero soy.
And not really. Y somos.
Y como somos—bueno,
eso sí es algo lindo, algo muy lindo.

We defy translation.
Ni tengo nombre. Nameless,
we are a whole culture
once removed,
Lolita alive for twenty-five years.
Ni soy, pero soy,
Puertorriqueña como ella
giving blood to the independent star,
daily transfusions
into the river
of la sangre viva.

LOVE POEM FOR NTOZAKE & ME

to the one and only Ntozake Shange

Because of you I believe
in sisterhood
and soulful sunshine
translated into song
accidental genius
and rainbow rivers
like the river that led me to you
Dreams come true
true love on wings of poetry
roaring African savannah lions
laying peacefully with the once hunted
butterflies dancing gracefully with the once haunted

Because of you I believe
in the peace found in healing
the healing that can only be found
in experience translated into words
translated into shared testimony
translated into bonds of true connection

And because I am one of those colored girls
who survived inescapable rites of passage
which compelled me to consider suicide
to then by God's mercy and grace
discover the you in me
who set her own self free
as I uncovered my own strength

in and on stages
found salvation within the pages
of a poet who survived to tell her story
and survived by telling it

Ntozake, thank you
for the courageous example to
find and act on the means
to reclaim the lost innocence
of my Black Boricua Bronxeña girlhood
to create a beautiful mosaic of dreams
shattered into a million fragmented pieces
to give birth to a new universe
of purpose and conviction
a work of art in an open sky of inspiration
for all the Black and Brown girls like me
born free
Born with the divine right to be
on this planet
to be loved
valued and
respected

Because of you
I am a poet
who believes
not in writing poems
on L-shaped desks
with lakeside views
but in birthing poems
on tile floors
back up against wooden doors

I am a poet who believes in creation
in writing poems
to inspire the next generation

I am a poet who believes in fire tears
to cleanse the soul
cascade down to make you whole
and healing thunder laughter

And I thank God that
the rainbow was enuf
to birth a thunder goddess
who birthed a rainbow
who birthed Ntozake
sunshine, moonlight and stardust
all over the place
as muses sparkled honey kisses
on your beautiful baby girl face

Ntozake, I love you

Pen to paper
salsa-dancin
Spanglish-speakin
soul-seekin
africana diaspora
diva

Ntozake, I believe in you

You are the iridescent rainbow reflection
constantly reminding me to believe in myself
You lowered rainbows into sewers saving

the lives of Black girls like me
sashaying colorful headwraps
hoop earrings, bangle bracelets
and sweet oil perfume

You sing survival
into words
into epics
into rainbow-colored
broadway lights
into the consciousness
of our time
our collective memory
our collective survival

To know you is a blessing
To be hugged warmly
To look into your beautiful coffee eyes
that whisper
This poem
this poem is for you
These words
this time
this breath
is for all the colored girls who considered suicide
but instead held their own candlelight vigils
in marble notebooks
Who fought demons all night
waiting for the arrival of first light
Who know that dawn is really a woman
the backdrop of a beautiful black sky
and a rainbow laying sexy on her side

Frost led me to you
and because of you, Ntozake
I know that sometimes
the greatest of poems
are birthed in the agony
of headaches, stomachaches and heartache
somewhere deep
within the quiet peace
of my soul

Poems that make me whole

Poems that set me free

Ntozake

Gracias.

HOMAGE TO MY HAIR

My hair is
powerful hair
mighty hair
goddess-like hair.

My hair can show you
the way to freedom
forever obstruct your vision
of internalized ugly isms.

My hair is the ocean at its wildest.
My hair is Olokun in a rage.

My hair is the untamed hurricane
of ancestral shame uncaged.

My hair is alive
beautiful
wild
and free.

My hair is the sun
forever
glistening.

1980

for the child victims of the Atlanta Child Murders

1980 wasn't special
except it was the year
I turned nine and became an activist
my child eyes glued to the six o'clock news

    fear floats in the swirls of 13 channels
        grows grows grows
      like the cold dead bodies of Black children
        into questions my mother does not answer

1980
    the year I learn against my fragile will
      the sting of hatred and
    wicked words that crush my spirit
    years before the word racism enters my vocabulary

1980
    the year between 1979 and 1981
      when more than forty Black children
    are kidnapped and
    slaughtered in Atlanta

  far away
    from away from the Bronx my mother assures me
  not far enough
  the danger zone is as close
  as the nearest television
  and for some odd reason
  close enough that we are no longer
    allowed to stray too far from the house.

1980
a year of morbid child curiosity,
a strange/need to know if
any more bodies of Black children
were found strangled or stabbed or shot,
if they had found the killer
or killers as they speculated the rise of KKK
sinister aspirations to wipe out
future Black generations.

1980
only one year in the span of
American childhood nightmares
where I'd dream myself
trapped in the black airless trunk
of a slow moving car
where I'd see my own child face
posted with the many small disappeared faces

looking so much like mine
mostly boys but some girls/hair braided and adorned
with rainbow-colored barrettes/barrettes like mine.

1980
another year of
no justice and no peace
the year before the Atlanta police found that Black man
with the thick glasses and the big afro and said he was
the killer, killing the dead count at 28
forgetting
about missing bones
doomed to forever remain missing
from their mommas and their papas
and a proper burial.

1980
the year my mother gave me a big white button
with bold green letters attached to a green satin ribbon
that read SAVE THE CHILDREN
that I proudly wore pinned to my school uniform
as I marched off to school/now part of the growing movement to
    save the children.

I felt somehow protected by this button
felt that I could save the children
and somehow save myself by wearing it
that somehow I was connected to all of the people
who went down to Atlanta to save the children/the activists and
    church leaders who
joined/the mothers and/the people led by hound dogs and psychics
    and even the New
York City Guardian Angels with their/red berets and black leather
    jackets.

1980
   the year
      I ran home after school
salty tears in my eyes

           What are you doing wearing that button?
Mrs. Mangione asked me in the schoolyard.

You're not bahhh-L-a-c-k?!

    (rolling the word black off her tongue like something
    you wouldn't wanna catch)

You're poor-tah-re-eeeck-can.

    (emphasis on *poor*/to put me in my place)

1980   just
the year of my first encounter with race
the year I start paying close attention to the news
the year I became part of a movement
the year I ask my mother,

    Is it true I'm not Black?

the year my mother tells me

          Puerto Ricans have Black, Indian
          and Spanish blood

the year I ask my mother,

> *Does that mean my blood is black too?*

the year she tells me,

> *Your blood is red like everybody else's.*

the year I gather a bit more evidence to not
          trust white people.

1980 wasn't special at all
except it was the year my mother made an activist of me
the year I proudly wore my button
the year I said nothing to that Italian lady in the schoolyard but
   went home looked in the
mirror and for the very first time said to myself

> *I, too, am Black.*

> *Save the children.*

ODE TO THE DIASPORICAN

Mira mi cara puertorriqueña
mi pelo vivo
mis manos morenas
Mira mi corazón que se llena de orgullo
y dime que no soy Boricua.

Some people say that I'm not the real thing
Boricua, that is
cause I wasn't born on the enchanted island
cause I was born on the mainland

north of Spanish Harlem
cause I was born in the Bronx . . .
some people think that I'm not bonafide
cause my playground was a concrete jungle
cause my Río Grande de Loiza was the Bronx River
cause my Fajardo was City Island
my Luquillo Orchard Beach
and summer nights were filled with city noises
instead of coquís
and Puerto Rico
was just some paradise
that we only saw in pictures.

What does it mean to live in between
What does it take to realize
that being Boricua
is a state of mind
a state of heart
a state of soul . . .

¡Mira!

No nací en Puerto Rico.
Puerto Rico nació en mí.

Mira mi cara puertorriqueña
mi pelo vivo
mis manos morenas
Mira mi corazón que se llena de orgullo
y dime que no soy Boricua.

POEM FOR MY GRIFA-RICAN SISTAH
OR BROKEN ENDS BROKEN PROMISES

for my twin sister Melissa, who endured it with me

Braids twist and tie
constrain baby naps never to be free
braids twist and tie
contain/hold in the shame
of not havin' long black silky strands
to run my fingers through.
Moños y bobby pins
twist and wrap
Please forgive me for the sin
of not inheriting Papi's "good hair"
moños y bobby pins
twist and wrap
restrain kinky naps
dying to be free
but not the pain
of not having a long black silky mane
to run my fingers through.

Clips and ribbons
to hold back and tie
oppressing baby naps
never to be free.

Clips and ribbons
to hold back and tie
imprisoning baby naps
never to have the dignity to be.

Chemical relaxers
broken ends/broken promises
activator and cream
mixed in with bitterness
mix well . . .

Keep away from children
Avoid contact with eyes
This product contains lye and lies
Harmful if swallowed

The ritual of combing/parting/sectioning
the greasing of the scalp/the neck
the forehead/the ears
the process/and then the burning/the burning

"It hurts to be beautiful, 'tate quieta"
my mother tells me
"¡Pero, mami, me PICA!"

and then the running/the running to water
to salvation/to neutralizer/to broken ends
and broken promises.

Graduating from Carefree Curl
to Kitty curl/to Revlon/to super duper Fabulaxer
different boxes offering us broken ends and broken promises.

"We've come a long way since Dixie Peach."
My mother tells me as I sit at the kitchen table.

Chemical relaxers to melt away the shame
until new growth reminds us
that it is time once again
for the ritual and the fear of
scalp burns and hair loss
and the welcoming
of broken ends
and broken
promises.

When the truth is that
Black hair
African-textured hair
carefree crazy curly hair
is beautiful
¡Qué viva pelo libre!

¡Qué viva!

NEGRITUDE

for Tato Laviera, Jesús Papoleto Meléndez, Juan Flores and Trinidad Sanchez Jr.

We be those Negroes
born to slave hands
resurrecting African gods
when transplanted to new lands
mixing ebonics
with spanglish slang

We be those Negroes
children of Yoruba y Ibo
bilingual and Indio
Afro-Caribes
masters of plantation work
race mixing
and Orisha spirit raising

We be those Negroes
creating jazz with cats
named Bird, Dizzy, Duke and Armstrong
Cubop Bugalu SalSoul searching journey men
Mongo Santamaría, Chano Pozo drum gods
and Celia Cruz
AZÚCAS!
Legends leaving our cultural footprints
on the muddy minds
of the mentally dead

We be those Negroes
creating Schomburg Museums of Black Studies
in Nuyorican Harlem streets
where we once danced
during zoot suits riots
to conga
maraca
bata
break beats
and Palladium massacres

We be those Negroes
drawn as Sambos and Jigaboos
by political cartoonists
who couldn't erase
the taste of
Africa
from Antillean culinary
magicians
creating miracles
with curries called sofrito

We be those Negroes
Younglords
Island Nationalists
Black Panthers
Vieques activists
Santeros
and Guerreros
brothers of Garvey
children of Malcolm
Black Spades
Savage Skulls

Chingalings
and Latin Kings

We be those Negroes
like Harvard-educated lawyer
Don Pedro Albizu Campos
stationed
in all Black regiments
learning the reality
of Jim Crow society
and their gringolandia
government race public policies
calling bilingual Negroes
Spics

We be those Negroes
before Sosa
before Clemente
before Jackie
giving Negro league
baseball legends
a place
under the sun
to call home
when no one else
would have them

We be those Negroes
dancing
moving
breaking
Egyptian
Electric Boogalooing

Locking
on concrete jungles
to Kool Herc Grandmaster Flash
Zulu Jamaican
Sound Boy systems
and aerosol
symphony backgrounds

We be those Negroes
Charlie Chasing / Disco Wizing
Rock Steadying
a dream called Hip-Hop
in Bronx backyard boulevards
between
casitas and tenements
with roaches for landlords

We be those Negroes
writing epics
like Willie Perdomo testaments
called "Nigger-Rican Blues"
and Victor Hernández Cruz
odes to "African Things"
hiding our dark-skinned
literary Abuelitas
with Bemba Colora
in places where the whiteness police
could never find them

We be those Negroes
denied access to Black Nationalist run
Karenga Kwanza poetry readings
because we remind the ignorant

of the complexity that is their culture
neither here nor there
not quite brown
not quite white
We navigate uncharted
waters
of Black identity boxes

We be those Negroes
Mulatto
We be those Negroes
Criollo
We be those Negroes
Moreno
We be those Negroes
Trigueños
We be those Negroes
Octoroons and Quadroons
We be those Negroes
Cimarrones and Nanny of the Maroons
We be those Negroes
Cienfuegos y Fidel
We be those Negroes
Luis Palés Matos and Aimé Césaire
We be those Negroes
Puentes
Mirandas
Riveras
Colons
Felicianos
Flores
Lavoes and
Palmieris

We be those Negroes
judíos
y a veces
jodíos
We be those Negroes
Dominicanos y Cubanos
We be those Negroes
Jaimiquinos y Haitianos
We be those Negroes
Panameños y Borinqueños

We be those Negroes
seeking freedom from
irrationality
in an age of nuclear
Goya families
and television
carbon copy clone
Univision / BET / MTV / Viacom
Slave children

We be those Negroes
known by many names
and many deeds
spoken of in secret
by African-American
scholars
in envy during their nightly
salsa
dance classes
as they try
to pick up white girls

We be those Negroes
Caribbean
Negritude
heroes
sometimes negating our destiny
but always finding
peace
in the darkness
of sleep

We be those Negroes
Negroes
we
be.

LUCUMÍ

para Freddie Moreno
(translated by Carolina Fung Feng)

Moreno
deja que tu leyenda
sea contada
alrededor de fogatas
no a través de cadenas
y látigos
pero a través de areítos
y sesiones de tambor.
El último de los Bakongo
el primero del
Toque de Bata
Sanidad de Ashé
Shaka Zulu

Ashanti
Dahomey
Princesa guerrera
Moreno
hablas en fuego
y te mueves
en ritmos del Clave.

El hijo
de Shangó
hijo de Loiza
espíritu de Boriquen
Afro-Taíno
ciudadano del Estado Libre Asociado
de Cubop
Tu memoria
vivirá
en las palabras
y en las obras
de los niños de Conga.

Moreno
deja que tu nombre de guerra
viva más allá de la oscuridad
de tu sombra.
Deja que aquellos que buscan la luz
encuentren reposo
entre la comodidad
de las notas de sinfonía
y los asesinatos del Birimbao.

Moreno
sabemos
y te queremos

porque tú representas
amor y paz.
En una época de oscuridad
cuando todo se desmorona
y el mundo ansía
la verdad de nuestra existencia.

No existe una mañana
sin un hoy
porque el hoy
es todo lo que algunos tienen.
Así que déjanos recordarte,
Moreno
nuestro hermano
nuestra reflexión
nuestro destino
nuestro amigo
lo mejor
de nuestro
pueblo latino
pa'lante
¡Siempre, pa'lante!
Moreno.

WE, THE CHILDREN OF JUAN EPSTEIN

for Juan Flores and Jose Irizarry

Somos
los hijos
de Juan Epstein
An island
in motion

transglobal nation
on the move
the Forgotten
and the Dispossessed
marginalized
colonized
yet still Dignified
Our suffering
can be heard
in Le Lo Lai
Scat Sessions
and Bugalu Breakdowns
Jíbaro
chants
and bomba
Barrio
Beatdowns
A Diaspora
striking back
Our seeds
are spread
throughout
the New World
from Nueva Yol
to Philly
to Chitown
to Massachusetts
and beyond
If you listen
closely
you can hear
the echoes
of an Afro-Taíno

people
the survivors
of 1898
Manifest Destiny
and Ponce Massacres

Somos
los hijos
de Juan Epstein
The Children
of Albizu
Betances
Bracetti
Hostos
Lebrón
and Flores
Our dreams
can be seen
in Supreme
Court
Sotomayor
Halls of Justice
and Bruno
pop
concert
Mars
festivals
Pantoja
Aspirations
and Mark
salsa
symphonies
from

bomba
to hip-hop
The Bronx
Fania
Boogie
B-Boys / Girls
We live
in Divided Borders
from the Piragueros
in Spanish Harlem
to the Alcapurria
Lady
on Grand Concourse
somos hustlers
entreprenuers
We will gladly
pay you Tuesday
for a mofongo
today

Somos
los hijos
de Juan Epstein
the offspring
from
a bad
episode
of Welcome
Back Kotter
a rerun
of the African
Diaspora
Latin Jazz

Masters
and reggaeton
pioneers
pop
culture
aficionados
preservers
of Nuyorican
poetics
Somos
los hijos
de Juan Epstein
our voices
are profound
and they
will be heard,
punto.

ARROZ POÉTICA

I got news yesterday
from a friend of mine
that all people against the war should
send a bag of rice to George Bush,
& on the bag we should write,
"If your enemies are hungry, feed them."

But to be perfectly clear,
my enemies are not hungry.
They are not standing in lines
for food, or stretching rations,
or waiting at the airports
to claim the pieces
of the bodies of their dead.
My enemies ride jets to parties.
They are not tied up in pens
in Guantanamo Bay. They are not
young children throwing rocks. My enemies eat
meats & vegetables at tables
in white houses where candles blaze, cast
shadows of crosses & flowers.
They wear ball gowns & suits & rings
to talk of war in neat & folded languages
that will not stain their formal dinner clothes
or tousle their hair. They use words like "casualties"
to speak of murder. They are not stripped down to skin
& made to stand barefoot in the cold or hot.

They do not lose their children to this war.
They do not lose their houses & their streets. They do not
come home to find their lamps broken.
They do not ever come home to find their families murdered
or disappeared or guns put at their faces.
Their children are not made to walk
a field of mines, exploding.

This is no wedding.
This is no feast.
I will not send George Bush rice, worked for rice
from my own kitchen
where it sits in a glass jar & I am transfixed
by the thousands of beautiful pieces
like a watcher at some homemade & dry
aquarium of grains, while the radio calls out
the local names of 2,000
US soldiers counted dead since March.
&, we all know it, there will always be more than
what's been counted. They will not say the names
of an Iraqi family trying to pass a checkpoint
in an old white van. A teenager caught out on some road
after curfew. The radio will go on, shouting
the names &, I promise you,
they will not call your name, Hassna
Ali Sabah, age 30, killed by a missile in Al-Bassra, or you,
Ibrahim Al-Yussuf, or the sons of Sa'id Shahish
on a farm outside of Baghdad, or Ibrahim, age 12,
as if your blood were any less red, as if the skins
that melted were any less skin & the bones
that broke were any less bone,
as if your eradication were any less absolute, any less

eradication from this earth where you were
not a president or a military soldier.
& you will not ever walk home
again, or smell your mother's hair again,
or shake the date palm tree
or smell the sea
or hear the people singing at your wedding
or become old
or dream or breathe, or even pray or whistle,
& your tongue will be all gone or useless
& it will not ever say again or ask a question,
you, who were birthed once, & given milk,
& given names that mean: she is born at night,
happy, favorite daughter,
morning, heart, father of
a multitude.

Your name, I will have noticed
on a list collected by an Iraqi census of the dead,
because your name is the name of my own brother,
because your name is the Tigrinya word for "tomorrow,"
because all my life I have wanted a farm,
because my students are 12, because I remember
when my sisters were 12. & I will not
have ever seen your eyes, & you will not
have ever seen my eyes
or the eyes of the ones who dropped the missiles,
or the eyes of the ones who ordered the missiles,
& the missiles have no eyes. You had no chance,
the way they fell on avenues & farms
& clocks & schoolchildren. There was no place for you
& so you burned. A bag of rice will not bring you back.

A poem cannot bring you. & although it is my promise here
to try to open every one of my windows, I cannot
imagine the intimacy with which
a life leaves its body, even then,
in detonation, when the skull is burst,
& the body's country of indivisible organs
flames into the everything. & even in
that quick departure as the life rushes on,
headlong or backwards, there must, must
be some singing as the hand waves "be well"
to its other hand, goodbye;
& the ear belongs to the field now.
& we cannot separate the roof from the heart
from the trees that were there, standing.
& so it is, when I say "night,"
it is your name I am calling,
when I say "field,"
your thousand, thousand names,
your million names.

SANTA ANA OF THE GROCERY CARTS

Santa Ana of grocery carts, truckers,
eggs in the kitchen at 4 am, nurses, cleaning ladies,
the saints of ironing, the saints
of tortillas. Santa Ana of cross-guards, tomato pickers,
bakeries of bread in pinks & yellows, sugars.
Santa Ana of Cambodia, Viet Nam, Aztlán
down Bristol & Raitt. Santa Ana.
Boulevards of red lips, beauty salons, boomboxes, drone
of barber shop clippers fading tall Vincent's head, schoolyards,

the workshop architects, mechanics.
Santa Ana of mothers, radiators, trains.
Santa Ana of barbecues.
Santa Ana of Trujillos, Sampsons & Agustíns,
Zuly & Xochit with their twin lampish skins.
Santa Ana of cholas, bangs & spray.
Santa Ana of AquaNet, altars,
the glitter & shine
of 99-cent stores, taco trocas, churches, of bells,
hallelujahs & center fields, aprons,
of winds, collard greens & lemon cake
in Ms. Davenport's kitchen,
sweat, sweat over the stove. Santa Ana
of polka-dots, chicharrones, Aztecs, African Fields, colombianas,
sun's children, vanished children. Santa Ana of órales.
Santa Ana of hairnets.
Patron saint of kitchens, asphalt, banana trees,
bless us if you are capable of blessing.

When we started, there were cousins & two parents,
now everything lost has been to you.
The house, axed & opossums
gone. Abrigette & her husband John.
& the schoolyard boys underneath the ground,
undressed so thoroughly by your thousand mouths, Santa Ana,

let that be
enough.

TEETH

for cousin Gedion, who drove us to Massawa

Two sisters ride down with us.
It is liberation day in Massawa.

The older sister is the color of injera; her teeth are big
      & stuck out.
The younger sister is a cinnamon stick.

Their almond eyes are the same.
Ink black hair falls beautiful down both their backs.

I see that you love one of them & change my mind
many times about who I think it is.

Months later, I will show their photographs to my father
who will laugh & say he knows.

"It is this one," he will say, surely, pointing
to the woman whose teeth stay, tame, in her mouth.

But what man would choose a woman
whose mouth looks stronger than his hands?

Know, Cousin, I pray there is love
between you & the older one
whose teeth might be bullets of ivory;

I imagine from this mouth:
      kites,
      rain,
      ax equal to lace, the yellow & lick

of a jar filled with
the sweet of stinging bees.

ODE TO THE LITTLE "R"

Little propeller
working between
the two fields of my a's,
making my name
a small boat
that leaves the port
of old San Juan
or Ponce,
with my grandfather,
Miguel, on a boat,
or in an airplane,
with a hundred or so
others, leaving the island
for work, cities,
in winters that would break
their bones, make old,
old men out of all of them,
factory workers, domino
players, little islands themselves
who would eat & be eaten by Chicago,
New York, the wars
they fought without
being able to vote for
the president. Little propeller
of their names: Francisco,
Reymundo, Arelis, Margarita,
Hernán, Roberto, Reina.
Little propeller of our names

delivering the cargo of blood
to the streets of Holyoke,
Brooklyn, New London,
Ojai, where the teacher says,
"Say your name?" sweetly,
& the beautiful propeller
working between
the two fields of my a's
& the teacher saying, "Oh!
You mean, 'Are-Raw-Sell-Lease.'"
Or "Robe-Bert-Toe"
or "Marred-Guh-Reetuh, like
the drink!" & the "r"
sounding like a balloon
deflating in the room, sad
& sagging. I am hurt.
It is as if I handed them
all my familiar trees & flowers,
every drawing of the family map
& boats & airplanes & cuatros
& coquís & they used their English
to make an axe & tried to chop
them down. But, "r," little propeller
of my name, small & beautiful monster
changing shapes, you win. You fly
around the room, little bee, upsetting
the teacher & making all of Class-310A laugh,
you fly over the yard, in our mouths,
as our bodies make airplanes over the grass,
you, little propeller, are taking over the city,
you are the sound of cars racing, the sound
of bicycle spokes fitted with playing cards
to make it sound like we are going fast,
this is our ode to you, little "r," little

machine of our names, simple
as a heart, just working, always,
there when we go to the grocery,
there in the songs
we sing in our sleep.

RUNNING HOME, I SAW THE PLANTS

On the way home, going,
with the hill & mammoth clouds
behind me, rushing to the house
before the rain, those beautiful Pakistani girls,
their faces happy as poppies, I thought, those girls
rushing home as I was rushing home.

Person, if you remember a thing I ever told you, please,
remember this.

As the first small pieces
of rain fell down,
glinting in departing light,
the beautiful girls were laughing, shrieking like
gulls, five or six of them (depending
on whether I count myself), the bright
& shining planets of their saris
lifting, just so, in the wind. I touch
my heart. I can't stop touching
my heart & saying, Today is my birthday,
for the beautiful clamor of the planets running home
beneath the gorgeous blackness of their wet & shining hair,
atop the gorgeous blackness of their patent leather hooves.
Today is my birthday. I know, now, the girls are planets.
I know, now, the girls are horses. & you—

NIGHT, FOR HENRY DUMAS

Henry Dumas, 1934-1968
did not die by a spaceship
or flying saucer or outer space at all,
but was shot down, at 33,
by a New York City Transit policeman,
will be shot down, May 23rd,
coming home, in just 6 days,
by a New York City Transit policeman
in the subway station singing & thinking of a poem,
at Lenox & 125th in Harlem, Tennessee,
Memphis, New York, Watts, Queens.
1157 Wheeler Avenue, San Quentin above which
sky swings down a giant rope, says
Climb me into heaven, or follow me home,
& Henry
& Amadou
& Malcolm
& Oscar
& Sean
& King,
& the night hangs over the men & their faces,
& the night grows thick above the streets,
I swear it is more blue, more black, tonight
with the men going up there.
Bring the children out
to see who their uncles are.

Dumas, Henry. "Outer Space Blues." *Knees of a Natural Man: The Selected Poetry of Henry Dumas.* Eugene B. Redmond ed. New York: Thunder's Mouth, 1989, 66-67.

MODESTO FLAKO JIMÉNEZ

GRACIAS MARGARITA AGRAMONTE

Ella aguantó mi maleta nueva
mientras lágrimas bailaban sobre su cara.

Olvidadizo, yo miraba
hacia los gigantes metales que se levantaban
mientras asustaban las palmas dominicanas
a decir adiós
hacia su gente.

Hechizado,
no me di cuenta de las señales.

Sus lágrimas eran tibias mientras nos abrazábamos.
"Tú vas a ver
a América," me dijo a mí,
"Compórtate bien."

Su último beso de protección fue mezclado,
con sus disculpas a los juegos
que no podía comprar;
sus últimas palabras de sabiduría,
"Tu abuela te comprará tu primer Nintendo."

Yo era indiferente a las preocupaciones adultas.
Mis ojos estaban llenos con los monstruos gigantes.

Pronto escapaba de su agarre, persiguiendo los monstruos.
Después de este punto pasajeros solamente.

Sigo extrañándola.
19 años, 4 meses, 9 días y sigo contando . . .
que no la veo.

THE CURSE OF THE GOAT

This goat is magical.
In various guises it has possessed
our maiden quisqueya through the years.

The first recorded appearance
in the grass of our country cane:
The goat stuck his flag in our soil
and made us take his name
la Isla Española.

When he moved on us
the great chief Caonabo
and our lady chief Anacaona,
our golden flower, our beauty, our warrior poet,
burned the trespasser's tower to the ground,
and La Navidad was stillborn.
But he still continued to move on us.
our spears were not enough
to fend off the advances of the Spanish goat,
the gold rush,
and Concepción de La Vega
grew and prospered.

Hatuey and Guamá raced ahead to warn the virgin Cuba
but the goat had tricks in abundance.
Simple smallpox infected
the Taíno.

And
because of his desire for sweets
the cane
infested the land.

The pure Pereskia Quisqueyana
became an endangered species.
The goat comes in different
shapes, sizes, forms.
The next time he appeared among us
as one of our own.
His disguise confused the land.

Falling under his spell, we embraced him,
the man who made the name commercial,
El Chivo,
the generalissimo.

With a malignant hunger
the many mouths of his cattle,
the devouring indiscriminate goat's maw of his ego,
destroyed all his homeland,
wanting to eat all the grass before it grew,
then shitting on the ground,
leaving nothing but emptiness
in a alluring but unearthly landscape with names like
"Ciudad Trujillo. Pico Trujillo."

When he was finally gone
old men shouted in anger
at the goat's corpse
their stories of abuse:

"My mother and father offended you,
so, not yet 13, you punish me
with a trip to camp La Cuarenta, your prison of oblivion.
'Take off your clothes dirty shit face aqueroso.'
Ordered the guard
I was a lucky child able to shout your name with love
and that's all that kept me safe
from being digested as your daily snack."

Finally now, my dear quisqueyanos
the Goat appears every 4 years
under the name of democracy.
We keep slaughtering the goats,
but then we serve each other goat stew,
we feed each other Hipólito and Leonel,
a meal that only makes you hungrier,
the new era of goat tricks,
corruption.

So many so greedy for a taste
of the drugs and money,
the new jewels and gold.

I understand
that we were the first ground zero, Mr. Díaz,
cursed from day one.
But I ask you
is there no way to restore the valor
of the Bayahibe Rose?

EL TAXISTA

para Felipe Natasha

Loco ver la vida a través de los ojos de Globo.
Para él, soy un mono en ropa de humano.
Para él, buscar el éxito en una nueva tarima
significa repudiar mi herencia,
me hace ser un fraude y un aspirante.

Buscando un préstamo para mi próximo show,
en una chaqueta a medida y mi zapatos Polo,
vengo donde él con una ofrenda de paz
con torta de queso y pan de banana.

La vieja mano grita disgustada,
"¿Mono, qué mierda es esta?
¡¿Por qué no me traes nuestro
plátano con aceite y agua
endulzada por el color
de años de bajo del sol?!"

Los españoles le cortaban las manos a los taínos,
si no ofrecían el tributo apropiado.

Él murmura, "Él no puede tomar con nosotros,
no hay blancos alrededor".
Me inclino respetuosamente, como un "mono leal",
y me retiro.

Confusión, enojo, decepción.
Solía admirar a Globo.
Él tiene su propia tropa, un hogar, una respetada familia.

Siempre está listo para ayudar a un vecino en necesidad.
Pero a yo explorando "diferencia" le da miedo.

¿Cómo le explico a mi raza que no hay raza superior?
Heredada esclavitud estabilizada en nuestras mentes.
Aunque el globo cambie, su mente se queda igual.
Se pregunta cómo, todavía, para él,
siendo astuto y utilizando tu cerebro
solamente equivale a ser un aristócrata europeo
que es dueño de esclavos.
está todo en nosotros,
cimarrón, mulato, incluso si usted no quiere, maestro.

Globo, ¿alguna vez nos miró como algo más
que fruteros, carniceros, bodegueros,
narcotraficantes, estafadores, tiguerazos,
o taxistas?
Globo, ¿motivas a tus niños a ser lo mejor?
o ¿te sientes feliz con que solo
cumplan con el estándar "dominicano"?
Por favor, Globo, escucha:
José Núñez de Cáceres, Junot Díaz, Julia Álvarez,
Jaime Colson, Juan Luis Guerra, María Montéz,
Arambilet.

Yo como plátanos y pan de banana.
Yo bailo en Kary's y veo Kaddish en la Armería.
En la noche, manejo un taxi
y cada tarde le enseño a los niños a escribir y actuar.
Todo esto
me hace Indio Taíno,
me hace dominicano,
me hace humano.

TITO MADERA SMITH

for Dr. Juan Flores

he claims he can translate palés matos'
black poetry faster than i can talk,
and that if i get too smart,
he will double translate pig latin
english right out of webster's
dictionary, do you know him?

he claims he can walk into east harlem
apartment where langston hughes gives
spanglish classes for newly arrived
immigrants seeking a bolitero-numbers
career and part-time vendors of cuchi-
fritters sunday afternoon in central
park, do you know him?

he claims to have a stronghold of the
only santería secret baptist sect in
west harlem, do you know him?

he claims he can talk spanish styled in
sunday dress eating crabmeat-jueyes
brought over on the morning eastern
plane deep fried by la negra costoso
joyfully singing puerto rican folklore:
"maría luisa no seas brava,
llévame contigo pa la cama," or
"oiga capitán delgado, hey captain delgaro,
mande a revisar la grama, please inspect
the grass, que dicen que un aeroplano,

they say that an airplane throws marijuana
seeds."

do you know him? yes, you do,
i know you know him, that's right,
madera smith, tito madera smith:
he blacks and prieto talks at the same time,
splitting his mother's santurce talk,
twisting his father's south carolina soul,
adding new york scented blackest harlem
brown-eyes diddy bops, tú sabes, mami,
that i can ski like a bomba soul salsa
mambo turns to aretha franklin stevie
wonder nicknamed patato guaguancó steps,
do you know him?

he puerto rican talks to las mamitas
outside the pentecostal church, and
he gets away with it, fast-paced i
understand-you-my-man, with clave
sticks coming out of his pockets hooked
to his stereophonic 15-speaker indispensable
disco sounds blasting away at cold reality
struggling to say estás buena, baby
as he walks out of tune and out of
step with alleluia cascabells,
puma sneakers,
pants rolled up,
shirt cut in middle chest,
santería chains,
madamo pantallas,
into the spanish social club,
to challenge elders in dominoes,
like the king of el diario's

budweiser tournament
drinking cerveza-beer
like a champ,
do you know him?
well, i sure don't,
and if i did, i'd
refer him to 1960
social scientists
for assimilation
acculturation
digging
autopsy
>
> into
> their
> heart
> attacks,
> oh,
> oh,
> there
> he
> comes,
> you can call him tito,
> or you can call him madera,
> or you can call him smitty,
> or you can call him mr. t,
> or you can call him nuyorican,
> or you can call him black,
> or you can call him latino,
> or you can call him mr. smith,
> his sharp eyes of awareness,
> greeting us in aristocratic harmony:
> "you can call me many things, but
> you gotta call me something."

JORGE BRANDON

poetry is an outcry, love, affection,
a sentiment, a feeling, an attitude,
a song.

it is internal gut expressing intimate
thoughts upon a moment's experience.

poetry is the incessant beauty called
a person by an action that takes form.

the smell of sand in water digging moon
the loving smile.

poetry is the mountain, the recital,
the reaction, the desire, to feel
right in wrong, to taste bitter
memory, to praise death, to mourn,
to call.

poetry, oh, poetry

beautiful novels in short-lived prose.

long live your concise aristocracy!

long live your detailed concrete forms!

long live the people who espouse you!

long live sentiments of love!

long live unending desires, on and on
forever on:

poetry poetry

a poeta called

the soul!

ANGELITOS EULOGY IN ANGER

angelito is my brother
can you undestand?
angelito is my brother

not that bro talk we misuse
but the real down
brother-blood-salsa   sangre de madre

angelito is my brother
dancing slow curves of misery
nodding slow-motion tunes
of alcohol dynamic soul   arrastrándose por las calles
           con su andar de ángel-loco

standing on the usual
corner the talk of all
the afflicition in the ghetto:
         se llevó el radio
         me escondió los cheques
         me quitó la cartera
         se robó el tique del ponchop

                              pero angelito lo pusieron
                              ahí mami, me entiendes

angelito was being sponsored
by soft legislators and by
the multi-million dollars
the racket is worth annually
and all of you loved the godfather
the all-time ghetto best film forever

                              me entiendes, papi
                              angelito lo tenían ahí
                              amedrentándoles las venas
                              mocosas sucias que
                              le imprentaron
                              a ese hermano mío
                              de sange vinagrosa
                              húmeda de esa sangre
                              descalza aguada
                              que cambió de roja a blanca

angelito was angered
by the teacher
    the preacher
    the liberal
    the social worker
    the basketball coach
that mistreated him and
didn't let him express
his inner feelings

                              a angelito le hicieron un trabajo
                              espiritual le echaron agua

maldita le mezclaron sus buenos
pensamientos le partieron el
melodioso cantar del cucurucú
en su cantar en brujos

angelito didn't get the chance
to receive an education or to
graduate from basic english
courses   no lo querían curar
because of that once a junkie
always a junkie theory i was
taught ten years ago when
heroine had not yet invaded the
wired fences of queens. all of
a sudden drugs reach queens blvd.

and all kinds of addiction cen-
ters popped off on my block to
cure them

y tú, condenao madre y padre
a veces te digo,
por dejarte convencer
sus cabezas
por sus caprichos
de más dinero
por parar de sembrar guineos
por traernos a este
maldito sitio
donde nos ultrajaron
los bichos de varones
las tetas llenas de leche
de mi abuela

los poderosos pezones
de aquella jibarita
que se meneaba poderosamente
que me hubiese
gustado agarrarla
con mucho gusto . . .
ahora, a esa jibarita,
me la tienen
como tecata flaca
perdida en su desaliento
andando de prostituta
abriéndole las patas
al viejo palo de mapo

and the other junkies
the real junkies of the
true definition of the
word junkie (the ones
who stumped your community
with high-class hopes shaded
by lack of real attention)
they profited died fat cats
and bought their way into
heaven

nunca los oí decir ni hablar
nada sobre ellos
zánganos aguajeros
sigan tomando cervezas
sigan mirando novelas
sigan criticándose uno a otro
sigan echándole la culpa solo.
a los padres

angelito sabía todo esto
entonces él en la perdición
de su muerte está más despierto
que ustedes. angelito me dijo
todo esto. cuando yo hablo
contigo
lo único que
oigo es el score de los mets

and the rest of you
so-called pretty-looking
bad so bad dumb young
spics are sleeping underneath
the $45-price of your pants

THE SALSA OF BETHESDA FOUNTAIN

the internal feelings we release
when we dance salsa
is the song of manu dibango
screaming africa
as if it were a night in el barrio
when the congas are out

the internal soul of salsa
is like don quijote de la mancha
classical because the roots are
from long ago, the symbol of cervantes
writing in pain of a lost
right arm, and in society today,
the cha-cha slow dance welfare

the internal spirit of salsa
is an out-bembé on sunday afternoons
while felipe flipped his sides
of the cuban-based salsa
which is also part of africa
and a song of the caribbean

the internal dance of salsa
is of course plena
and permit me to say these words
in afro-spanish:
la bomba y la plena puro son
de Puerto Rico que ismael es el
rey y es el juez
meaning the same as marvin gaye
singing spiritual social songs
to black awareness

a blackness in spanish
a blackness in english
mixture-met on jam sessions in central park,
there were no differences in
the sounds emerging from inside
soul-salsa is universal
meaning a rhythm of mixtures
with world-wide bases

did you say you want it stronger?
well, okay, it is a root called africa
in all of us.

COMMONWEALTH

no, not yet, no, not yet
i will not proclaim myself,
a total child of any land,
i'm still in the commonwealth
stage of my life, wondering
what to decide, what to conclude,
what to declare myself.

i'm still in the commonwealth
stage of my life, not knowing
which ideology to select.

i'm still in the commonwealth
stage of my life, all of us
caught in a web of suspension,
light-years away from the indians'
peaceful enclaves.

i'm still in the commonwealth
stage of my life, observing
the many integrated experiences
we took everything
and became everybody else.

i'm still in the commonwealth
stage of my life, but there's
not enough hatred in our hearts
to kill each other or to draw
blood for too long, ours
is a mental search
carved through a mainstream of options

but yet, somewhere
in the commonwealth, we all yearn
to feel our strengths,
to show our ultimate,
to find common wealth among us,
to close our eyes,
to find the total silence, silencio, silence,
to find . . . not one thing that unites us,
even in silence we are still
in the commonwealth stage of our lives,
so let's touch hands, friends and foes,
and stay together to hear each other's
sounds just for one moment, let's stay
tucked together, and maybe then, less
options, maybe then, hope.

NEGRITO

el negrito
vino a nueva york
vio milagros
en sus ojos
su tía le pidió
un abrazo y le dijo,
"no te juntes con
los prietos, negrito".
el negrito
se rascó los piojos
y le dijo,
"pero, titi, pero, titi,
los prietos son negritos".
su tía le agarró
la mano y le dijo,

"no te juntes con
los molletos, negrito".
el negrito
se miró sus manos
y le dijo,
"pero, titi, pero, titi,
así no es puerto rico".
su tía le pidió
un besito y le dijo,
"si los cocolos te molestan,
corres; si te agarran, baila.
hazme caso, hazme caso,
negrito".
el negrito
bajó la cabeza
nueva york lo saludó,
nueva york lo saludó,
y le dijo,
"confusión"
nueva york lo saludó
y le dijo,
"confusión".

LADY LIBERTY

for liberty, your day filled in splendor,
july fourth, new york harbor, nineteen eighty-six,
midnight sky, fireworks splashing,
heaven exploding
into radiant bouquets,
wall street a backdrop of centennial adulation,
computerized capital angling cameras
celebrating the international symbol of freedom

stretched across micro-chips,
awacs surveillance,
wall-to-wall people, sailing ships,
gliding armies ferried
in pursuit of happiness, constitution adoration,
packaged television channels for liberty,
immigrant illusions
celebrated in the name of democratic principles,
god bless america, land of the star
spangled banner
that we love.

but the symbol suffered
one hundred years of decay
climbing up to the spined crown,
the fractured torch hand,
the ruptured intestines,
palms blistered and calloused,
feet embroidered in rust,
centennial decay,
the lady's eyes,
cataract-filled, exposed
to sun and snow, a salty wind,
discolored verses staining her robe.

she needed re-molding, re-designing,
the decomposed body
now melted down for souveniers,
lungs and limbs jailed
in scaffolding of ugly cubicles
incarcerating the body
as she prepared to receive

her twentieth-century transplant
paid for by pitching pennies,
hometown chicken barbecues,
marathons on america's main streets.
she heard the speeches:
the president's
the french and american partners,
the nation believed in her, rooted for the queen,
and lady liberty decided to reflect
on lincoln's emancipatory resoluteness,
on washington's patriotism,
on jefferson's lucidity,
on william jennings bryan's socialism,
on woodrow wilson's league of nations,
on roosevelt's new deal,
on kennedy's ecumenical postures,
and on martin luther king's non-violence.

lady liberty decided to reflect
on lillian wald's settlements,
on helen keller's sixth sense,
on susan b. anthony's suffrage movement,
on mother cabrini's giving soul,
on harriet tubman's stubborn pursuit of freedom.

just before she was touched,
just before she was dismantled,
lady liberty spoke,
she spoke for the principles,
for the preamble,
for the bill of rights,
and thirty-nine peaceful

presidential transitions,
and, just before she was touched,

lady liberty wanted to convey
her own resolutions,
her own bi-centennial goals,
so that in twenty eighty-six,
she would be smiling and she would be proud.
and then, just before she was touched,
and then, while she was being re-constructed,
and then, while she was being celebrated,
she spoke.

if you touch me, touch ALL of my people
who need attention and societal repair,
give the tered and the poor
the same attention, AMERICA,
touch us ALL with liberty,
touch us ALL with liberty.

hunger abounds, our soil is plentiful,
our technology advanced enough
to feed the world,
to feed humanity's hunger . . .
but let's celebrate not our wealth,
not our sophisticate defense,
not our scientific advancements,
not our intellectual adventures.
let us concentrate on our weaknesses,
on our societal needs,
for we will never be free

if indeed freedom is subjugated
to trampling upon people's needs.

this is a warning,
my beloved america.

so touch me,
and in touching me
touch all our people.
do not single me out,
touch all our people,
touch all our people,
all our people
    our people
        people.

and then i shall truly enjoy
my day, filled in splendor,
july fourth, new york harbor,
nineteen eighty-six, midnight sky,
fireworks splashing,
heaven exploding
into radiant bouquets,
celebrating in the name of equality,
in the pursuit of happiness,
god bless america,
land of star
spangled banner
that we love.

MIXTURAO

for English only

we-who engage in
western hemispheric
continental spanish majority
communally sharing linguistics
in humanistic proportions

we-who integrate
urban America
simmering each other's slangs
indigenous nativizing
our tongues' crusing accents
who are you, English,
telling me, "Speak only English
or die."

We-who grassroots
and jíbaro dialectics
yodeling Mexican riddles
chicano 'ese' talk
creole caribbeanisms
black negroid textings
african twisting
european colonizers'
oppressive repertories
savoring new vocabularies
who are you, English,
telling me, "Speak only English
or die."

We-who create continental music
elaborate universal jazz
rhythmic tonalities
vallenato oilings
gospel-rap soulings
brazilian portuguesa
bonito bolero
mayan songs soothing
quebecois hard rock
patois aging
andino cumbias
world-wide tango curvings
merengue-calypso
mating-mixing dancing
tres por cuatro cubanties
con los pasos firmes de aztecas
who are you, English,
telling me, "Speak only English
or die."

we-who are at peace in continental
inter-mixtures
do hereby challenge
united states isolationism
anti-immigrant mono-lingual
constitutional bullets
declarations telling us to
"speak only English or die"
"love it or leave it"
spelling big stick carcass
translations universally excluded
multi-lingual multi-cultural
expressions "need not to apply"

who are you, English,
telling me, "Speak only English
or die."

so enter our multi-lingual
frontiers become a sharing
partner maybe then I might
allow you the privilege
to call me a tremendous
continental "MIXTURAO."

NIDEAQUINIDEALLÁ

de que I know yo si sé
backnforth here soy de aquí
regreso dicen y que what
aterrice o acá o allá

my first name is de aquí
my last name is de allá
my last name is nideaquínideallá
yet to be defined
evolucionario hybrid

backnforth here soy de aquí
cannot be defined
cannot be categorized
cannot be pasteurizao
cannot be homogenizao

what's my new name?
¿cómo me dicen?
regreso a mi tierra native

me llaman y que what
le contesto somos
we are the children
immigrant/migrantes
our madres cutting
blood crowns entering
fronteras wired fences
nuestros padres wrinkled
foreheads peso of dollar
an hour miseria
our uncles and tías
flesh-skinned manos
see-through cemented
tenements hard core trabajo
mis hermanos and sisters
open-preyed borders
societal disasters

de que i know yo si sé
in my yet-to-be-defined
birthplace homeland
dual citizenship accusations
indignations differentiations
pesadillas de callas
intellectual displacements
transplanting raíces
aquí no acá yes aquí allá
backnforth no sé si maybe
in between schizophrenia
cultural ataques in all
directions hip-hopping
nightmares paralyzing
incertidumbres frenéticas

aterrice o acá o allá
child of western hemispheric
creations ancestral inheritors
not knowing past three
previous generations
my boricua sobrenombre
original by parent's birth
nuyorican by geographic
migrational displacements
caribbeanic by folklore
hispanic by culture
latino by mutual promotion
urban by modern necessity
offspring indigenous dialectics
too many hats to wear
too little time to square
qué vida what a life

My first name is de aquí
u.s. of a limbo confusion
insignias of apathy
prejuicio subtle racism
minority status

My middle name is de allá
constant anti-nuyorican
anti-latino born wedlock
in u.s. soils bilingual
problemas not me anymore
we in all of us ustedes
siempre malnombreándonos
we fight not-to-be brainwashed
so se acabó el relajo

stop mental disenfranchisement
my last new latest name:

        nideaquínideallá
        impossible to blend
        impossible to categorize
        impossible to analyze
        impossible to synthesize
        our guerrilla cultural camouflage
        survival linguistic construction
        at emergency moment's notice
        complex afirmaciones parametric
        principles fermenting
        secretive universal
        garabatopandegato pan
        continental yearnings
        complex heringonsa
        de mi hablar

        nideaquínideallá
        escríbelo junto
        sin letra mayúscula
        gracias

TWO POUNDS, NIGHT SKY NOTES

For Aiden

        After reading "Little" by Alfred Starr Hamilton

how fragile the pocked moon
crumpled sheaf-skin
stretched over living bone v paper

when he was
new   a halting

      sliver heart

within sister palms
a curled body
aching to suck

moon-cream
crater lips cracked
for whimper

rattle   this death
silence stones
he was

regolith
basaltic spray
      fountain leap!

of voltage ash
he was falling knock
still

SOUTHWEST PHILADELPHIA, 1988

Our eyes focused on swirled vats:
vanilla ice cream, then cherry water ice,
more vanilla,
cherry for a tower of red
and white stripes that melted
into pink after heat stroll.

We had to wait for tall, plastic cups,
like all the brown
kids, while Papi grumbled.*
Counter girls sucked their teeth,
gloved their hands
but we never noticed that then.

Children with stain history—
my brother, fair-skinned and universal
prize, and me, Black and not—
walked the block with the evidence there,
cherry crystal-flecked jackets,
happy. Papi held our hands,**
brooding the cost.

---

*then raged "Miss, why we always gotta wait? We were first. My children were first!"
**only for us/ Blackness was catching/ the neighborhood/ pecking ravens in flight/ us
  them

MALDICIÓN DE BORIKÉN A LOS LEÓN: LA CIEGA EN PARAÍSO

most recent vessel (*i never trust*)   stilled-pool brujería (*what i see in blur*) no future gazing   sino que al punto (*i catch myself wearing you*) ahorita in contours   textures in (*twining*) even (*then i cannot depend upon sight*) my disappearance   (*the melding*)   and returning renewed.   i mourn   buried bluster wind (*i do not know which*)   la arena empaña este cuerpo (*offering*) rough care   (*a life of*) i char (*deep down*) beneath sun massacre (*a wonder*) then drown in blood kelp   (*new sea glass glitters*) barracuda teeth (*tumble without you*) sharpness (*color pulse pinpoints*) acá el espacio me controla (*woven greens gather   spread   dissemble-retreat*)   bruma-bruja   (*murk above*) quieres el mar   toma   (*iris the field   clouds tipping scar   this sight*)

TANGO CRIOLLO

Toss aside the Panama hat with its black band and feather,
and take her as you always take her, the woman,
the death: hard and quick. Embrace her close,
chest to chest, her eyes a pain-dare or lowered orchid.

Spin.   Her legs are bridges to open and cross,
fly her pointed heel, criminal, seductive. You lead
the retreat, train her to follow like a dog
you beat until she loves you. The cawing crows

fly. Your hand, all cracked leather, but smooth
as a dandy who bathes in milk water each evening.
Each pivot, a sailing across the cold depths
that sucked your mother's people down but not her.

She walked stinking from the sea with gray flesh,
shark teeth stuck at her mandible. She pulled
them out and danced, a tango into the son
with the kind of fist that could kiss a woman cold.

Throngs came. Violence, the spectacle. Lust,
the tool to draw your redness out. From between her thighs,
to another her's mouth. On and on, the dance.
When my great-grandmother lost her legs to quaking,

you tipped your white hat, boarded the boat,
to plow the sea, plow the stage, a woman.
No name. The children: kicks in their glitter.
And when she died, the dancer-wife with bones

of puss and clack, the news was weeks in arriving to New York.
You, weeks more with the woman, who only gave
you daughters. On to Puerto Rico, to the boy,
scrounging for scraps in dust. You taught him to dance

and toss aside the gray hat with its white band and feather,
set the white scarf swish down, folded just so
to enchant the leg called destruction,
and how to dance with a woman called death.

BULL | MACHETE | BULLET | LAUREL | TIME

Alejandro

Alejandro

Alejandro *

ale ale to call bull to deathly dance
matador flight of color in the sand

---

*Llámale

tight golden embroidery for skin
        a suit to take a life
Alejandro you are not the matador
you are (their) beast
in Central Valley fields
your hands slick with pesticides
cracked by vine prick, dust and sun
you harvest another man's bounty
careful to not touch your eyes
        don't touch your eyes
fruit flesh can blind a man
and has done so to many
gone the gold of dawn on upturned tender
green leaves, beauty before bowed
back and sweat

    "There is no victory without pain."*

            Alejandro

Alejandro   *Alejandro***

we are the beast together
I know what it is to be asked
        What are you?
The prod and pull of hands
on skin, through hair
as if to catalogue me for auction
        here be a good [insert subjugated identity here]
                breed her out for labor***
even my unborn descendants
know inquisition

---

    *Lolita Lebrón
    **el nombre de hermanas y hermanos
***shithole

                    Alejandro

Alejandro   *Alejandro**

spectrum of brown
you picked up and shipped back
to unrooted land
that which floats
in your genetic memory
not ingrained in thumb
print circles unspooling
in time
                        how many wait
                    in deportation cells
            dancing fluorescent light patterns
                    shackles in glare
            because they don't have the papers
                        flimsy
            to carry, born here or there

we beasts set down for slaughter
Walmart, corner store, walking a street
to buy rolled cigars or Skittles
we breathe too much
            must be put down

            "I grew up in the segregated south in the 50s and 60s
                and I can't tell you how scared I am right now"**

                    Alejandro
                                        when will we be free
                    Alejandro
                                        when will we be free
                    Alejandro
                                when will we all be free***

---

*con más fuerza
**Patricia Spears Jones
***Llámale como amante

my lover is human
but his hand be dove wing

my lover is human
to love I must be human
I love you, human
Alejandro we can be human
give our human to one another
we battle march cry our tears
like warriors
political statement to be
emotion forward
in a world that would want us beasts
numbed to bleed out
with chalk outlines our only story
written in dust perked for wind
warriors are not numb
we feel deeply
bare our tears with our knives

Alejandro

when will we be free

Alejandro

when will we be free

Alejandro

*when will we all be free**

"There are many things that can only be seen through eyes that have cried"**

dream with me the day when dawn
touches those same tender leaves

---

*Llámale a la eternidad
**Oscar Romero

and we do not fear disappearance
of body, the disappearance of so many
bodies, children whose fathers or mothers
do not come home one unexplained day

La Migra, La Policia the un-ordering
of blood orders

Jesus!

Jesús!

Holy Mother!

Power within!

Nothing beyond!

dream with me land
space
cool cloud of breath
still blue morning
place for children
to play
skin their knees
cry swift
run to their fathers
mothers
know the certainty of cozy
until elder eye-spark dwindles
of its own accord

Alejandro

when will we be free

Alejandro

when will we be free

Alejandro

when will we all be free *

---

*Juntos, me gente

CHOCOLATE CITY LATINA

1

Daddy
taught me to merengue
when I was three
The rhythms blurred
with the Motown do wop
a salsa and *Fingertips* cacophony
Instead of Marin
there was Coleman's
slant-eyed, cocky grin
and the low down
rumble of his African
laced with black bottom cadence
covering the rolling r's
and labia loaded lengua
de Boricua
Swallowed whole
como un pez
done backstroked thru the Bermuda Triangle
grazed the Hudson Bay
and breaststroked around the Great Lakes
to sun on the banks of the Detroit River
The lure still caught on my uvula
pulling me forward
in a Temptation strut,
a Supreme swivel
hips loose and mouth open
a wet note, caught, and reeled in
do wa, do wop

the hesitant swish and clip
of the serrated gourd and scraper
urge the beat on
the undercurrent, a cupped palm
splayed fingers
pounding the tight skin
of a tall drum
like the hard snap
of young black men's fingers
in front of corner stores
on 12th Street
before the fires
do wa, do wop,
swish
a canto for decades of overcoming
covered by smoldering Bushes,
and bumbling Fords
who yielded
blackened hulls and ghosts
that sing falsetto
as each building is razed
to open space,
hosts to phantom teepees and
red women, like the Taíno
squat before huge mortars
grinding grain
their translucent figures
mingled with oil drum fires
and old young men in rags
who warm their calloused hands
over acrid smoke.

2

In the bleakness of winter
I discovered seers of beauty
who supped with Ché,
laughed with Fidel,
and sang like Langston
After bathing in the rains
of El Yunque and
dodging bombs en Vieques,
they lost themselves
in the mire of slums
and mass transit
Their songs solder my two selves
together, symmetrical, the steel band
runs the length of my body
up the center of my face
Fingering the scarred space,
I let the silence speak
and feel the rhythmic chant of those,
like the Taíno who came before,
Sioux, Lakota, Ojibwa
the unchanging rhythm of a hallowed drum
and moccasined feet against packed earth
Voices deep, a hum
joining the do wa, do wop, swish, swish
as the walls fall
thud, thud, thud
nuts and bolts
poured into a Tupperware bowl
A cloud billows out
like the Hudson's building implosion
and I am covered in the dust of the ancients.

THIS POEM IS ABOUT GOD

The Anglos have always feared death
believing they would burn
for past sins
or suffer the white void
having trampled so many earthly souls
in their quest for worldly goods

they fear the scent of ancestors
the salt fish spray
or sun dried clay
that lingers in places
that fish or clay
would never be

they think that to say
is to be
as in I am alive,
and that is all that one needs
as though,
one is not touched
by inaudible forces

to say that I am dead
to slaughter me with rope and blade
then burn the carcass
is not to destroy me
for, if ever I was alive
and nurtured one soul
then I am again

in the grains of sand squished between
a child's fingers,

the energy that rises from a conga,
the shine of sweat and semen
between a lover's legs
great burning gulps of air
after a brisk run
I am replenishing,
renewing,
continuing
the cycle of all living things

collecting time and space,
energy and atoms,
until I am whole again
and ready to begin
yet, another descent.

MIS HERMANOS

My brother works for Allstate
lives in Sterling Whites, Michigan
and always sells the most
flags for the VFW
He makes love to an anglo
every night
and wears a coiffure
that irons out the waves
as his perfect basso profundo
obscures the rolling
lengua de Puerto Rico

My brother works as a mechanic
for a mafia-run garage in Manhattan
They call him Mike

when his name is Guadalupe
The pomade he uses
to press down the kinks
gives him the look of painted plaster
and the Anglo he makes love to
every night
washes the grease stained
pillow cases in lye soap
He forces his belt
to the last notch
accentuating the brawn of his torso
and brags about
how good his bosses treat him
as he clips the beeper to his belt

My brother doesn't work
he listens to country western
and drinks muchas cervezas
at night
in the back of his pick-up
w/the Anglos he meets in the bars
Sometimes he picks fruit
but worries that the sun
will make his mestizo skin
too brown
He speaks Spanish sometimes
when he's making love to the Anglos
porque las chicas
think it's sexy
but to nuestros padres he always
says that we are Americans
and should hablar inglés solamente.

HOME

Silence, if not for the palpitation of the water against the steel hull of the ship as it heads away from the coral shores and out into the openness of the blue-green water. He is slender, erect. Resplendent in his black skin and white robes, he stands on deck near the rail. He leans far over the rail, but his hands are strong and the muscles in his arms tense as his hands grip the bar.

His smile is remorseless as he glances back at the island remembering the childhood spent racing along its beaches, wet sand squished between toes and the hot sun on a bare back. And later, the breathless burning of exertion quenched by the cold milk of coconuts plucked from shallow water.

I am the wind. I touch his face; lick his lips. I am the island; I blush as his eyes caress my beaches. He remembers me; I am his mother. He remembers the shelter of my palm leaves, the feel of my firm ground under his long, most elegant feet. I am his lover, he remembers the trickle of my fresh water over his tongue. I am the sun; I warm the bush of his hair and press myself against his back. I can feel the flesh of his back warming to me. I am the wind; remember me, remember me, I whisper close to his ear. He smiles and my love flows all over him. Don't leave me; I whisper close to his lips. Nothing. Don't leave me. I whisper again. His brow furrows. He looks at my greenness—all loose and grown over—he looks at the pale sand of my now untrodden beaches—at the glinting waters' reflection that causes him to shade his eyes. He looks at me once more and then he turns his back on me.

I am the wind and I am motionless.

Come back to me, I begin. Come back to me. Nothing. He stares out over the ocean—in another direction—away from me. Come back to me I say. He says nothing, does not acknowledge me. Come back to me I shout as he heads towards the other side of the ship—further away from me—where he cannot even see me. Don't leave me I cry. Don't leave me and he pretends not to hear. His long strides take him further away and I—who art the wind—fight to hold him. His bare feet grip the deck and for an instant he struggles well maintaining the balance he developed on my back—with my care. Will you come back to me—I ask in low moans trying to maintain a semblance of decorum. You my most loved of sons, my most cherished lover. Will you come back? But he continues to fight, straining against my caresses flailing at my kisses.

I will not let you go, I scream, unable to stop myself as I wash over his feet loosening the grip with a bit of slime and pull him forcibly into me and he plunges down down down. I can feel him—his warmth in my coolness—but he continues to struggle. I will not let you go I say to him—Will you stay? But he says nothing and continues to flail himself against me. He is trying to reach the top—the breathing level—but I push his head down playfully like I used to when he was a child and just learning to swim. Maybe he will remember my touch, my waters, maybe he will remember me. But he continues to fight, to hit against me. I can feel his anger . . . his . . . he fears me! I am saddened as I pull him closer to my center, refusing release.

SONG FOR MY FATHER

Ricky Ricardo es mi padre
his hair, thick and black
pequeño de cuerpo como los indios
and eyes, profundo, como el cacique
wise and uncertain
the persistent alto of his voice
a Taíno keening the song of a cantor
remembering
the rustle of perpetual greeness
the heat and thunder
of a hide stretched tight
over a hallow core
                        Ba ba looo Ba ba looo
calling the orishas
like the hi de hi de ho
of another brother
Cab's loose white suit
a shaman's robe
his wide mouth dare
teasing
papi's tight-lipped restraint
as Cab fingers
the long golden chain
                        Ba ba looo
lazy lips and hooded eyes
complete papi's César Romero leer
torment of frosted gringas
todo el mundo
Cain't be no Chano Pozo.
Rosano Brazzi's throaty laugh
heralds another conquest

masking Pozo's pain
cupped hands scrape and pound
the black son's rhythms rise
                    Ba ba looo Ba ba looo
remembering
horses and men
Christoph's raiders ravaging
the land of the Caribe,
home of the Arawak
los puertos ricos
cuando un día malo
could cost a hand, a foot, a life
fragile people, dead, dying
grafted to the blood of Africa
stained by the blood of Castile
                    Ba ba looo
the merengue shuffle
a veiled ghost dance
summoning Yemayá
mother of the sea,
waters churning, rumbling
rushing up to meet Changó
fists clenching lightning bolts
hair strung with meteorites
bells, rattles, drums
the crow of a rooster
sounds roll and crash
creating that roar in his head
                    Ba ba looo
sanity is
the winded drone of a war conch
the whistle of a flute
carved from an enemy's bone

or a retreat
to a nest of wide hips
sloping breasts,
cinnamon sweat
and coconut breath
                    Ba ba looo
coquís trill through the night
like slick brown stones
they rest in watery shade
their bodies home
por los espíritus de los indios
co-quíí, co-quíí, co-quíí
their song
a kaddish in bolero guise
solace is a mound
of mango-colored woman flesh
he pulls it closer
burying his face in her warm scent.

WADE

A black man's head

Look at that boy's head twirling off of his neck.
Look at that boy's head; it's a top in the sand, ballerina skull.
Look at that crimson flourish. Look at that defiant mouth.
Be careful when you touch that pretty face. He might bite you.
You know them niggers like to play possum.

Look at all that blue on black. Look at all that red
on top and red at the bottom. We beat him so good
his forehead turned green.

We wringed his washcloth neck
as soon as he fixed his lips to smirk.

Take this tongue. Stuff those cheeks with rocks.
Sink that empty head in the river.
Let the fish make a castle out of that face;
Let it sit, open jawed on a throne of rocks,
trying to use bubbles for voice.
Let us see if god will trouble the water.

AMIE-RICA SEES A THERAPIST

We spill their blood as a sacrifice to their gods; we throw their bones to
*   learn what will become of them*
The fractals of blood splatter, or inkblot, she interprets them as
Destiny manifested: here is your self-determination.
You know what your skin means!

Fractals of blood splatter or inkblot, she interprets them as
one test in her psychiatric evaluation.
The hypocrisy of post-race demonstrated by manic mulatta,
    Amie-Rica:
If you don't like the effect, don't produce the cause!

One test in her psychiatric evaluation is listening to what she has
    to say:
Their skin is the reason all bad things happen to them.
There is a fundamental order in laying black boys down.
We spill their blood as a sacrifice to their gods; we throw their bones to
    learn what will become of them.

MAMA'S LEGEND

for Lena

Whetstone

Remember when hurricane David made Mama's roof flutter
like a convent girl's uniform skirt?
David rolled Mama's roof down the street like an empty crocus
    sack.

I heard that all the women in town came with
gifts of salt fish and greens,
or balancing dasheen and fig on their heads.
Their husbands came to the yard as soon as the rain stopped.
The men worked all day to keep the sky
from taking the rest of what Mama owned.

This was after her husband had died, after he left her with 9
    children
and land they would never claim.

There was plenty talk when Mama married him, you know.
He was man whose cheeks would turn smelter red. He had
    whetstone eyes and furnace
hair. She bore him 8 mulattos but only 1 of them could pass;
that's how Black Mama was.

They say Mama's eyes were the size of nutmegs.
She could make a thieving man empty his pockets without
    swinging her cutlass.

Mama's swing was immaculate! Her cutlass was always sharp, oui!
But the sharpest thing Mama owned was behind her teeth.

They say Mama found love while breaking sugarcane stalks.
Amid the clatter of steel wounding air,
she met a man whose eyes could sharpen her tongue.

DAME UN TRAGUITO

para Tato Laviera

It is clear to see that Jesus was a conguero
beating back bango skins 'til his palms bled
bloodshot Rorschach red

No need to put an accent over the *e* to know
who he be—Claro que sí

Pah Pa Pah Pa   Cu Cu Cu-Roo

That he sang backup Boogaloo for Obàtálá
Swore by the hypnotic effects of a bolero

caught in the throat of a rising sun suddenly
sinking—a tecato's jones coming down

on 110th Street & Lexington Avenue
in the crusty eyelash of El Barrio

That he multiplied wine by sending his little cousin Pipo
to cop a few bottles from Pepo's bodega

where he kept a muscatel stash just beneath the
alabaster statuette of San Lazaro &

Bustello can urn of Doña Chicha's ashes
atop the register with the taped faded Polaroids

of his pregnant tía in Ponce & his songless tío
with the afro the size of Saturn in Sing Sing
inked up from head to toe

It's plain to see that Jesus spoke in 4-4 time
& guaguancó

that he tapped his dusty rusty patent leather
zapatos to a rhythm only the children
of Africans & Indians understand

bailando con Yemayá   buscando la claridad

Singing: *El agua limpia todo*

O was he born in a manger or Morrisania Hospital
The critics will ask their silly questions like social

workers dumb to the reality of the times
But Jesus will pay them no mind

nor will he adhere to the census takers
giving the side-eye to tax collectors

The only numbers he cares about come out
in New York or Brooklyn

so he could buy his baby a new pair of shoes
so he could walk on water—dried puddles of old wino piss

or tap his toes trying to mimic the sound of dominoes
click or ring fingers slapping against the stiff neck

of beer bottle to once sun-baked viejitos in guayabera
shirts & Panama hats, shouting—¡MANTECA!

Con cerveza breath working his arms & legs
into a sweat-drenched rum-stench rumba
furious frenzy as if despojando

saying to no one & everyone in particular
what he begins to hear reverberating

break dancing bomba planting
plena in his inner ear—

                              ¡Fíjate!

BROKE BAROQUE

        I was a lucky stiff
stuffed in a garbage bag
        with a Day-Glo toe tag
the size of a Winnebago
        Parallel-parked against
a callus so thick and red
        you'd swear it was a blowhard
Right-wing televangelist
        screaming holy Jesus hell or high water
about the end of the world
        and the second coming
of Burl Ives on 5th Ave & 34th St
        Oblong objects have always been
my Achilles' heel
        It's no wonder I heard

a squeal
       when the orderly
tried to put me in
       the freezer but couldn't
get past my ankle
       that got rankled
in the coroner's report
       He said I was left
for dead
       in the slums of Calcutta
in the favelas of Rio de Janeiro
       in the tombs of Timbuktu
in the wounds of South Bronx fumes
       and Biloxi blues
on a nowhere man cruise
       My head was a cardboard box
my liver an anthill of the Savannah
       Manna from heaven so hard
nearly knocked me upside down
       but I survived with
my wits about me
       A roguish lout going
toe-to-toe with the best of 'em
       from the ass-end of a bottle
of cheap perfume
       Drunk off the flames
of fruit of the looms
       where to my surprise
I surmise
       the cries of wine resides
in a dark alley
       in broad daylight

tapping the bottle for residue
　　This is how my pulse
was taken
　　in exchange for
bacon
　　They say the poor would make
prime choice ribs
　　Tell that to Eve
when you see her

POEM FOR VÍCTOR HERNÁNDEZ CRUZ
WHOSE WORDS GIVE SALSA TO BLUES

chingchingchingching-ta
chingchingchingching-pa
parrah paa parrah paa
parrah paa paa paa
snap attack
arawak
rum rico
on your back
music in your
thighs
black latin love
in your eyes
coked out streetcorners
taíno africano
work choreograoher
boogaloo shangó of the streets
knockin off similes & metaphors
with a flick of your
maraca hips

chingchikiching chikiching ching ching
   pbraa pbraa-pbraa
   pbraa pbraa-pbraa
ghetto incantations
rhythmic concrete jungle
libations
w/ the hot salsa funk
& sweat of love of love
of love for the beauty
of the people, their various
nuances & attitudes
livin life on the avenue
sending congabongo magic S.O.S
to an ilsand
that is their heart
their musical pulse
life's beat
pumpin blood into
rhythms
geographic hypnotic
trance of the
afro taíno dance
cuchifrito bacalao
mouth watering
merengue feet
& clava hands
paahm paahm-paahm paahm
música para los santos
de paz poesía
amor amor
& vida

MY FATHER IS A BROWN SCAR

My father is a brown scar
on a white bedspread,
a pincushion stapled
together with needles,
a slab of flesh
with tubes going
through him like
turnpikes, driven
to this last bed
by a brain that
popped like an
egg. His nails
are immaculately
kept, his arms
map out his
dumb youthful
wasteful trackmark
days full of arrogance
confusion and rage.
My father is a beanbag
slumped in a corner,
his mouth wrenched open
to receive holy communion
from the world of medicine
and science, the world
of mechanical breathing
and silence. My father
looks good looks boyish
in his white hair and
overnight shadow.
My father is a brown dot

in a sea of infinite white space.
My father is a memory I wear
on my face.

ARRIVAL

Steroids turn my mother's hair from black to white
in less than a year. My mother's family would have

loved for that to happen to the skin my sister
inherited from her father, an anonymous black doctor/donor

from Baltimore my mother got with to feed her fix.
My sister's voice and my mother's

colliding in my head as I think about the July day
I picked my mother up at Reagan National.

She left her common-law husband after thirty years.
He'd leave her home tied to an oxygen tank and

go off to Puerto Rico and take up with another
woman who could cook and clean and cater to his needs.

Everything my mother did for him—and work at Walmart
and clean office buildings on the side, where she thinks

she got pulmonary fibrosis inhaling chemicals for
twenty years, scarring her lung tissue into dry sponges.

He kept pushing her to sign away her half of their house.
A broke-down aging narcissist finally met his match;

he must've forgotten that she was street smart
and he, a compromise with her ego;

how a woman settles for a man out of some survival instinct.
I can't believe I allowed this man to keep me from

my daughter for all these years, she tells me.
You lost a lot of time, I say, trying to return my sister's favor

and bring *them* back together.
Curbside at US Airways' arrivals terminal my mother's

in a wheelchair looking tired and helpless, an airline
oxygen tank strapped to the back of the wheelchair. She's in a

white and blue flower-print blouse and navy knit slacks and the
white shoes of someone that lives on an island near water and sun.

I hand her a yellow bouquet and a green oxygen tank to
add to her Great Escape curbside wheelchair portraiture.

Within a week she is in the ICU at Bethesda General
holding the hand of a dying woman twenty years her senior,

assuring her *everything is going to be fine, just fine.*
Her life continuing to be a Fellini film even as it

rolls on to the credits and the word *finis.*
Months later I'm wheeling her around the mall, the

rehab center's wheelchair giving my forty year-old back
a first-time golfer's workout. The nurse on graveyard shift,

who pumps her full of steroids and late-night diabetic snacks,
says to me, *She's gained a few pounds.* I want to say, *No shit.*

Instead I say, *Yeah—and her hair is getting whiter.*
I'm taking her out on the town to get her hair cut and nails done,

then a rare picture together and then a late lunch—all the shrimp
I'm allergic to she can eat. I'm toasting her girl's night out

with a glass of red wine and in the middle of our dinner,
her oxygen tank runs out. I'm off to the parking lot,

trying not to panic.
I come running back to the table with the second one,

trying to figure out how to work the valve.
Somehow the gods have aligned themselves

on this sunny September Saturday afternoon—
I used to work at a hospital, the waiter says,

teaching me the righty tighty left loosey routine,
my mother's breathing never skipping a beat.

In a couple of months we will sit down and have our first
    Thanksgiving
together where she will tear up the duck unlike an old woman
    with a

bad heart diabetes kidney problems bronchitis and a third of her
    lung capacity.
but she paces herself and the burning logs on the fireplace light up
    her face.

She finally tells me what happened the night she gave birth to
    me; how the
doctor was without answers to why I was so sick, screaming
    uncontrollably

from the womb of an incubator. *I finally broke down and told him I
    was on drugs,*
she says. *I was scared—but I had to tell him. I didn't want anything to
    happen to my*

beautiful baby boy. Relieved, the doctor turns and tells her, *Thank
    you, Ms. Gonzalez—*
You just saved your son's life.

BROKE CELEBRITY (CULTURE)

Paparazzi
    follow me
in and out
    of cardboard boxes
They stalk me at the
    unemployment line
Snap
    shots of me
as I sit
    along the curb
peeling crusty
    scabs from

my high-heeled
    callused feet
They have me pose
    for photo-ops
outside welfare hotels
    Even have me
hold up hunks
    of government cheese
like award-winning statuettes
    They treat me
like a pampered pet
    some privileged poodle
whose poop doesn't stink
    Snap and point
their fingers
    Have me turn
and bow and
    smile
I gladly do
    as they say
and end up
    in all the rags

JAMÓN Y QUESO

"En la espalda de mi padre, con ropas prestadas, vine a América."
—Li-Young-Lee

Mi padre perdido en las calles de New Jersey
planta la memoria que ahora invento
Es el verano de 1969
él camina por estas líneas
que doblo como mantel precioso
Ordena un sándwich
de jamón y queso
(por cuatro años consecutivos)
Luego
Green salad
(caminos del Cibao donde la nostalgia se regresa)
Black coffee
(sin la azúcar melodiosa el resto no pasa aquí)

Mi padre camina sombra lerda en la tinta
nos mira extrañado (a mi memoria y a mí)
Tengo cinco años
me duele el portazo que nos abisma
Aprendo a escribir mi nombre

¿Qué hago en la parte escondida de su vergüenza?
Cruzo las calles desoladas de Paterson
asida a la fotografía de mi padre

En los apartamentos
viven como colmenas gentes forjadoras de sueños

Comienzo
a engordar la idea de un mundo ancho que se desborda
Por estas calles anduvo
lleno de vida el cadáver de Allen Ginsberg
Entusiasmada
inflada de esperanza comienzo a
bordar imágenes nuevas
en el mantel donde mi padre inscribió
  fábrica
    sudor
      invisibilidad
        jamón y queso
          jamón y queso
            jamón y queso
              jamón y queso...
sigo bordando como la que no quiere la cosa
Allen Ginsberg y yo tete-a-tete
Nada hay que nos separe
hablamos el mismo idioma
Le leo un poema de desolación
él ríe con dientes imperfectos
Somos camaradas Allen y yo

Por la otra esquina
imponente
poderosa doña Aída hila mi nombre
para que todos sepan que he llegado
Para que no se me olvide

La soledad pesa en la memoria
Mi padre llega de la fábrica perdido en sudor
viene recitando un poema
reclamando las calles de Manhattan

las calles de cualquier pueblo que camino
Me trae de la mano
No estoy segura si es a él
o es a ti
a quien amo profundamente en este instante, Allen

¿Por qué me meto en la memoria
que mi padre disolvió?
Jamón y queso les contaba
jamón y queso
(por cuatro años consecutivos)
Invisible
mientras yo aprendía a escribir mi nombre

Vengo de la mano de Allen Ginsberg
mano de mi padre
mano de doña Aída
mano mía esta que
borda en el paño ancho de un país que se desborda
acostumbrado a las ropas prestadas

Espejo claro de identidad múltiple
que nos trae a mi padre y a mí
(Él ha jurado jamás dejar el Cibao
yo le sigo trayendo en la memoria)
Se quita el zapato izquierdo
Descubre el lugar donde antes
el dedo más largo nos unía
Se lo han amputado para salvarle la vida
Agarro el símil
Sé a que viene esta memoria
Carne magra   oscura
por la que viajo a New Jersey

Algo comienza a dispersarse
se desborda
inunda los apartamentos
que habitan los forjadores de sueños
Salgo sabiendo a donde voy
Aprendo a caminar con sandalias
del brazo de mi padre que ya no está aquí
Vulnerables
a carne viva nos amamos más

Encuentro mi sitio en las calles de New Jersey
y me vuelvo a casa
—casa inventada entre la nostalgia y el perdón—
Planto memorias que mi hijo luego inventará
Al jardín viene a visitarme el fantasma de Allen Ginsberg
hasta osa cuestionarme el buen poeta
y me sonrío
Le leo un poema que habla de regreso
regreso malabarista como el de Li-Young-Lee
Ambos sabemos viajar en una espalda
ancha
robusta (a pesar del tiempo)
Ambos sabemos el secreto de la carne magra
oscura   podrida   que nos mantiene vitales
Somos voces que saben de donde nace el silencio
voces que se alzan a través de los tiempos
Nosotros los hijos de la memoria
Viajeros con raíces
   Viajeros con raíces
      Viajeros con raíces
         Viajeros con raíces   inventores de memorias

CARA SUCIA

Nació de pie como un augurio
Presta a la batalla nació
El cordón tres veces anudado al cuello
Arrancó de cuajo las raíces a su madre
Dos azabaches brillantes
desafiantes como el Diablo los ojos
Caimito morado
A plena luz del día hizo sombras
Piernas abajo con un grito de sirena se lanzó

De pie como un augurio creció
Con la tinta de la mala suerte
La abuela no quería una niña morena
de pelo crespo burlando la raza
Otra marca incrustada en la estirpe
Otro pelo sediento de vaselina
El discurso bajo el ala
En lugar del pan trajo desgracia

El mundo no quería otra niña morena
Otra piel cantando salves en los montes del Cibao
A la junta vinieron todos
a mirar la afrentosa criatura
La que nació de pie
con la piel morada azul marino
envejecida por las horas
Anudado al cuello el cordón invisible
El diagnóstico insalvable
Mil veces maldecida criatura
La que nació de pie
dicen que antes de desprenderse
mordió el vientre de la madre

Desapercibida jamás ha de pasar
Escandalosa presencia
Escandalosa piel
Escandaloso el pelo
Se pasea por las calles
Fuerza no hay para detener
a la que nació de pie
con la piel oscura
con los ojos brillantes
el discurso bajo el ala
Ángel negro voz cantante.

EL CORTE

The Haitian Massacre, which took place in October 1937, is also known as El Corte (the cutting) to Dominicans and as Kouto-a (the knife) to Haitians. At the order of Dominican dictator Rafael Leonidas Trujillo, Haitians and Dominicans of Haitian origin, living and working at the Haitian-Dominican border, were systematically killed by members of Trujillo's National Guard and hired thugs. Estimates vary, but anywhere from 15000 to 30000 people were killed.

Twenty thousand tongues curled up
at the bottom of El Masacre awaken
In imperfect rows they march toward
the Presidential Palace in Santo Domingo
El Generalísimo afraid of his own shadow
begs the moon for white light
In agony he powders his face
His biggest fear?
The fermentation of skin and bone
The sudden rise of ancestry

Twenty thousand tongues curled up
inside his French-style uniform
tear down the place brick by brick

How do we break the curse—stop his shadow from casting
    dummies?
Decked in white his paws go on raping virgins
His rotten sugarcane pocks poison infested holes
on the island's feeble body
He litters the earth
    litters the earth
        litters the earth
Or is it that unfathomable crime
fertilizes the conscience of those who have one?

Should we make stiff wax miniature figures of El General?
minus his sad penis of course?
Should we burn them on the edge of El Masacre?

Each woman he raped
each man he slit to filter hatred in
comes up from death
See the beautiful ones surfacing from the bottom of time?
Each gets plastered tightly in the heart of another

Come on down
Come on down see the fantasy island
where history hums like a tamed dragon
We have this habit of carrying our dead with us
They stick to the bottom of our tongues
We sing with them from sunset to sundown
They rise from the bottom of El Masacre
We don't bury our dead   We don't.

CROSSING EL MASACRE

At five I knew all about war
and about strolling in the meadows
under the ochre embrace of the sun
I knew I was a warrior
Only warriors understood El Masacre
flowed one way then the other

Each time we parted the water
my father would smile and say
"This is how we know God"
His words leaping
from one side to the other
My voice tugging at the mountains

He would say if you write a poem
that lashes from there to here
then we could part the water again
So I kept writing over the curled softness
blowing ripples
my poem a bulky dribble of foam rising

The echo of Papa Doc shouts from the palace
seeping through the bones of dead black dogs
their hair spills and covers the swollen curves of Haiti
She cries for all her dead children
The ones from here the ones from there

I am the one on deck as the ship parts red waters
I am the one writing this poem
that lashes from there to here
But there like here is an abstraction

Little fish jump on board mourning
what I take with me

Hear my plea
If you go there or if you come here
decayed bodies will lure you
The forceful hand of dictatorship
will bend you mercilessly
You will drink red over and over
An unquenchable thirst will play
its lonely song in your throat

The Tonton Macoutes
will tear down your house
Papa Doc will kill you
with a glance of his spectacles
I knew that at five

Caravans of women walk over the water
They all wear red scarves
that float like flags in the wind
Red flags waving sorrow
My eyes dive to fetch skeletons
I am a warrior—remember?
But even here high on the deck
I stand in danger of dying too
Papa Doc can turn his head and shoot me
with his black spectacles

This poem keeps singing the devastation
of the land and I see it
I am all the little girls from the bateyes
Our mothers cross the river
shaping red memories

We dance in grief's spectral flood
Ripples shooting down the bodies of two maidens
look at me now   haunted face
dancing alone
Haiti's grief clawing the warrior I am

I can't hear well what I must say
but I can no longer pretend god sparks me
I am deaf
   blind
      unable to earn my breath

I write
Let the flowers come up from the river bottom
Let the hibiscus bloom only for them
Let this poem sing the shame
Sing the shame Sing the shame

This is how we know god.

JESÚS PAPOLETO MELÉNDEZ

A SAN DIEGO SOUTHERN/AFRICAN NIGHT

(O i have no opinion
                    of What My Eyes See! . . .)

:There's a black man,
                    A man whose skin is black
                                        —the color,
                                                    BlacK!
Running across The Street
        in the middle of the night;
                        BlacK NighT!
                            Only the flickering lights of business
                            buildings
                                                    ,still
                            burning in the night(
                                            like the eyes
                                            of obese monsters)
                    And the stars,
                                of course   —They
                                                    in their distance
                    are out tonight;
                                Quietly knowing,
                                Unsaying a word.
THE TRAFFIC LIGHT CHaNGeS—
        So Now, The Color RED is Against
                            HiM—WHO crosses The Street!
                            POLICECAR
                                    cruises   by . . .   And
                                    SeiZe HiM!

                                             (BlackMan)
                              & FLaSHeS
                              itS LiGHtS
                              BRiiiiGhHtTtT!!!!!!!!

¡¡¡In the Middle of the Night
RED&OrANGe/BlUe&WHiTE!!!
LiGHTS!!!
                              THEY cut HiM off at the pass
                              Of the corner of a sidewalk/UP
                                             Against!
                              TheCARRRR!!! MOTHER!!!!!

HiS Hands on the hood
    He is forced to spread his legs A/ParTWIdE–Like this
                              THEY Dare call it Eagle!
    So THEY could search him up good, To make sure
                              There's nothing up his sleeve
                       The/re/s/no/thi/ng/u/p/hi/S/m/i......
n/D!
            :THEY take his wallet ,from out of him/
                       Removing the papers ,from the person
            :THEY tell him to go sit in the car/
               In the memory of the back seat,
                       Looking out the window like that, perhaps
                                    resembling a bird

And He obeys THEM,
               HE does
    What HE believes that THEY say/
                       It is dead night.
                       The night is dead.
                       There are not too many people
around,

walking
,with their opinions on hand
:"Art!
for Art's sake!"

(And i think;
How difFerent this is
from, "SomeWhere Else"
where, a Soldier would demand
for the same kind of rights
In a foreign land,
dressed in camouflaged fatigues
with an Uzi
slung over his shoulder,
saying
"YOUR PAPERS! YOUR
PAPERS! LET ME SEE YOUR PAPERS!!!"
,except
for those   ,mostly
in cars
going home
from the long days
they've just lived
in the lengths
of their lives
/tired
from the things
that they do
with their lives,
And/ThereForeTheyAreInGreatHurries
Be....lieveIt!
Be....lieveIt!

YouBetteRBe....lieveIt!
Be....lieveIt!)

Nonchalantly tossing
lighted cigarettes
from out their
open windows
            watching
the world go
down the drain(
            bye)
stepping harder
on the gas
when they see
the lights
turning
from yellow, to red,
                  They
already traveling
beyond the speed
of anybody walking,
trying desperately
to be
the first to
get
to
the other side
of a brand new street
which they've seen
before,
at the corner
of which
are
2POLICE

& 1 blacKDude
imprisoned in a trance
& a light
turning
from yellow, to ReD!
                (My little sister says
                        about her visit with me here
                                :"The lights don't give you enough ti)me
                                to
                                chew yo
                                ur gum
                                &cross the
                                street!"
                                                ,She
                coming from a real Cool/CRUeL Metropolis
                having thus acquired an acute UNderstanding
                        of the danger of crossing a simple street,
                                                for a girl, She says
                "As soon as you step out to cross it
                The lights start blinking for you to go back!
                It's a car's world out here!
                Pedestrians should drive!"
                                TheBlack peDestrianMan

                                                                sits

                        In the POLICEMAN's CAR
                        with his BiGBlacKHanDs

                                                        down

                        in front of HiM

                                                moping,
                                                sort of
                        For TheCAUSE! of his BlacKsKiN
                                                —THaT

though it blended with
the color of this NiGHT,
It failed
to cloak HiM from THEIR SiGHT!

And
THEPOLICE,
WoMan,
LaDy,
CoP,
is sitting in the front seat
(preTending)
that it is Her duTy
to be doing her nails
,While
holding on to the leather of herGun,
touchingIt,
ListeninG..
To Every ThoughT that HE has
To Think
:This BlackMan,
HiS Black Pride, Fuming
within
hiS BlackMan's Feelings
(sitting
in the back
seat
of a
STraNGeMaN's
CaR!)

Outside,
The Air is Cool ....   :Thus is San Diego,
A City most noticeable for
Its Lovely Days
of
Perfect Skies
(iF

you ignore the factories
where BomBs are born
& ,Therefore, THE TARGET
That carpets the floOR)
,And ToNighT....
is a beautiful night
To Be Lived
& enjoy in your being.............!

THEMANCoP

rests languidly,
leaning against the
roof of his car
,Observing the tranquility
of a RedLightDIstriCT's ACtiVity
ReMarKing,
"How smoothly America funCtions
free from Crime,
at
Peace" (
while, POLItICIans seek Votes
in the childish arms
of
loving prostitutes)

THEMANCoP calls
                THEBoYS
                        ,Back at the Ranch
                            To see how the BallGame is going
                                —& if anybody thoughT
                                to leave him a sandwich
                                for when things go
        BORinG
                ,And while he's at it
                        (& picking his teeth with a knife)
                    He asks THIS COMPUTER
                THEY'VE got over there (with a VoICE like a woMan
                                of aNAnDRoGyNous souND)
                    If sHE'S
                    Ever Heard of this WiseGuy

                                            HE'S got
                                in the backseat of the Car/
                            If "HE" EverEver
                                    ,Ever Did
                        AnyThing!
                        AnyThing, WronG
                            In HiS Whole Loving Life/
                                AnyThing/AnyThing!
                        As aBlackMan/Child
                                    in this World
                        WITHaCRIMINALMIND!
                        —Anything, Anything!
                                    "Are You Sure?!
                                    —What's The Score?!"

THE ANSWER IS . . .   NO!!! . . . /&/SO!!! . . .

THEMANCoP must   write HiM a ticket, According to

"TheProPerProCeDurE"
                    (Thinking)
                          :If this were a windy city
                           HE'D run HiM in
                                for spittininthegutter!
                                    ....&TOHELL!
                    WITHtHEWoMEN
                    SCReeeEEEEaMINGGGINALLEYS(
                                        some)
        Reluctantly,losing,virginities
                            ,while
                                the blood of their taxes
                                pays
                                the way
                                    forthewagesofSin
                                        &Preachers
                                        are left
                            to argue
            withtheMeanFaceoftheWind!

Now, THEMANCoP calls
        TheBlacK, bOY
to come out
from out
of the car,
            real easy, like slow
And sign Here
On the line
To say
That I
Gave yoU
This,
And ThaT

YoU
Took IT
And, Now
U
N
D
E
R
S
T
A
N
D
ThaT
YoU Owe
"The
Good
PeoPle"
Of
This
Fare
City,
    Truly
    America's Finest
    Fair City,
35 Bucks
Of
Your
Hard Earned
How
Ever
It
Is

That
YoU
Get
IT
Cold
Cash,
BECAUSE!!!
YoU DiD
Cross
The
Street
While
The YelloW
LighT
Was
A-BlinK-InG
And, Then
DiD
Turn
A-ReD
By
The Time
YoU-A-GoT
To
The
Other
Good Side!
And, So HE Signs
HiS NaMe! . . .
On
The
Paper:
The NaMe . . .

HiS Mother
Gave
To HiM,
The NaMe!....
By Which
He Is
KnowN
On
The
Face
Of
This Earth,
The NaMe! . . .
By
Which
GOD
Will Know
HiM
As Well:
CAPITAL X!
And HiS Fingers
are All on the pen!
        O!HiSBlacKFinGer'SPrinTS!
Are On
The Piece of Paper
And On
The Hood of The Car
And On
The Back of The Seat
Where HE WePT
HiS TeaRS
And
HiS TeaRS

Are NoW LeFT
Where
HiS ShAdOW
Once Sulked
And, For This
Even IT!
Refuses
to
walk
with
him
just now, No
not now
It fades
in
the
depth
of
This Night,
      "OH! WHERE IS HOME?!" . . .

                THEMANCoP
                gives HiM
                TheTickeT
                withPride
                like a piece of ArT
                but itaint
                TearingiT
                from out of a book
                of them.

And, NoW, "THE COMPUTER"
Has Devoured HiS NaMe! . . .
           And, *"SomeWhere," "SomeWhere!"*
               No One Knows Where

                              —It is smacking its lips
                                   & waiting for dessert!

AND IT WILL NEVER FORGET!

NO! IT WILL NEVER FORGET:
The NaMe! . . . Nor/the/Height/of/Said/MaN
Nor the Weight of HiM
Nor the Color of HiS Eyes
Nor the Color of HiS Hair
Nor the Color of HiS Skin
Nor the Number that is His
Nor The Age of This MaN as He Ages
Through Time
                    —This BlacKMaN
                         ¿WHO?
                         . . . at 2-30 in the morning/One
                              dark and lonely, Good Morning!
       was detained by THEPOLICE
BeCause!!!
!!"The 'DistinCtive' Color
!!!of a LighT
!!!was
!!!AGaINST/HiM!"

We Must Be Thankful ThaT
                    ThE DiFfErEncE, HeRe
                              ,from AnyWhere ElSe
                                   In This World (is)
       ThaTThisBlacKMaNis
,Finally set,

                    on the leash of his f , reedom to go
                    about,D,oing his   bu, si, ness   in

·◈· 251 ·◈·

                              pursui,   t   of   the
                         ha,pp,y,n,es,s he dreams, in his w
                              i d e   o   p   e   n, d mind
                                                    —AnyWhere ,ElSe

HE WOULD HAVE BEEN SHOT • RIGHT ON THE SPOT
    • FOR BREAKING THE LAW!!!

So, TheNicePOLICEMANWoMANCoPs
                having, Thus
                        Completed Their DuTy,
                                drive away, with their lights
                                        swallowed up
                                in the eyes of the monster
                                        ,Whom(?)
                                They've Sworn:
                        ToProTecT&ToSerVe
                                WithTheirLives................Owns
                                                        the
                                                        world
                                                        going
                                                round

&TheBlacKMaN,   goes
                        slowly, across the street
                                (contemplating,This)

ANDTHELIGHTSHAVENOMOREOPINIONTOUTTERINHISFACE!
BuT NoW!!!—HE IS CURRRRRRRRRRRRRRRRRRRRRR
RRSSSSSiNG!!!...
POuNDING theAiROfTHeNIGhT——with HiS VoICE! :
I-KNOW-I'M-NOT-WHITE!!!-I-KNOW-I'M-NOT-WHITE!!!-
I-KNOW-I'M-NOT-WHITE!!!-I-KNOW-I'M-NOT-WHITE!!!-
I-KNOW-I'M-NOT-WHITE!!!-I-KNOW-I'M-NOT-WHITE!!!-
I-KNOW-I'M-NOT-WHITE!!!-I-KNOW-I'M-NOT-WHITE!!!-

I-KNOW-I'M-NOT-WHITE!!!-I-KNOW-I'M-NOT-WHITE!!!-
I-KNOW-I'M-NOT-WHITE!!!-I-KNOW-I'M-NOT-WHITE!!!-
I-KNOW-I'M-NOT-WHITE!!!-I-KNOW-I'M-NOT-WHITE!!!-
I-KNOW-I'M-NOT-WHITE!!!-I-KNOW-I'M-NOT-WHITE!!!-
I-KNOW-I'M-NOT-WHITE!!!-I-KNOW-I'M-NOT-WHITE!!!-
I-KNOW-I'M-NOT-WHITE!!!-I-KNOW-I'M-NOT-WHITE!!!-
I-KNOW-I'M-NOT-WHITE!!!-I-KNOW-I'M-NOT-WHITE!!!-
I-KNOW-I'M-NOT-WHITE!!!-I-KNOW-I'M-NOT-WHITE!!!-
I-KNOW-I'M-NOT-WHITE!!!-I-KNOW-I'M-NOT-WHITE!!!-
I-KNOW-I'M-NOT-WHITE!!!-I-KNOW-I'M-NOT-WHITE!!!-
I-KNOW-I'M-NOT-WHITE!!!-I-KNOW-I'M-NOT-WHITE!!!-
I-KNOW-I'M-NOT-WHITE!!!-I-KNOW-I'M-NOT-WHITE!!!-
I-KNOW-I'M-NOT-WHITE!!!-I-KNOW-I'M-NOT-WHITE!!!-
I-KNOW-I'M-NOT-WHITE!!!-I-KNOW-I'M-NOT-WHITE!!!-
I-KNOW-I'M-NOT-WHITE!!!-I-KNOW-I'M-NOT-WHITE!!!-
I-KNOW-I'M-NOT-WHITE!!!-I-KNOW-I'M-NOT-WHITE!!!-
I-KNOW-I'M-NOT-WHITE!!!-I-KNOW-I'M-NOT-WHITE!!!-
I-KNOW-I'M-NOT-WHITE!!!-I-KNOW-I'M-NOT-WHITE!!!-
I-KNOW-I'M-NOT-WHITE!!!-I-KNOW-I'M-NOT-WHITE!!!-
I-KNOW-I'M-NOT-WHITE!!!-I-KNOW-I'M-NOT-WHITE!!!-
I-KNOW-I'M-NOT-WHITE!!!-I-KNOW-I'M-NOT-WHITE!!!-
I-KNOW-I'M-

SISTER

para nuestras hermanas

have you seen the revolutionary sister
rappin to the masses of poor /
      she talks about revolution /   change
      she talks about redistributing wealth
      to all

      she's read Mao   & Marx   Che & Lenin
      she's true /   for real
      she believes in what she does
      she loves /

          she loves you /
          she loves her people.

she sleeps little /   works hard
sometimes her eyes show it
she tries to hide it /   she smiles
she's friendly /   loves children
she talks with junkies
& understands

      she's pretty /   beautiful shape
      she's a woman
      & she loves.

she'll die /   loving
loving you.

      / i understand you want to lay her.

MESSAGE TO URBAN SIGHTSEERS

HEY YOU /   sightseer
from smalltown, nowhere, u.s. of a.
bring your head
                down
        /your eyes off those TALL business buildings

look-a-here sightseer/   sightsee
i'm a sight
        /a sight to be seen by your sore eyes

sure, i'll be your guide
        /wanna send a friend a picture postcard?
here, take this one/   that's me/my brothers
                my mother/my father
                my aunt/my uncle
                my sisters/our cousins
                & our dog
we all live very near one another/
the same apartment

oh, you think it's cute
the way my youngest brother sits on our dog?
we don't.
actually he thinks rover is a horse /
no, no kidding
he really thinks rover is a horse
        :he wants to be a cowboy
        i think he'll be a soldier riding horseback
        on some tank

do you really like the family pose?
it was taken on our fire escape/   it collapsed
just as we all entered the house
                                        /nobody hurt

but since last summer
the people across the street
have had the ugly view of our apartment
    that there wall is our wall to wall
                                        —nothingness

last winter/   when it snowed
all the kids from the neighborhood
came up to my house and we skied in my livingroom

come on/   sightseer
i'll take you to my house
you can sit in the livingroom
with your feet in my bedroom
and your elbow in the kitchen
come dinnertime   we all can gather round
the table
the floor
the beds
the fire escapes
the halls
the toilet
the bathtub/   & eat our food

if we run out of plates
we'll use the dog's bowl the ashtrays
the rats' poison dish
the pots & pans
small corners on the table

and our hands   to cup our share
of one thirty-seven cents
can of spaghetti   divided by family

come on/   sightseer
don't be a fool
take advantage of my hospitality

oh don't leave/
i ain't tell you bout me doing homework
while roaches gather round
to get their education/
                    kind-a-makes me feel
                    like doctor dolittle

and when we flood the sewers/   turn on the hydrants
and make like jones beach
while junkies   taking people off
so theys can get their daily fed

HEY YOU/   sightseer
from smalltown, nowhere, u.s. of a.
bring your head
               down
          /your eyes off those TALL business buildings

look-a-here sightseer/   sightsee
i'm a sight
          /a sight to be seen by your sore eyes
by the eyes of the o. e. o.
by the eyes of the world
by the eyes of the stars and moon

look-a-here/   LOOK   LOOK GODDAMNIT
I'M INTERESTING!!!

¡HEY YO/YO SOY!

Hey!
   Yo! . . .
     Yo! . . . Yo! . . .
Hey-ey . . .
      Yo! / Yo! . . . Yo! . . . . Yo! . . .
   Yo! / Yo! / Yo! . . .
         Yo! . . .
Hey-ey!
     Yo! / Yo! . . . Yo! . . . Yo! . . .
   Yo! / Yo! /Yo! . . .
        Yo! . . .
            Hey-ey! Yo! . . .
              ¡Yo Soy
                Puertorriqueño, Bro! . . .

That's Right, Ése
That's What I Say, Jefe
        Que,
I, too, Am PuroPutoÚnico,
      Uniqueó, Ése

      Just Like You, Like You
         Just
      Like You, Ése Ése
          Que
     I Am Me,
      Que
     I Am You

As You,
Am Me—
Que,
Hey!
Yo!
Yo Soy
Puertorriqueño, Bro!

Que,

It Is A "*We*" Thing -
It Is an Así
Thang!

:A Whole, Huge
Nosotro Trip
that governs this Ship,
el Planeta Earth,
—that gives Us Birth—
in *Multi Colors*
of the Universe!

And,
Everything That I Be
You Be, Too!
También,

Se

Dice, Así
Ése

BeCause
BecauseBecause
BecauseBecause
Because*Why?!* . . .
BecauseBecause

BecauseBecause

           BeCause*Why?!* . . .

    Because of Love
       of A *Love so* deep
          deep
       that still it seeps
         seeps
      within Us deep
         deep,
        yet still
          it *seeps* . . .

Que Mis Raíces Son
      de Ése, Ése
   Nativo Taíno
    Indigeino
  de Paraíso,
     bailando ritmo
      ritmo Africano,
          Que Fue
     Violado
       por un
     Anti-Cholo
   Españolo:

   Therefore, Latino
  Therefore,
    Why
    My Hair grows
     —So, Bro! . . .

¿Comprende Vu
        What I'm telling You?! . . .

Que Soy
        a Modern *Latin*
        from el *Barrio Manhattan!*
                ¡¿Y, Qué?! . . .

This, *Thing,*
        RACISM!!!
                is an Unnatural schism
        that makes You
          part of a SyStem
                        that puts you
                        in its prison
                                For almost
                                NO Reason
                                        ¡¿Y,Qué?! . . .
                                That allows
                                        For KiLLing
                                                Your Own!
                                                        Ése!

                        That allows
                                For KiLLing
                                        Your Own!

'Tis, *It's the*
        SeaSon . . .
                for a good Reason
        To Show Cause,
                For What Cause!(a)

You would KiLL
KillKill!!!
Your Own Brother, *Ése!*
Ése allí . . .
y
Ése allí . . .
Ése allí . . .
y
Ése allí . . .

ComprendeMí!!!–
Ése allí,
y
Ése allí . . .
Ése allí,
y
Ése allí . . .
ComprendeMí!!! . . .
Ése allí,
y
Ése allí . . .

E. ETHELBERT MILLER

PANAMA

in the early twenties
a boat brought
my father to america
his first impressions
were spoken in spanish

years later when he
had forgotten the
language he could not
remember what he had

seen

TOMORROW

tomorrow
i will take the
journey back
sail
the
middle passage
it
would be better
to be packed
like spoons again
than
to continue to
live among
knives and forks

JUANITA

when she was small
she wore the lipstick of her mother
face made older with powder
like the pictures of movie stars
cut from magazines
the blonde ones she taped on the wall
next to jesus

SPANISH CONVERSATION

in cuba
a dark-skinned woman asks me
if i'm from angola
i try to explain in the no spanish i know
that i am american

she finds this difficult to believe
at times i do too

SOLIDARITY

for Roberto Vargas

when trees bend funny and out of shape
when lightblue skies turn blueblack grey
hungry winds will
knock behind the bellycaves
of coffee-colored strangers
and hurricanes will come
and speak no English

THE SEA

neruda once told me
that i should visit the sea
that to know a wave is to love
is to come and flow from one to another
the sand is like our hearts
so many parts to care for
so endless and yet it touches the sea
as one

AJA MONET

UNA OFRENDA

Vermilion wax seeps soft
down a braided back of wick
the mischievous flame swallows
small devils rendered helpless
shadows tremor the parquet
how we rid a room of virulence
tug a cork from deep copper wine
and pour toward the mestizo priest
hospitality defies sin, a spineless
bruised banana lay near
the lanterns gutter, a gift
for the double edged hatchet
warrior   marooned in the projects
hid in the holy hood of our crown
doused our bodies in albahaca water
blessed by sandhog saints
abre el camino
as hellish hipsters sip on Brooklyn brew
we   the stop and frisked spirits
haunt these streets
handcuffed with bicycles
while they litter their laughs
maraca our wrists at city hall
to thunder the gods from their
tenement altars
venture to gentrify our heaven
and wage a war with a witch.

GRANMA

Wind propels your body across the canvas clairvoyant woman sails
the traveling sea waves hiss and stretch it's jaw rare roar of
revolution kissing the belly of a boat luminous creature of loss born
of men mistaking light for power what song do we sing to journey
the liveable land of heart weary and faint conviction babbling the
brow did it rain? the voyage becomes compass of justice well crafter
bravery you who face the fear of vanishing so that we may ascend
tell me, witch woman how did you not forsee our family breaking
apart or did you mistake the horizon for arms?

LEFT BEHIND

what she do with her hands, she destroy with her feet

In those days women did what they were told she said
a valley rooted in the humid air of the world
where trogon spectators recite in periwinkle toss
over Guantanamo sapphire sea, the scarlet-chested bird
flies below a turmeric sun, discovers portals in crops of sugarcane,
snivels on her husband's Finca. Where is the new Cupid fires?
In the night, she shakes down the stars for fugue.
A Kingston hummingbird comes to her
in a dream. She swaddles her nine-month-old son
in the arms of a maid. A daughter here, a daughter there. I will
    return
she said. Not before grandchildren though. She goes,
a poinciana tree grows in Brooklyn, shades both the pigeon and
    the owl.
Men need search my heart. I am unimpressed by creatures
    without wings
for whom love is not a drifting she said.
Mother is an earthly word.
Beneath her.

❧ ANTHONY MORALES ❧

CLASON POINT ANGEL OF THE BACKPARK/CLASON POINT ANGEL OF HOLY MERCY

toss guts in grass
throw wrappers in trash

y'all sound the same
each kingpin asking for change in lane

damn shame elephant sprinkler flying
stuck on ground

fools cut school to burn
within security of 4 fences 4 exits

peek over shoulders
visitors never protected

he got muck you got fire
what's good session

dead them
leeches fall when autumn rushes

slugs crawl slow
blink antenna eyes
bucks blossom butterflies

sneak into backyard bbq
all kin created from cups of concrete

benches turn to couches
catch breeze and breathe
bittersweet bronx river mist

risky hanging too long
daydream until sunset

slide thru drive by
daps light up peace fully unto you
make moves for future reference
keep stepping

remember bad times and good luck
this play area closes after dusk

****

where are all your friends
gone in smokesession wind

mañana will begin
once you wake from being asleep

story and noble
been praying for your salvation
while you addicted to damnation

lord will whisper bendición

but your hearing so affected by loud
even if singing redemption song
still couldn't read sign language subtitles

who will title you mister or miss
doña or don

chukkas grow roots
longer you hang on corner
each night going in
got gassed seen ghosts gave greys
pushed back fade
further than you could succeed

take another homie away
who will grieve who left
breath baited hook
flaming vicious verses

fast fame extinguished
ashes blown off precious clip

unconscious casualty of community's catastrophe

not blasphemy
begging forgiveness when infested with wicked demons
pushing you to praise almighty dollar as all you believe in

answers within your grasp
as long as your grip calm holding cement storm

new dawn next chance all sins forgotten
thinking you low sky watching

living lonely
love needs limpieza

when it rains/we get wet weather
hope in our bones
our goretex umbrella

pa'lante gente
we can make it out
this puddlelicious porquería

ANTI GENTRIFICATION SPELL FOR THE BOOGIE DOWN, OR PSALM FOR THE BURNED OUT BRONX, OR THE BLOCK PREVENTS DEVELOPERS' INVASION

don't be a hood tourist
poverty voyeur

rent a blood hang with local
so wolves won't smell food

Soundview was known as Aquahung
run by the Snakapin tribe
Sinawoys killed Anne Hutchinson

factorization can multiply
poverty times benign neglect times

gentrification times eminent domain
Cross Bronx over community

divided from Jonas Bronck
split by Robert Moses

subtract us so cluelessly

no matter what your parents said
you wanted to explore origins of Black Spades Zulu Nation

stroll past Stevenson home of dropout alumni
Pun Drag on Remy 3rd

Lord Tariq told you wipe your feet
when you step in the house
uptown baby

sample Story Ave's finest

fried frustration struggle smorgasbord
buffet of bullshit won't ever be bored

snack on Kee Hing combo
better than dead lunch meat
sitting stale at hot millz

enjoy intoxicating cheap thrills
loose dollar dutches
varieties of ice cold 2 L easys

history only reaches
as far as you can remember

reveals faint fossils
but blunt guts is all that remains
right next to bloodstain on bench

was Wesley thinking
about how white men could jump in junior high

was Andre Harrell thinking of Uptown Records
once he felt new jack swing

what was Sonia Sotomayor's concept
of justice marching through dark hallways of Bronxdale

when did Kemba think he could truly
crossover as he started cooking
at Watson while Cory Gunz and Slugga Lee
had a sour freestyle session

Afrika Bambataa made peace squashing beef
between rival crews killing each other

saw the planet rock from
turntable rotation at maximum speed

let the breaks create brand new universe
all from the Boogie Down

bulldozers blast remnants of tenements
fiends' ghosts scatter

doing monkey flips on playgrounds
with no merry go rounds

only spiderwebs on slides alphabet bricks
tagged claiming CPG PNO SMM Nine Trey territory

neighbor love
where mamas and wifeys serve customers
then wish you a good day

once upon a block party cookout
for all the families with enough burgers and buns

for everyone to sip dark from red plastic cups
and burn loud until pigs
arrest without permit

sunday morning baked bread
after first homily to learn history from the sky

let's enter the Bronx 1st original public housing project
Clason Point Gardens
46 buildings 2 stories each
architecture is astounding
be aware of your surroundings

please don't feed the natives
restless starving stomachs
empty minds jewels might make them jump outta windows

land on soft swamp land
snatch privilege from hands
absolutely trading places

bright orange bulb color vintage distinct district
instant photographic drastic dramatic

tragic magic happens in CPG
shadow ghetto theatre
spontaneous eruption conniving corruption

gas them with your outta town
antics bammer bochinche

with your luxury revenge is guaranteed
how easily we smile and bleed
situational comedy turned horrific

won't get too specific
pleading fizith
intimidation would be stimulating

please don't yelp this
avoid this caserío tour at all cost if you can help it

outta here on next gypsy cab
another parts unknown

unfriendly visit could drown in
shallowest puddles of orchard beach

reach from University to Gildersleeve
from Gun Hill to Brook

back to
Clason Point
need quilombo's courage
stake claim to what little we got

can't bring peace or cameras
sunset at Story and Soundview is glorious

busfare don't give hood pass
you don't have permission to tell our stories

ABUELITA ABUELITA NO LLORE MÁS
ABUELITA ABUELITA EN SU VIDA PRAY FOR PAZ

for Melba Burgos

off that guagua aérea
señor, por favor que no me mortifiques

factoría hustle
sewed lace luxury undergarments by day
opened & shut down Latin Quarter by night

una mujer en Nueva York
bailando until new morning

ritmo más profundo makes you sing along
release all that pena each song

large family in Spanish Harlem small apartments
dreams squeezed into Brook Avenue roach motel railroad
prewar buildings born for arson insurance

hard to preach que pasa power
when children starving

cornflakes with water
ketchup sandwich bacalaíto for breakfast
yucca for dinner

may the Lord be with you always
feeble sinners
don't trespass sister or misjudge brother

grandma's hands crotcheted Lares flag
collecting dust in back of closet

pushed past parched desert
constant conversation with Dios
from blessed mouth to beloved ears

no more boogiemen to fear
except monstruos malcriados
don't say Cruz Casillas 3 times
instant ghost appearance

corner contagion of deadly distraction
top of head to bottom of toes
heard glorious gospel according to Babita
before canela eyes close

shielded us from hood frights
in dawn's distance
city skyline horizon 2 train to rikers then riverside church
after Harlem state building to Empire antenna

hardwired heart holding on to hope
one kiss of bony knuckles
faith begins to float

sunrise to midnight
echándolo pa'lante
always polite

negra linda
your smile is a kite
flying from highest cascada en El Yunque

able to see Guzmán Abajo
and look up at constellations above Borinken
oye, Babita, por favor
can we hear you laugh again

AFRO LATINIDAD, OR CARLITO BROWNIEST

unfettered/better jet like a ghost/walking on/damage
engrained/no more asking what's wrong/can tell before/bust that
package/o some of that loud/lion with alleycat heart/scratching
for next scrap/widening gap or closing chasm/not what but how/
desires shut down/insistence before introducing/intentions/
splendid spending/suffocating screams/in done dreams/forgot
first lines/tumbling towards triumph/shrug shoulders/at
origins/don't be mad/at the margins/kicking/same invisible
football/landing on back/looking at soft sky/answers in
rotation/trust tried escaping/ astral projection has limitations/one
day/have to open eyes/ instead letting world thin/dirty water
dilemma/disinfect doubt/ reflection of a colonized
nation/searching for autonomy/what would Melba do/with all
that independence/over night/align all the plugs/so capital could
stay charged/but this community been/ cracked portrait/collecting
dust/on a shaky shelf/found on curb refurbished/so
nervous/frequency distorted digital glitch/critical
switch/jíbaro/defiende lo tuyo/ownership begins/when you
recognize roots/sunk deep beneath/western white supremacy only
surface/unravel generations/splitting after breaking up/what we
thought would lift us higher/hope crippled by capitalism/
lingering after effects/like insecurity inertia/ego sealed in
envelopes/organized in old shoeboxes/every starrcade/great
american bash/wrestlemania/summerslam/survivor series/royal
rumble/recorded on dusty vhs from unlocked cablevision box/
something to look forward to/during deadly week/bad vibes/

stacked by mailbox/in project lobby/remove one brick/whole
building might fall down/took bus to beach/almost
ended/drowning in tears/don't know who/might love or kill
you/intricate negotiation/nimble mechanism/somehow mañana
still living/when that sun dice despierta/must get up/rise how
ancestors determine/trademarked pa'lante 2 step/as you summon
familiar spirits/dedicated devils/want to add illegitimate debt/to
guaranteed death/if you never listened to/this man/how can/you
be/his best friend/no sir/i cannot accept this atrophy/praise
merely a trophy/certificate in frame/displayed in clason point
lane/to remind self/how far we came/may not want/to face/don't
look/the same/anyone examine/picture like no way/that's
you/what happened/coño/lots of sessions/couldn't remember/if
tried/be thankful/you survived/where's the satisfaction/if solo
star/dolo at bar/huffing to heal/bleeding horizon/proven
pathetic/ won't let them see/pour up more rum to revitalize that
ritmo/ have you moved on/surrounded by same people/family
stayed here forever/o can life be/on just this/another
night/yesterday became tomorrow/faster than we forgot/what the
plan/for today was/to leave/but couldn't move/stuck mafucka/off
too many henny nut crackers borrowed loose & i'm saying though
light ups/can't waste away/if you stopped getting wasted/basic
fams/ what you chasing/not outside/muscles grow from constant
motion/will your corazón/ get more brolic/if you let your peanut
head/turn honey roasted

PRACTICING FADE-AWAYS

—after Larry Levis

On a deserted playground in late day sun,
my palms dusted black, dribbling
a worn, leather ball behind my back, this loneliness
echoes from the handball courts nearby.
Nearly all the markings—free throw lane, sideline,
center circle—rubbed to nothing.
A crack in the earth cuts across the schoolyard,
jagged as a scar on a choir boy's cheek.

Twenty years ago,
I ran this very court with nine other
wanna-be ballers. We'd steal
through peeled chain links, or hop
the gate, to get here: our blacktop Eden.
One boy, who had a funny pigeon-toed set shot
and a voice full of church bells, sang spirituals
every time he made a basket,
the other boys humming along, laughing,
high-fives flying down the court.

And a boy we called 'The Sandman'
for how he put you to sleep with his shoulder fake or drop step,
over six feet tall in the tenth grade,
smooth talker with an itch for older guys' girlfriends.
One Sunday morning, they found him stabbed to death
outside the Motel 6, pockets untouched,
bills folded neatly against his beautiful cooling thigh.

And 'Downtown' Ricky Brown,
whose family headed west when he was two
but still called himself a New Yorker,
who never pulled from less than thirty feet out,
and could bank shots blindfolded.
He went to Grambling, drove himself
crazy with conspiracy theories and liquor,
was last seen roaming the French Quarter, shoeless, babbling
about the Illuminati's six-hundred sixty-six ways
to enslave the populace.

At sixteen, I discovered
Venice Beach, with its thousand bodybuilders,
roller skates and red thong bikinis.
I would stand on the sidelines and watch
the local ballplayers, leaping and hollering
quicksilver giants, run and gun,
already grown into their man bodies,
funkadelic rising from a boombox in the sand.
Now, all I hear are chain nets chiming as I sink
one fade-away after another,
the backboard, the pole, throwing a long shadow
across the cracked black asphalt.

What the nets want must be this caress,
this stillness stretching
along every avenue, over high school
gymnasiums and deserted playgrounds,
and the ambulance drivers drifting into naps
back at the station house.
What the boys who ran these courts wanted was
a lob pass high enough
to pull them into the sky,

something they could catch in both hands
and hang from,
long enough for someone to snap
a photograph, to hold them there,
skybound. Risen.

HOW TO SPLIT A COLD ONE

Olvera Street, Los Angeles, CA

Mira los zopilotes, my uncle Beto tells me.
Everywhere you look, vultures.
His voice cuts through camera shutters
and the shuffle of Birkenstocks,
across counters covered by Mexican flags,
maracas and mariachi figurines.
I betchu these gabachos think Pancho Villa
is a congo player from East L.A.,
and La Raza is something you shave with.
A blond boy in a Speedy González tank top
snaps a shot of my uncle's middle finger.

When I was last here, I was the boy's age.
Those were the days Uncle Beto refused
to speak Spanish, blasted Pat Benatar
from Camaro tweeters and wore blonde hairs
splayed across his varsity letter
like soldier's brass. I hold my laugh
long enough to pay for a Zapatista T-shirt
and a Jimmy Baca paperback when he takes me
back to my own high school days:
High-top fades, flip up shades
and leather Back to Africa medallions.

Jokes about the week I changed my name
to *Juanito X*, and stopped eating chorizo.
Oh, so now you're ready to be Mexican?
The silence hangs heavy between us
like the T-shirts flanking the cashier,
a slogan slung across the chest
like a bandolier: *DRINK CULTURA!*

Last time we were here, my afro
was as big as my body. My grandmother
bought a clay jar like the one shattered
by a Texas cop's buckshot
when she first came up from Aguascalientes.
When we got home, she filled it
with cool water and offered me a sip.
I tipped the jug, grains of sand
swimming across the crooked borders
of my teeth, and spat across the kitchen floor.
*That's the earth you taste, M'ijo. The land
we come from. It's good for you.
Now drink.*

Beto and I step out into the sun. Dry.
Thirsty. A west wind brings us a tray
of carne asada, the kind Grandma used to make
on Saturdays just like this. The kind
Grandpa taught me to wash down
with tall bottles of Corona. Without words,
we walk over, seat ourselves and
hard-think drink orders. Without words,
we face each other, reading the menus. Words
like Corona and Cultura
simmering in closed mouths.

RENEGADES OF FUNK

I.

When we were twelve, we taught ourselves to fly,
to tuck the sky beneath our feet, to spin
the world on fingertips. To pirouette
on elbows, heads and backs, to run away
while standing still. So when Miss Jefferson—
her eyebrows shaved then painted black, the spot
of lipstick on her one good tooth—would praise
the genius Newton, I knew then to keep
her close, to trust her like a chicken hawk
at Colonel Sanders'. I refute your laws,
Oppressor! I'm the truth you cannot stop!
Busting headspins on her desk, a moonwalk
out the door. Referred to Mr. Brown's
detention. All them try'na keep us down!

II.

Attention: Rhythm's why they keep us. Down
      in Memphis, bluesmen beg the sky to pour
down liquor. Empty bottles, barren hands.
      A pawn shop banjo gathers dust. Guitars
sit idle, songs forgotten. Ghosts come late
      to find the crossroads cluttered, strip malls now
where haints once hung. The young, it seems, forget
      the drum and it bled, the dream and how
it fed the mothers on the auction block.
      But rhythm's why they keep us. Rhythm's why
we've kept up. Cotton fields and backs
      that creak, a song for every lash, a cry
on beat and blues sucked dry. The strip malls bleed
      the ghosts from banjos. Hollers caught in greed.

III.

The ghosts. The angles. Holocausts. The need
to shake these shackles, field songs in our bones.
As if, at twelve, we knew all this, we named
our best moves free: to break and pop-lock, blood
and bruises marking rites. We'd gather, dance
ourselves electric, stomp and conjure storm,
old lightning in our limbs. We thunderstruck
maroons, machete-wielding silhouettes
reject the fetters, come together still—
some call it Capoeira, call it street-
dance. We say culture. Say *survival*.
Bahia's berimbau or Boombox in
the "Boogie Down": a killing art as play,
an ancient killing art to break us free.

IV.

O Lord, send somethin' down to break us free,
said send us somethin' now to set us free
swing low Your chariot to rescue we.
The calls went up in every blessed field.
The people shouting, singing in the fields.
They lit the torches, compromised the yield.
This earthly house is gonna soon decay,
said look like Massa's house gon' soon decay.
I got my castle. Where he plan to stay?
Some waited in the hills till nightfall came,
an exodus of thousands. When night came,
they built their fires, sang into the flames:
Upon the mountaintop, the Good Lord spoke.
And out His mouth came the fire and the smoke.

V.

The art of spitting fire? How to smoke
a fool without a gun? We learned that too.
We studied master poets—Kane, not Keats;
Rakim, not Rilke. "Raw," "I Ain't No Joke,"
our Nightingales and Orpheus. And few
there were among us couldn't ride a beat
in strict tetrameter. Impromptu odes
and elegies—instead of slanting rhymes
we *gangster* learned them, kicking seventeen
entendre couplets just to fuck with old
Miss Jefferson, the Newton freak. Sometimes
we even got her out her seat, her ten
thin digits waving side to side, held high
and hiding nothing. Where our eyes could see.

VI.

And we knew nothing but what eyes could see—
the burnt-out liquor stores and beauty shops,
mechanics' lots, abandoned, boarded up
pastrami shacks where, seemed like everyday,
we used to ditch class, battle Centipedes
and Space Invaders. Gone. Or going fast.
What eyes could see was flux—the world, and us,
and all we knew, like smoke. So renegade
we did, against erasure, time and, hell,
we thought, against the Reaper, too. We left
our names in citadels, sprayed hieroglyphs
in church. Our rebel yells in aerosol—
We bomb therefore we are. We break therefore
we are. We spit the gospel. Therefore, Are.

VII.

     The walls are sprayed in gospel: This is for
the ones who never made the magazines.
     Between breakbeats and bad breaks, broken homes
and flat broke, caught but never crushed. The stars
     we knew we were, who recognized the shine
despite the shade. We renegade in rhyme,
     in dance, on trains and walls. We renegade
in lecture halls, the yes, yes, y'all's in suits,
     construction boots and aprons. Out of work
or nine to five, still renegade. Those laid
     to rest, forgotten renegades, in dirt
too soon with Kuriaki, Pun and Pac—
     I sing your name in praise, remember why
when we were twelve, we taught ourselves to fly.

SHERMAN AVE. LOVE POEM

A street sweeper rounds
     the corner, headlights
stretching a mans silhouette
     across the cool brick
of a brownstone. A window
     rattles, creaks, lifts open
from his rib and a woman
     steps through, pushes

off the ledge. Doesn't flail,
     doesn't scream or scratch
at passing brick. Mid-flight,
     she lies flat, spreads her
swollen shadow onto
     a fire hydrant. She is sure

as gravity. The man
       crossing the street, all rib
and open eye, clutches
       his Koran. Read in prison
how pregnant women
       would dive from slave ships.
Thought then, and believes
       now more than ever: this is
the one true act.

THE CORNER

Hard rain and reggaeton score the night. On this block here,
at this hour, when even alley cats know to keep in shadow, backs
to the wall and ears piqued, the few renegade rain-soaked heads
you come across are here on business. Transactions and sales,
give and take in the marketplace of the moon. If you wait
long enough, they say, you can hear the hellhounds' bay. The
     cross-

roads—in the swollen tongue of work-weary bluesmen across
geography and generations. Hoodoo Land. 'Legba's turf. It's here,
they say, where Robert Johnson sold his soul to learn the sweet
secret of conjuring moonlight from string and wood. When back-
roads all seemed to lead to the same place, men fresh from their
     cells
came to strike deals on a new start in life, to get ahead.

Take this young boy, JoJo. Fresh out the joint, before he'd head
anywhere near his mama's house, he'd run straight here. Across
the street from the carryout and check cashing spot, he'll peddle
his rocks to anybody who pushes past. Even little Ebony. Hear
she was prom queen once, drove the young boys crazy back
in the days before JoJo caught hold of her. How the weight

melts from face and neck. How skin cankers, and blood and sweat
crust corners of lips licked only in wet dreams. How she gives
    head
now by the dumpster behind the church, fucks, how fast five bucks
find their way back to JoJo's hands. And Jesus, on a stone cross,
watches it all from on high. How it begins, ends and begins
    again here.
on the corner. Tonight, rain clouds bruise the sky. JoJo sells

like a man with plans, as if he can buy his way away. Sells
as if he were the first to have such ideas. As if *moving weight*
wasn't just a new name for an old dream. When his mama was
    out here,
they called it *pushing*. By the time his daughter's head
can fit its first wig, they'll be calling it something else. The cross-
roads has seen it all. Seven hundred sixty-two JoJos, JoJoing back

to the days of fire-can crooners, doo-wop daddies and off-key back-
up singers, warming hands and running from the rollers. As if
    their cells
were hardwired for trouble, they'd find new lines to cross and
    cross
again. And find themselves back on the courtyard, lifting weights.
or back on cots, crumpling "Dear John" letters, slipping heads
in and out of nooses. After years locked down, they all end up
    back here.

Maybe you've seen how they come back—years lifting or losing
    weight,
thugs turned sissy or cell-block Muslim, some with heads
full of schemes to cross the system, some half-dead. Always,
    always, here.

TROUBLE MAN

It's the bone of a question
    caught in your throat,
pre-dawn sighs of the day's
    first traffic, shoulders like
fists under the skin. Say
    it's raining this morning,
you've just left a woman's
    blue musk and duvet,
to find devil knows what
    in the world, your wet collar,
to thin jacket, no match
    for pissed off sky gods.
And say this car pulls near,
    plastic bag for passenger
slide window, trading rain
    for music. Marvin Gaye.
And maybe you know
    this song. How long
since a man you called father
    troubled the hi-fi, smoldering
Newport in hand, and ran
    this record under a needle.
How long since a man's
    broken falsetto colored
every hour indigo. Years
    since he drifted, dreaming
into rice fields, stammered
    cracked Vietcong, gunboats
and helicopters swirling
    in his head. Years since
his own long walks, silent

returns, and Marvin's
many voices his only salve.
	He came up harder than
you know, your father.
		Didn't make it by the rules.
Your father came up hard,
		didn't get to make no rules
graying beard, callused hands,
		fingernails thick as nickels.
You were the boy who became
		that man without meaning
to, and know now: A man's
		life is never measured
in beats, but beat-downs,
		not line breaks, just breaks.
You hear Marvin fade down
		the avenue and it caresses you
like a brick: Your father,
		Marvin, and men like them
have already moaned every book
		you will ever write.
This you know, baby. This
		you know.

RAQUEL I. PENZO

MY BROOKLYN (IN RESPONSE TO GENTRIFICATION)

My Brooklyn taught me that light-skinned girls who speak
    Spanish are Puerto Rican,
and dark-skinned girls who speak
    Spanish are from Panama
That meant girls who looked like me but weren't Puerto Rican
    or Panamanian tried to
pass as Black girls whose parents came from parents that had
parents who had a
"Massa" as a parent, until my Spanish betrayed me

My Brooklyn taught me to be friendly to my neighborhood drug
    dealer. They will look
after your car, your daughters, your safety
They will have your back if it came to that
They will patrol the block and keep other, more dangerous drug
    dealers at bay
They will never sell to your kin

My Brooklyn taught me that women with bowed legs were
    whores, that too much sex
spread their thighs in an unnatural way
I'd end each day praying my untouched thighs would always
    kiss each other goodnight,
that no one would notice me, that I would never wear that label

My Brooklyn taught me that Black people were scary and white
people couldn't be trusted and that if I just stayed inside and
watched cartoons and baseball and novelas I wouldn't be

mugged or raped or end up pregnant like that little girl up the street—she was always outside playing

My Brooklyn taught me that of all the Christians, Catholics were the most hated, and of all the Catholics, the colored ones were low on the totem pole, and that at the bottom of the totem pole, the Spanish Catholics were the most punished; we had to repent for our color and language and passion, and maybe perhaps for adding Adobo to everything

And my Brooklyn taught me that everything and nothing I could ever want resides in this borough. That I could come home again, but my room would no longer be my room but rather an office or a den or a Starbucks. That my memories are for sale. And that no matter how many years pass, there will always be a yellow cat sleeping on the bread in the bodega across the street

THE TALK

There were men in Mami's bed for as long as Daughter could
  remember.

Like,
the one who knew all of Daughter's
favorite candies and always had the
sleepy eyes and the thin mustache.

Or,
the one with the brand new white car,
all tricked out with speakers on top of
speakers, tinted windows and spoilers.

Or,
the one with the salt-and-pepper hair
and telenovela good-looks,
who only stuck around for a very short time:
here one day, unceremoniously gone the next.

There was, of course
the man that made Mami's belly grow big
with Sister, the one that lured everyone off
to a snowy town with promises of
family and security

And,
the one who helped make Daughter;
he hadn't been around since the beginning,
instead traipsing through the lives of other
Mamis making Brother after Brother
after Sister after Brother

But when it came to Daughter,
men were strictly forbidden.

"No boyfriends," said Mami. "Boys only want one thing."

TEN-POUND DRAW

On your first day in London
you learn
that if you want to be loved
on the first night
in more than one position
you have to help with the cooking.

On your second day in London
you learn
that the best way
to get your smoke on
was to first find out
where the dark faces live.
You ride the Tube to Brixton Station
and find them all over the world
living at the end of the line.

At the top of the escalator
brotherman sells incense and oil,
sends orders into his cell phone
you think, *Righteousnouss*
must be a booming market.

The black girls the block girls
the black girls on the block
wink, smile and insist
that you are Pakistani &
you tell them that you are Nuyorikistani
so you talk like this *y como* like

that y *como* like *kikireeboo tan*
bella, no doubt, it's all good,
I am all of that if you want me to be
but do you know where one can find
a ten-pound draw?

No luck find the parliament funk &
Roger from Reading said you just can't ask
for a dime bag, so you buy ten bottles
of Egyptian musk and show Brotherman
the thirst in your eyes.
He leads you to the smoke
for a small finder's fee.

You are willing to take these chances
in spite of the suspicious glances
but just in case, you buy a Big Ben postcard,
address it to the Crazy Bunch c/o El Barrio
and you write:

Yo, if I don't make it back home
I was thinking about ya'll
when I went to Brixton
looking for a ten-pound draw

THE NEW BOOGALOO

There's a disco ball
spinning starlight
on the New Boogaloo

Tell Sonia
that the bombs

are ready to drop
that the soneros
are ready to sing
to those flowers
that did not survive
Operation Green Thumb

Tell Dwight
that the renaissance
he's been waiting for
is ready to set up shop
that dreams
are taking responsibility
for themselves

Tell Marcito
that painters are eating piraguas
sitting on milkcrates & kicking it
with poets
who are bored
with keeping it real

Tell Rosalía
that the Reverend Pedro Pietri
is on the rooftop
handing out passports
because the spaceship casita
is about to take off

Oye, mamita
no te apures
que como like a Brook Avenue
bombaso, we're gonna make you dance

Que como un cocotaso limpio
we're gonna make your head rock

So tell Pachanga
that Si No Hablas Español—bienvenido
that Si No Hablas Inglés—bienvenido

And don't forget to tell Domingo
that we're gonna shoot it up
mainline, mainstream,
mainland, underground
until we catch your vein
So take this sound
to your grave and tell the whole block
that a *bámbula* building session
is about to begin
& it's gonna be like two church boys
talking loud on the subway
praising the Lord
in the New Boogaloo—
    check it:

¡Pero que son!
I know it was the Lord son
Eso que mira, you know what it is fam
We keep the Bible real because
he wants me to learn sun
because he told me sun
to bring my notebook sun
Y mira I was like whoa
when the Reverend Pedro
was waiting for me
with a passport
and he told me

that this time
we all gonna die knowing
how beautiful we really are

LOOK WHAT I FOUND

So I was walking
to the reading
when I saw
two brothers talking
in front of a church.

Brother One
talked about his platonic
relationship with Jesus, Sunday
miracles & baptized dreams.
He said, *I pray. I pray*
every day and I pray
every night.

Brother Two
egged him on with a
speak & say that.

Then, for emphasis, Brother One
said, *You hear me? I pray*
every day & night.

When Brother One saw me approaching,
he lowered his voice to a hymn, waited
until I walked by and said,

Even
when I'm high.

SHOULD OLD SHIT BE FORGOT

Papo the Poet
started kicking a poem
while Dick Clark
put the city to count

Once again we pledge
down for whatever until the day we die
love forever it takes sixty seconds
to forget the one who left you
waiting at the bus stop

And Brother Lo said:

All that shit you talking
sounds good but let's rap
on the thirty dollars
you owe me

I hear you I hear you, I hear
what you're saying
We boys, we should be happy
when big ass disco balls
drop on our drunk resolutions

Father Time says
he's only gonna smoke
on weekends

New Year cornets
are swept off the street
like old friends

Champagne corks richochet
off ballroom walls

Roast pork burns while we
puff & pass in project halls

Bullets kill El Barrio sky
to celebrate holding it down
The same ole same ole shit
we promise every year

Fuck it
Pass the rum
It's cold out here
Who wants some?

You could say please
You could freeze
Whatever
Happy New Years
Feliz Año Nuevo

I'm out her for a reason
not the season
should old shit be forgot
and all that good stuff
but I want my money
before next year

SIDE A (3:2)

You switch to a velvet booth, a short-circuited
tombstone solo wears a cosmopolitan smirk—

Who is that copping pleas talking about
they haven't played that tune in a while?

Today is heavy-footed, branch-dumb, old
standards grill the last call & outside

The skylines, the skylines are consumed by
one. Two. One-two-three—

Time to dig historic in that section of the circle
where high call answers question with song.

Yes, Poet, I heard you.

And then what happened to Shorty Bon Bon?
He gave his last breath to Viejo San Juan.
Is it true what they say about Shorty Bon Bon?
No bird sells his wings, no sonero his son.
O, read me those poems about Shorty Bon Bon!
He buried his drum in La Plaza Colón.
O, tell me what happened to Shorty Bon Bon!
He lost his junjún in Viejo San Juan.

You lived on dreams & pauses for a whole take.
Whenever prayer shocked your fate lines, Buddha

sang for pennies & his song blubbered the heavens,
the heavens went quiet with his laugh. The rocks

in your path were unemployed & there was enough
space for a second life—sounds like just as it is—

only way out was to be about something.

You—fly-guy with the hard hands, blade-swimmer,
don't know if you heard but this horse is ready.
Gather your clouds & pearls, eagle-colt, glass slipper,
bitch mink, evil-faced guitar wail, O bongo, O
agogo, kundalini & caduceus—clack-clack, oye
como va, check my bon bon something nasty.

It is true—since birth your ears have been close
to the curb—for every initiation, a costly exit.

Recall the way bodies rocked, heads nodded,
summers were fertile for fib stacked upon fib.

A platoon of funerals & shipwrecks marched
to pure end, wreaking spleen-to-spine havoc.

Still, you scraped dead skin off your fingertips—
all those hot beats & not one to go home with.

Youtar on the fence & mesmerized sin, sneak
attack & crossfire—O, no, Voice, you dead flower
—before you go, grab my cowbell, my clave can
divide by three & conquer-by-twilight—O clave,
go, combust bleachers, warrior-call—thug-trychel,
hang from my neck & party all night long.

MIGUEL PIÑERO

A LOWER EAST SIDE POEM

Just once before I die
I want to climb up on a
tenement sky
to dream my lungs out till
I cry
then scatter my ashes thru
the Lower East Side.

So let me sing my song tonight
let me feel out of sight
and let all eyes be dry
when they scatter my ashes thru
the Lower East Side.

From Houston to 14th Street
from Second Avenue to the mighty D
here the hustlers & suckers meet
the faggots & freaks will all get
high
on the ashes that have been scattered
thru the Lower East Side.

There's no other place for me to be
there's no other place that I can see
there's no other town around that
brings you up or keeps you down
no food little heat sweeps by
fancy cars & pimps' bars & juke saloons
& greasy spoons make my spirits fly

with my ashes scattered thru the
Lower East Side . . .

A thief, a junkie I've been
committed every known sin
Jews and Gentiles . . . Bums & Men
of style . . . run away child
police shooting wild . . .
mother's futile wails . . . pushers
making sales . . . dope wheelers
& cocaine dealers . . . smoking pot
streets are hot & feed off those who bleed to death . . .

all that's true
all that's true
all that is true
but this ain't no lie
when I ask that my ashes be scattered thru
the Lower East Side.

So here I am, look at me
I stand proud as you can see
pleased to be from the Lower East
a street fighting man
a problem of this land
I am the Philosopher of the Criminal Mind
a dweller of prison time
a cancer of Rockefeller's ghettocide
this concrete tomb is my home
to belong to survive you gotta be strong
you can't be shy less without request
someone will scatter your ashes thru
the Lower East Side.

I don't wanna be buried in Puerto Rico
I don't wanna rest in Long Island Cemetery
I wanna be near the stabbing shooting
gambling fighting & unnatural dying
& new birth crying
so please when I die . . .
don't take me far away
keep me nearby
take my ashes and scatter them thru out
the Lower East Side . . .

THE BOOK OF GENESIS ACCORDING TO SAN MIGUELITO

Before the beginning
God created God
In the beginning
God created the ghettos & slums
and God saw this was good.
So God said,
"Let there be more ghettos & slums"
and there were more ghettos & slums.
But God saw this was plain
so
to decorate it
God created lead-base paint
and then
God commanded the rivers of garbage & filth
to flow gracefully through the ghettos.
On the third day
because on the second day God was out of town
On the third day
God's nose was running
& his jones was coming down and God

in his all-knowing wisdom
knew he was sick
he needed a fix
so God
created the backyards of the ghettos
& the alleys of the slums
in heroin & cocaine
and
with his divine wisdom & grace
God created hepatitis
who begat lockjaw
who begat malaria
who begat degradation
who begat
   GENOCIDE
and God knew this was good
in fact God knew things couldn't git better
but he decided to try anyway
On the fourth day
God was riding around Harlem in a gypsy cab
when he created the people
and he created these beings in ethnic proportion
but he saw the people lonely & hungry
and from his eminent rectum
he created a companion for these people
and he called this companion
capitalism
who begat racism
who begat exploitation
who begat male chauvinism
who begat machismo
who begat imperialism
who begat colonialism

who begat wall street
who begat foreign wars
and God knew
and God saw
and God felt this was extra good
and God said
VAYAAAAAAA
On the fifth day
the people kneeled
the people prayed
the people begged
and this manifested itself in a petition
a letter to the editor
to know why? WHY? WHY? Qué pasa, babyyyyy?????
and God said,
"My fellow subjects
let me make one thing perfectly clear
by saying this about that:
    NO . . . COMMENT!"
But on the sixth day God spoke to the people
he said . . . "PEOPLE!!!
the ghettos & the slums
& all the other great things I've created
will have dominion over thee"
and then
he commanded the ghettos & slums
and all the other great things he created
to multiply
and they multiplied
On the seventh day God was tired
so he called in sick
collected his overtime pay
a paid vacation included

But before God got on that t.w.a.
for the sunny beaches of Puerto Rico
He noticed his main man Satan
planting the learning trees of consciousness
around his ghetto edens
so God called a news conference
on a state of the heavens address
on a coast to coast national t.v. hook up
and God told the people to be
COOL
and the people were cool
and the people kept cool
and the people are cool
and the people stay cool
and God said
Vaya. . . .

THE MENUDO OF A CUCHIFRITO LOVE AFFAIR

la ruca
juanita rosita esposita
they called her mexicana rose
con piel de canela
pelo darker than bustelo café
eyes big like rellenos
color of a ripe avocado
her lips tasted like seasoned mangos
and her body was sweet as coconut milk
this menudo of beauty
made my taco nights
burn like jalapeños
sí señor . . .
my heart was a tortilla

then one riceless beanless night
after a heated chilly pepper tequila fight
she left
left me like a burnt pork chop
for a chitlin' hamhock buckwheat eatin' man
who wore a watermelon wallet &
a collard green conversation
disturbing my macho machete pride
so that la mancha de plátano
reminded me that I was a weak mondongo
my love . . . my life . . . my pride was a burnt chicharrón
a cold mofongo
a melted piragua
I turned into a hot tamale
state of rage
an alcapurria gone insane
when I saw these two enchiladas
in a pastelillo embrace
so in my pasteles envy
my tostón jealousy
that my salchicha-eyes spied
the chorizo the mad morcilla drive
así fue que fueron
traspasados los dos bacalaos
and now with my burrito strike
displaying my quenepa pride
in my tamarindo smile
I remember the pegao and the uncooked taste
of the frijol menudo of my cuchifrito
love affair . . .

NEW YORK CITY HARD TIME BLUES

NYC Blues
Big time time hard on on me blues
New York City hard sunday morning blues
yeah
junkie waking up
bones ache trying to shake
New York City sunday morning blues
the sun was vomiting itself up over
the carbon monoxide detroit perfume
strolling down the black asphalt dance floor
where all the disco sweat drenched Mr. Mario's
summer suit still mambo-tango hustled
to the tunes of fiberglass songs
New York City sunday morning means
liquor store closed
bars don't open 'til noon
and my connection wasn't upping
a 25-cent balloon
yeah
yeah reality wasn't giving me no play
telling me it was going to be sunday
24 hours the whole day
it was like the reincarnation of the night
before when my ashtray became
the cemetery of all my lost memories
when a stumble bum blues band
kept me up all night playing me cheap
F. M.
dreams
of hard time
sad time

bad time
hell, we all know times are
hard
sad
bad
all over
well I thought of the pope
welfare hopes
then I thought of the pope again
whose sexual collar musta been tighter
than a pimp's hat band
yeah
that brought a warm beer smile to this
wasteland the mirror called my face
ya see
I left my faith in a mausoleum
when my inspiration ran off with
a trumpet player
who wore doubleknit suits and stacy adam shoes
this girl left me so broke
my horoscope said
my sign was a dead dog in the middle
of the road
yeah
the morning will be giving up to the noon
and soon I'll hear winos and junkyard dogs
howling at the moon
made the shadows
dance
at jake's juke saloon
as a battalion of violet virgins
sang tunes
of deflowered songs

men poured their
fantasies of lust into young boy's
ears
car stolen
whizzed by
crying hard luck tears in beers
the love conflict of air-conditioned
dim-lit motel rooms
rumpled sheets with blood stains
explain
my yesterday night of mind
the winter fell as hard
as the smell of a brick shithouse
in the hot south
Om . . .
but the hawk seeped into my home
chillin' my bones
Om . . .
it didn't hear my incantation
there has to be an explanation
wasn't it true
when you
Om . . .
you are one
Om . . .
make me warm
Om . . .
is part of god
Om . . .
make the cold wind stop
Om . . .
perhaps if I
Om . . .

stronger
Om . . .
louder
Om . . .
LONGER
OMMMMMMMMMMMMMMMMMMMMMM
it don't work
Om . . .
I feel like a jerk
I'll try once more just to make sure
OMMMMM
maybe if I pleaded on my knees
to J. C.
he'd take heed of my needs
and melt the icicles
from the tears in my eyes
but it was still cold
I'm told if you sing
"I'm gonna lay down my sword and shield
down by the river side . . . down by the river side"
I get no signal
maybe if I do it bilingual
"en la cruz, en la cruz yo primero vi la luz"
oh come on chuito
have a heart
take apart the winter winds from me
please . . . J. C. . . .
OM . . .
en la cruz
down by the river side
10 hail marys I offer
and 5 our fathers
but the cold was no further

than before
I should know its very rare when
a prayer
gets the boiler fixed
OMMMMM
yeah
New York City december sunday morning
was whippin' my ass in a cold-blooded fashion
treatin' me like a stepchild
putting a serious hurting on me
watching me bleed
thru my sleeves
as I tried to get high
shooting up caffeine without saccarine
that some beat artist sold me down
on eldredge st.
yeah
but that's the ghetto creed
that the strong must feed
yeah
brotherman
everything was happening faster than the
speed of sound
my whole seemed like it was going down
I wonder who ever wrote that tune
about being back on top in june
nigger forgot about september and december
now that's a month to remember
when each cold day becomes like a brick wall
and you're the bouncing ball
yeah I kept seeing my fate being sealed
by the silk smooth hands of the eternal bill
collector

who keeps rattling my doorknob
pressing my avon ding dong bell . . .
my pockets were crying the blues
telling me that I ain't fed them a dollar in years
and was it clear that they couldn't hold
any more unpaid debts . . . traffic tickets . . . or promissory notes
and hey that was when I wished I was back in
L.A.
laid back
L.A.
kick back
L.A.
smog town
hollywood . . . driving down to malibu
hollywood U. S. A. . . . hey hey USA hollywood
seedy-looking film producers smile at you
over a burrito with taco bell breath
explain the plots to fellini movies
they ain't ever seen
hollywood . . . down to malibu
at two a.m. if you get tired
of cal worthington shit-eating grin
you walk out on him hit santa monica blvd
and watch the manicured thumbs caress the
homosexual airs of rolled up jeans and silver buckles
as westwood camaro rides very slow very low
down western ave
where neon lights scream
the latest kick in adult entertainment
masturbation
enters your thoughts
when pornographic stars with colgate smiles
whisper

inane
mundane
snides of flicking your bic
or I'm nancy fly with me national
well I'm going nowhere got nowhere to go
going nowhere fast
got me a couple of dollars a few dimes
and plenty of time
go into some bar on alvarado
and temple listen to some mariachi music
or stroll into some dive joint off sunset
sit in some naugahyde booth
with some dishwater blond
with sagging breasts
wearing a see-thru blouse
and listen to all her 1930 starlet dreams
as she smokes all my cigarettes
sure what have I got back at that
refugee from a leprosy colony hotel
but a one station a.m. radio
feeding my neurological cells
with those south street philadelphia blues
she wants to cruise thru griffin park
no, thank you
I'd rather listen to linda ronstadt instead
and the bartender tell dirty jokes
and his customers recite 12% alcoholic aluminum
recycled viet nam horror stories
reading the signs of our times
the obituary of a dying society
the folktales of yesteryear's gonorrhea
history
hollywood going down to malibu

malibu . . . pretty people and fonzi T-shirts
flex their muscles spreading spiritual bad breath
and joe namath perfume
yeah
but i'm in new york city
crying the junkie blues
welfare afro hairdos sprout out
of frye boots
yeah punk rockers hitting on you
for subway fare three times
soon the mohair slick lines
at penn station are getting impatient
wanna get home
to alone
make the scene with a magazine
or with a plastic doll
'cause the missus got another headache
gaze at the farrah foster poster
that adorns his horny teenage son's walls
yeah these days always
have a way of showing up
like rubber checks
I wish I could cop a bottle of muscatel
stroll thru the bowery with a pocket
full of wino dreams
but sunday morning in New York City
for the junkie there ain't no pity
we just walk the streets with loaded dice
and hear people say there goes miky
miky piñero
they call him the junkie christ . . .

AFRO/RIKAN

sounds like Black Boogie Down/howling/into Moshulu
Parkway/for answers, scratching at this/twilight /hybrid/skin.
Watching Static Shock while/eating rice and beans, proof
borders are in the bartering./Prove you know every/word to 50
Cent's *The Massacre*/and how to salsa/enough/to make the block
moan./They heard you ain't got/no/rhythm, didn't even play
Biggie at your birthday. You even seen every episode of
Martin?/Remember *The Brothers García?*/Do you/you ever been
baffled/by your/own Spanglish/how it tries/to lick the moon/
clean of its grays/knows how hard it is to be/a smudged
shade/instead of a real color./So jealous/of not knowing/you/
you boast/unknown/lineage to be enough.

WEPA: BABEL TONGUE

Duma says I have the heaviest puerto
of a *muy rico* mouth, the richest gums
from the sand streets. Excitedly,
my tongue claims currency, tries to bribe
its way past the borders of another's skin.

Yet, chained on an island of saliva, lengua stares
at the inverted tower of my throat, thinks
God, what I would do to climb that skyless cielo.

THE PUERTO RICAN MAID RESPONDS TO KENDRICK LAMAR'S YELL

after u

disculpe, but
you remind me of a house
i had in San Juan, all open doors
with

that same sound to their hinges.

i still hear them, voices
across the ocean; i stare too long
at what i left behind, fold paper
into envelopes, and sail
change until i return.

tengamos que limpiar
our mouths every once in
a while to make room for our
sanity, and i left home too,
feet staggering from my tongue.

your words look just like a clumsy
leaving Kendrick, pobrecito, no hay
mucho tiempo.

Pero, what choice did we have?

GABRIEL RAMÍREZ

RESILIENCE

my uncle went to buy cigarettes
in a supermarket owned by
the Dominican mafia &
men he scammed were watching
the cameras. they grabbed my uncle,
took him to the back & sent everyone home.
they tortured him till sunrise. beating him
close to death with anything they could find;
their hands weren't enough.
they knocked him out, threw him in their car &
wanted to bury him alive. my uncle woke up &
fought his way out a car full of men with guns.
he limped far but not far enough for them to miss.
a dog barked until the police came.

at his wake

he looked as though
he had died in his sleep.
not a cut or bruise
on his face. all you could see
were his swollen knuckles;
eight shiny mountains
you can find his spirit
slamming dominos
so hard they fused
with the earth.

years later the FBI found the three men who killed my uncle
in the Dominican Republic. in court the murderers said
he just wouldn't die.
he was one tough son of a bitch.
he was hard to kill.

WHAT I LEARNED IN U.S. HISTORY CLASS

America's first
word was murder.
America found
a gun. America
wasn't breastfed.
America is still
raping it's mother.
America don't got
no daddy. America
is a bastard child.
America went to church
on Sunday. America
was baptized in Native-
American blood. America
smoked crack in confessionals.
America beats it's wife.
America don't know love.
America lost it's mind
in the Atlantic ocean.
America thinks "America"
is it's real name.

ALIVE=BLK

i'm the only one in my family
who claims to be alive. my family
acts like no one in our ancestry
was alive. i have relatives who don't
like people who are alive. i've gone
through life not knowing i was alive.
not knowing alive had to be
what i looked like. i had to teach myself
how to be alive. i was taught those who were
alive would rather be dead or will die
due to unnatural causes. i was presented
with a book of my families' ancestry.
a woman's first name was Africa.
how much more alive could she have been
in a book full of dead people?

THE LEGENDARY LEGS OF THE RODRIGUEZ WOMEN

Unequivocal with his observation,
a New Orleans accent and a smile
the stranger comments, "Nice stems"
quickly passing by my shoulder,
creating a small breezy respite from the stale heat.

My cheeks respond in gratitude,
with thoughts of my mother
and the legendary legs of the Rodriguez women,
mythical like Ithaca and Helen.
The genetic heirlooms
from a grandmother I never knew
as 1970s pictures framed in sunflower yellow
document my mother standing on beauty pageant stages
in stilettos with an audience of wishful suitors
and envious women.

Instinctive like writing names on wet sand
I touch the brown flesh and muscles below my knees
wonder if Carmelita ever thinks of my mom or me
when she inspects the variant blues of her veins,
slips on silk stockings, dances to Tito Puente,
wades in the water we call home.

PAINTED WALLS

Possessed by the spirits of renaissance artists
I paint over walls

    beach sand hues over red delicious
    memories embedded
    in the irregular shaped corners
    of my bedroom   sanctuary   office
    mommy's special timeout place

and years of masonry experience
continues as I build new facades
hallmarked with est.-in-1983 bricks
based in shame carried daily
like my unborn child.

Shame wrapped around me like a sabana,
worn like my mother's favorite perfume
its scent enmeshed with mine
as I inhale and exhale
the toxicity of childhood silence

eat, drink, sit and talk with shame
like the siblings I never had,
fuck it until I get love out of it

forget it ever existed
in the palms of an alcoholic mother
and bruises on four-year-old skin

forgive the wife for not calling the police,
believing she was the dirty bitch

he claimed with each slap to the face
and bruises on thirty-four-year-old skin

stare at it in the mirror
figuring out how to let it go
like an offering
left on the doorstep
of the ocean.

GARCIA FOLKLORE #27

Located between the boundary
of the Atlantic and Caribbean Ocean
a tide swept the two-year-old child
commanding her body like an ancient sacrifice.

But the young mother disagreed
for the child had many lands to explore,
stories to pen, books to read,
hearts to conquer, stories to learn from.

Swooping the breathless infant
from the ocean's hands
with a mythical strength
she saved the child

but the bones in the mother's back
always remind her of the day
she fought the ocean and won.

SOLITARY ENCOUNTERS

His intellect reminded me of Spanish Harlem,
unpretentious but resonating,
as he discussed the gentrification of boyhood memories,
the irony of Paine's title Common Sense,
coined the term déjà vu history
when another child disappears, a shooting becomes rudimentary,
a person beaten for kissing the wrong person.

His philosophy on how the world works
reminded me of the Bronx,
unafraid of who he offended
as he revealed why he carries a knife
wherever he goes, why he will never marry
a woman named after a cocktail
and why provocation is sometimes necessary.

He doesn't remember the inappropriate joke
we simultaneously smiled at, our goodbye hug
awkward like undergraduate sex
when hands don't know where they should go,
or how I stared at him longer than I should.

LOUIS REYES RIVERA

NO HOLE IN PUNCTURED POEM

there's no hole in a punctured love poem
cause everybody writes
from the twinge on the loose
with a grip on the twinge
in the crawl of a groove that is missed
through the middle of the marrow in the breast
from the breast in the middle of the bone
everybody hears the willow.

There's no hole in a punctured poem
cause everybody loves to write
with the touch of the brush
from the tingle of a touch
in the brush of the breath
with the stroke of a tongue
in the middle of the space thru the middle
of the space from the drumming in a breast
in the middle of the breast in a drum
everybody hears the willow.

There's no puncture in the hole of love
cause everybody is a poem
from a whisper to a riff
in the honey and the scent
with a fever in the spin
from the honey and the scent

in the lacing of a stich
with the stiches in a tune

thru the rage from a sting with the two
in the middle of a strum from a smile
on our breast we two in the middle of
a strum with a pang in our breast us
too in the middle of embrace we become
                              the willow
        listening to a song.

"THE ADVERB"

to the degree of being broke
i am an adverb
        lost to the treachery of growling waves
            that slurp & push & roll against my worth
yet loudly I ring the song of a longing heart
on a hungry vessel calling bells out at sea
        rouunnngg.
        rouunngg.
the fifth rung sound/
here
the adverb
more poor than a metaphor's bell bottom
undulated sway from side to side
        ship's men working decks
        climbing sails
        hoisting rigs with spars astern
        the promised pay that time forgets
        the scorched skin the sun bemoans—
yes. i concede there's some room for me here
but below the deck
        sweat stench & captured cargo
        jealously vie for the smallest

breath
space
between
bodies
planks
tiers of iron links interlaced & dragged
by the constant threat of watchmen's whips
    cracked!
    crammed
    aching oarsmen
pulling the weight of the future rowed in their hands
    the only pay these muscles ever get:
        a glint of sunlight daily
        a cup of wormslop seldom
        & a bucket filled with water salt
        to wash away the guilt of merchants
        hounding the labors of men

my place in the world is here/with them
but only within the scheme of an adverb
wanting to be clearer than the wind
that howls thru their stomachs
harboring for attention
    an adverb/
barely grabbing an ear to hear
a lonely sound hungrily refusing to concede
attached to acts that help describe
what must happen on shores that rattle in chains
from where the report of thirtieth or third
poetically simple soul tossed to the seas
ruptured in ports
hanged on a poplar near some alien beach
forgotten by the sons of sweat

now hidden in a secret vault
now openly exposed/
        the adverb
the one that speaks to stir or serve
wrenching voracious
war word on nerves
to minds blown cold
the part of our speech that pains as well
longs as much to be more sensitive
to touch my place among the scrolls.

"LIKE TOUSSAINT, SO MARTÍ"

always there was talk of Toussaint & Martí
always is a basic chord to guide the tone of wanting
always in the present a romantic song is heard,
like the echo of Lempira
strapped upright on a jesuit pole
refusing the gates of heaven
while a torch was set to wood,
or the inflection of Hatuey
spitting in the face of cackling flames
fanned by coats of arms & catholic priests,
or the sounding call of Tecun Umán
staring at that lonely cloud above him
cursing the torrent of fire tormenting his flesh
rejecting the promise of paradise & popes

even while the breastplates of brigands stood
& laughed amid Mayan tears & burning scrolls
the stoking embers of hallowed bones & crackling wood
the sacrament of monks preying over ashes of resistance,
there was already talk of Toussaint & Martí,

of voices rising with machetes
that once in canefields swung beneath the lash
now stalking the forests of thunder & rain,
now swinging at the throats of colonial greed
now climbing over martyred men thrown
against the mouths of cannonblast & rifle fire
muffling the gasp in Napoleon's roar
widening the gash of liberation lanced by
the bladder of carlistas & the blabber of cortés

Toussaint, the trunk of a tree
branching from the slash & burn of slaves no more
spreading his arms embracing Maroons
like the separated fingers of a calloused hand
now formed into fists pounding against the breath of death
& like Toussaint, so Martí,
that poet/apostle residing atop
the sores in our hands where destiny
once again speaks on behalf of voices drowned
by the coffers of greed & the din of merchants' wares

yet even before fallen trees rose & bled
even before Guarionex & Caonabó raised the chains
around their wrists & prayed that Huracán
full of downpour & conviction
cast a well of waves upon
the docks & decks of prison ships
whirling waters crushing mast & sails
to set them free among St. Vincent's Black Caribs,
there was already talk of the coming of Martí
bringing back the scattered branches of cedar wood
& cherry blossoms to strike the might of bayonets
& birth the nodes of hope upon the womb of earth
no longer torn by maggots

the dream of a wondrous dawn
echoing the song of a planet bursting freedom
amid wielders of machetes
in Cuba & Ayiti, Martí & Toussaint
dragon trail & dragon head
pushing through the vaginal walls of conflict in contention
& reared by the first band of cimarrons claiming mountains black
where rituals forged between Arawak and African
long ago had given rise to the timbre of Makandal
urging the waters of every river's mouth
escape from the soil of savannahs enslaved

the sharp stones of planted spikes
tearing through the clamor of shackles broke
ditch dug holes hovering below
the hidden wreath of branch & leaf
covering the snares that lie in wait
along narrow trails of dust & hills
where Boukman drinks the blood of goats, passing his cup
and urging each swear to turn the earth into a friend
listen to Toya teaching Dessalines
          about spear

                              chucks & slingshots
                         musket fire arrow shaft
                      plunging deep slicing cut
                   sharpened picks & makeshift ax
come to greet Old Nanny fatting bullets fired back
redcoat throats caught in the midst of holy ground
blest by yesterday's faith in Toussaint & Martí
who studied & plotted the direction of wind
taught & stirred the pages of expression
giving shape to the substance of our course
where neither england nor france nor spain

or even the states of northern hate
could stop cajole distort abort
the revelation of revolution on the brink of Caribbean seas.

EXCERPT FROM "CU/BOP"

they came
& they met
in the harrows of big apple slightslice
on the corners of lenox & third
down inside brooklyn harlem after hour grind spot
with their trumpets & axes
bongos & timbales
maracas & congas
chops & drums
bass & piano
bleeding needing emerging
mambo kings & bebop monarchs
mondongo fare & chittlin roast
like   yuca
        yuca
                yuca tenango
yuca yuca yuca tenango
peas & rice
greens & grits
hocks & rinds

THE DISDIRECTED

Some folk think that poet
is but another word for star
where star don't mean to signify

beyond the glitter & the glimmer
of cold coke
cocktail glasses clicking
up against the hard vein sweat
of who you know
& how that knowledge could get me into bed
with someone who might rub me
if you please
>   dust
>   rust
>   slowly
>   solely
nothing else but sheen or shine
making out like substance & sustenance
have no place beyond the deadly force
of cut throat yester-rape
where the mundane shame of pain
looks to them like crusts of shadows
falling into disrepute
but that ain't what a poet is
& stars just seem that way
to those who look
but cannot see
exactly what they checking out . . .
musicians on the run
the people & their sweat
still & slow
who sour
sweetly near romantic pools
neath salt bed seas by curaçao
in the midst of devastated nueva york
>   newport
>   newark

running toward the edge of hell
at every corner of the road we call
                              right here:
        a hemisphere of slaves
        now kept as household maids
        with hairnets wet & woven
        like the pubic curls
        of wombless tubes
        got cut & sliced
        like the olla or an oven pot
        cooled to simmer til it's hot
I said
some would think that there ain't nothing else
but glitter gut
stardust versifying lyricists
who glut the gleam of gotten gain
measured by a gutter cup of
get what's mine or steal what's yours
cocktail sipping
evening gown
hard-on pants of beaded braids
bread with butter
vegetating knitted shawl

Oh, but I paid 600 dollars to have my hair . .
fixed(!)
like spaded cats that can't create
a child their own
like the studyless who
hawk up on a benevolent phrase
from those who hunt down anything
& once absorbed
call it mine(!)

or like the unstudied undersullied wouldbe
groups of disdirected poets
tuning up on trite like lines
they'd never lived
       never tasted
       never known the pain thereof
lacking keys in tune with insight
vision staling from a beamless search
lacking grace to dig down deep
inside the pit of
constant climbing
elbow rubbing
searching for a coattail pulled
a cocktail lost
but never sit beneath their guiding stars
to question what it was
preceded hate
confused with doubt
unclear &
tearing at the fibers of illusion
like the way some think perhaps they came
upon the earth selfcreated

but they never even read a book
that didn't lie
or steal or con
the sanity & sanctity of breath
& never once have tried to excavate
the question & the meaning
of the dance that comes with song
or use their eyes to see or sense or feel
beyond the question & the meaning
of sparkling rays pulsing to perform

while every throb of thirsting
                    searching
                    thinking being knows
that nommo prophet keeper of a narrative pursuit
means that poet is a struggle for
a glimpse of light
a grope for hope
urging war against deceit
but studyless & wouldbe,
no direction in their dance,
they dis the fact that
star is just another word for sun
imploring heat speeding
past each wave of night imploding
from the energy of dusk
creating rise & giving voice
to one more poet
who ain't no way like elbows
to be rubbed or snubbed
but is indeed a pulsing push
of constant growth & pain
reminding us we're all just flesh
& real enough
to sit beside & ponder.

WITNESS: IMAGINATION

"inside each & every third eye
is the Ocean of Imagination
with no bottom to reach
no shoreline to touch
no limitation self-imposed

"& it is here
in the deep of what we see
where capacity resides
to dream & seek
create & shape
blow the breath of life
& raise into existence
the insides of our we
taking you & me
everywhere within ourselves
to trek & tread
those distant tracings that rise beyond the moon
overpass every planet in the sky
undertake any star & state
that would bind us into borders
bound by fixed condition
tricking us to so believe
we cannot claim the order of the day
or change our destiny ourselves

"But imaginate the possible
:if, out of the forward urge
of somehow since we issued forth
growing out from nothing
into something given birth
from nowhere into somewhere we reach Did
standing on the cusp of what & when
then certainly from here
we can get to any other there & in the flow of self-determined
   move
we can change & shape the course of Now!"

BONAFIDE ROJAS

NOTES ON THE RETURN TO THE ISLAND

i was there
watching the ocean
splash against the
new walls of
cabo rojo
that change
every season
the old walls fall
into the ocean
displays new
colors of seafoam
sliding down
ever so gently
josé tells me
new stories
of the west coast
of puerto rico
i would've
never known

i was there as
the lighthouse
that stood
majestically
overlooking
the caribbean sea
closed & quiet
hoping to find
someone before

border patrols do
to warn them
there is colonialism
here, be weary with
the poison they pick
who warns them
to not cross
the mona passage
& shines a light
for them & tells
them to be careful
border patrol
is more ruthless
than the sharks
circling their boat

i was there
climbing down
the rocks hoping
i don't fall
& have my
face ripped
apart by the
boulders &
earth made
schrapnel
i can see
the ocean
talking to
yemayá
happy to see
me be baptized
in these waters

of playa sucia
rising out
with seaweed
in my hair
i smell the salt
taste the water
the rocks clip
my feet
i don't care
i was there

i was there
at a bar in
río piedras
with urayoán
talking about
our respective
adolescence
from the boogie
down to around
the corner, drinking
medalla & listening
to really bad
bands pretend
not to care
while the crowd
was happy to
see their friends
on stage & imagine
they've made it
we repeated
the word borracho
& it became

the word
of the night
we met up
with yarimir
at another bar
& talked about
music & the
universe
all the while
i watch
hundreds of
teenage
puertorriqueños
having their
first beer, first
kiss, first hangover

i was there
in santurce
on avenida juncos
at the very first
queer rock show
at el local
i drank medalla like water
the bands sounded
like they loved the misfits
& early los angelels punk
urayoán & josé miguel
were there too
& drove me home
swirling across the street
like an erratic dolphin
tailgating a drunk cop car

mimicking their moves
& somehow we made
it home in one piece
the next day i went back
& saw the writings
on the wall
i was there.

THIRTY WAYS TO LOOK AT A NUYORICAN

I.
i do not wake up to roosters
i wake up to construction sights
& the noises of the buses

II.
english was fed to me
by my televised babysitter

III.
i barely know what oceans look like
orchard beach & brighton beach do not count

IV.
i buy rice & beans in cans, i know how
to grow culture but I don't know how to grow food

V.
my skin is pale, my cousin's skin is black
we are called white boy & negro
at the same time at the same table

VI.

i do not know how to hotwire a car

VII.

i have a fear of needles, so being a junkie is out
but being a thief (only sometimes)

VIII.

i have more books than articles of clothing

IX.

as i remember it, i've been called jewish
more times after i turned twenty-one
for whatever reason

X.

i do not believe in haircuts
until i cut my hair again

XI.

when riding the train
everyone can be nuyorican but
most are new yorkers

XII.

i constantly get lost in queens

XIII.

i once walked into a riot
& immediately walked out

XIV.
excelsior

XV.
my son & i watch
cartoons all day

XVI.
people make fun of me for not knowing
how to drive then they visit NYC
& completely understand why

XVII.
police have stopped me for looking
too out of place, i was standing in front
of my building

XVIII.
when in london, searching for the puerto rican
flag is like finding a needle in a brick wall

XIX.
spanish does not make a nuyorican
english does not make a nuyorican

XX.
the nuyorican dances in their sleep

XXI.
pedro, papoleto, miguel, sandra, louis, jorge, tato & bimbo
walk into a bar & performed magic, performed beautiful magic

XXII.
my obituary is not written yet

XXIII.
when i returned to puerto rico
everyone stared at me when i spoke
i think it was because of my accent

XXIV.
nuyoricans look like everyone
nuyoricans look like no one

XXV.
my son was born in chicago, lived in harlem,
moved to detroit, is puerto rican & irish
but i keep his heart in the Bronx

XXVI.
i am like every puerto rican
i am not like every puerto rican

XXVII.
in the middle of the bandera
is the heart of nuyorican
ask Betances

XXVIII.
el morro is more famous than
the empire state building

XXIX.
a nuyorican & a puerto rican
walk into the bar & they both
ask for a cuba libre

XXX.
patria. libertad. sangre.

REMEMBER THEIR NAMES

the evening whispers
a flickering flame & the streets
of spanish harlem are quiet

you can feel it change on 116th st.
where la marqueta is staring down its roads
& sees the faces bleaching with the gentrification

1st ave. is being tidal waved with bull's-eyes
on the corner children hold signs that say
libertad but you understand it as something
that has to be freed or liberated
so you introduce a slow invasion
instead of self preservation

salsa isn't as loud as it used to be
the congas are quiet
the bombas have been defused
but there is still a resistance in the streets

we are looking for pedro pietri
to give us our passports
so we can detach ourselves from ourselves

if you don't recognize our birth certificates
then we don't recognize your citizenship

we wander through the streets of our memory
looking for julia de burgos
in the concrete of our tongue

where is el barrio?

here we stand on lexington ave.
battling for our self respect
& have our names recognized
that we are a part of a tradition
of beauty that has been here since the 40s
with a beautiful array of black & brown faces

this is not the "upper upper east side"
this is not "spaha"
this is not "upper yorkville"

we will not let nyc be transformed
by real estate developers for the sake
of free market capitalism

we carry the weight
of the young lords
on our shoulders,
filiberto is screaming
from the rooftops
but no one hears him
because the 6 train is too loud

we hear the gunshots
they are killing our leaders

but the community doesn't
know their names

we are the children of lolita
raised in a city with
a skyline taller than god

we are looking at the stars willie perdomo
told us about but the space has been brought by home depot

2nd ave. holds the blood of our history
betances, brugman, bracetti & rojas
are standing on the corner with their
fingerprints redder than red staining
these streets with a legacy
that has to be remembered

this is not the first time someone
has tried to take what's ours
on an island, we have seen this before
columbus, the united states military
robert moses & his eminent domain
we are not nomads

where we lay our guayabera is our home
arrest the politicos who say they defend us
but do not walk with us
the ghosts of our nationalism
are on columbus ave.
holding their bodies riddled
with radiation & bullets

their names are carried
by our breath

by our strength
by our hearts

we speak their names
with love & gratitude
for their struggle & commitment
to our progression

de hostos
cofresí
de diego
gonzalo marín
matienzo cintrón
mattei lluberas
ramírez medina
rodríguez de tió
ríus rivera
ruiz belvis
schomburg
valero de bernabé
zeno gandía
fernández
águila blanca
albizu campos
cancel miranda
vázquez
canales
canales
canales
coll y cuchí
collazo
corretjer
delgado

matos paoli

santos

torresola

viscal garriga

marqués

vélez rieckehoff

margenat

soto vélez

rodríguez-trias

palés matos

barceló

berríos

boschetti

mari brás

brown

concepción de gracia

ramírez

dávila

escobar

gerena

de lourdes santiago

lloréns torres

torres

torres

rodríguez orellana

pedreira

poventud

thomas

lópez rivera

rivera

rivera

pérez

morales

let these names rename these streets
let these names be our conduit to our fighting spirit
let these names remind us that
we are a continuation of a battle that has
been everlasting since our first breath on borikén.

MOTHER

tonight
> you sleep on a
> bed that is not yours, in
> a room you did not decorate
> people

> who work
>> here, you do not
>> know their names, they call you
>> by your surname, patient number
>> your chart

this has
> been a long road
> everything hurts, feels broken but
> be patient, i know it seems like
> it won't

> ever
>> stop, but it won't
>> last forever, you think
>> of how your body has failed you
>> betrayed

you for
  sweets, gave you high
  blood pressure, developed
  new routine of pills, insulin
  but this

  will not
      be your song, this
  will pass, diabetes
  is another chapter in your
  life like death,

deadbeats,
  migration, like
  single parenthood, like
  marriage, wild child teenagers, this
  will pass

THE OLD NEW STORY

  this new
  story is not
  new, we go where no one
  wants to go then everyone wants
  to go

  then we're
  pushed out slowly
  by greedy landlords &
  eminent domain, spoiled kids &
  big dreams

of the
big city, making
it, they walk with their new
entitlement & scoff at the
old man

who's been
here longer than
all of us, call the cops
on him for playing the same song
he's played

every
saturday, but
the new entitlement
doesn't like that, doesn't under
stand it

this new
story is old
we've gone through before
we've wrote this before & no one
listens

they brush
it off as, "change,
can't stay the same, it's life"
they say, "it is what it is, that
is life"

i do
not agree, i
refuse to believe that,

defend what you have created,
have loved

have built,
from the ground up
no one wanted your streets
before you, you have thirty years
in it

defend
the street that loves
your childhood like a sling,
act like you care, that your home
matters

THE CREED OF A GRAFFITI WRITER

we strike at night
the streets of new york
is our canvas

we hide in the shadows
when the pig patrol strolls
by the moon gives us our
only source of light

we are the addicts of aerosol
the krylon can clan
the rusto patrol
we are the german tip spraying
backpack wearing
black book carrying

magnum pilot tagging
the wack toy buffers

we are the brigade of bombers
mounting on our midnight mission
of colorized madness
the color blending
spray paint & mind-melding maniacs

we are the ghetto picassos
the modern-day matisses
the artistic shakespeares
that tear white walls in half

we are the street canvas killers
with one quick splat
of an ultra flat black
with silver outlines
& yellow highlights, perfected
during 3 a.m. night skylines

we are the crews that redecorate
building walls with wildstyles
burning people's imagination
with motions of the can
the walls wailed words of life
through the sight of krylon colors
on the streets of new york
we bomb city blocks
rocking throw-ups on top of window sills
while standing on top of garbage cans

we are the ones who set
bronx-brooklyn expeditions
in traditions of nomads
we go where no man's can
has sprayed on walls before

our names are found on
high-rises, bridges & building roofs
our plans are waterproof
shockproof and foolproof

we are the tye dye tone tint
marauders that wrote manifestos
on black walls with a silver uni, sg-7
& white pentel markers

we mark the many lands & train stations
our tags rag black books & cardboard
scratched on windows & train doors
stickers slapped over any bastard
you had beef with but only in self-defense

we gaze at our glossy words
& lose ourselves in arrows & 3-d shadows
we are the 12 oz prophets
that wrote prophecies with
our hieroglyphics to help
people understand us

it is simply the love
of seeing our name on the wall
it is the symbolic value
of feeling important

in a world we are lost in
it was the outlet that introduced
art into our way of thinking
we wore baggy jeans
hat to the back & army fatigues
when we ventured on our
trip of blending bombing wonderland

the street was our canvas
when art brushes & stencils
don't matter only liquitechs
& spray paint, the toxic aroma
that entered our bloodstream
on nights when we froze our fingertips
writing upside down with the can
pushing all the paint out

feel the wrath of graff
when society calls us vandals & delinquents
that's why your child wants to be just like us

we bomb your door to tell you our name
it's a shame you erased our
high-rise artistic motion trains:

the far rockaway/lefferts A
the outside D, B & Q in Brooklyn
the coney island F
the canarsie L
the J, M & the Z over the williamsburg bridge
the N & the R in queens
the 1 & the 9 in washington heights
the 2 & the 5 in the bronx

the new lots 3
the jerome 4
the westchester 6
& the flushing purple 7 train

now we reign on your law
the ink scribe scribbles on your forehead
then pronounces you hip hoply dead
the 4th son of hip hop
overshadowed by technic tabled microphones
& puma gray suede complexion tone
there is no hip hop without graffiti only rap
so we wrap our hands around cans becoming one

our motions are studied by anthropologists
making money off our art
the spritz on clean canvas can
be hazardous to minds
when your eyes can't understand
the buck wildstyle alphabet
sunrises call for travels
homeward bound

we are the ones that make
the clickclackclickclackclickclackclickclack sound
with a can on new land
when a tag could get ourselves shot

we are the artistic poets
that perform magic with spray paint
& just call ourselves writers.

A WOMAN THAT WRITES

1. este es mi rebaño
dos crías
dos hombres que los aman, los protegen
uno de mí
otro del lado mío

y una mujer que escribe

2. el logos
el lobo de la luz
la cosa que siniestra se restriega
por las imprimaturas
la criatura de tal categoría
la ley que aún no permite decir
he de parir
como quién dice
he de pensar

3. la mujer
debe alejarse de las ritmias
debe ella ser el mismo ritmo, marea de sangre
cantarle tan solo a la vaina que la envuelve

la vagina que es
el vehículo

ser tan solo cuerpo
o tan solo tinta

¿todavía?

4. que no de mí
ni del fragmento de las sangres que componen
esta soledad

no hay tal soledad
ni tal compañía,

la que pare
sabe ese misterio

la que escribe y pare sabe
que las cosas son esto y lo otro a la vez en cada esfera
en cada estancia de lo que existe

tinta lo uno,
sangre y tripas de ombligo que atan y que sueltan

todo se escribe
los símbolos son las ganas de parir lo propio como igual
y no llegar más que al simulacro

5. los hijos son
el amor como una tinta
la tinta como un amor hecho
de algo más o menos corredizo.

6. ¿pero qué es lo corredizo sino las cosas que existen
que sino la huida?

la gente que se alimenta de la entraña y después parte

que sino este aparte de puntas en los dedos tecleando

la naturaleza muerta de los platos
en el fregadreo

el marido nuevo leyendo internet
los hijos dormidos, echados en la noche de su ensueño?

para la mujer que escribe; ¿es esto lo extraño?
¿es esto su hogar?

coño, pero cuánta soledad, ¿cómo se aguanta esto?

sin la trascendencia
escribiendo con el todo en el cuarto.

7. ¿a qué aspira la mujer que escribe?

¿a qué canal de luz?

¿a qué reconocimiento?

si nunca jamás podrá volver a ser la insensata
ya lo ha sido

    ya parió dos veces y creyó en los hombres, en la familia
creyó que se acababa la eterna soledad
el andar solitaria y vertida sobre las cosas

nadie nunca aplaudirá

nadie confiará en la entereza del logos que la habita
con razón y con hijos
el logos la ha deshabitado —a veces piensa
ella no aprendió a renunciar
y ahora es el vehículo de una gravitación que fue
si acaso una promesa para otros
afrodita y psique. la muerte en los ojos del nacido

nadie que pasa por eso suele pensar —dicen—
ella los ha oído

nadie que se ha abierto en sangre y placenta y que pasa por eso
tiene accceso a lo alto
lo suyo en la tierra, las tripas, los piojos

lo suyo (si acaso) son los hijos que duermen mientras ella
  escribe a su lado.

¿así que a qué aspiro?

¿al tibio olor del innombrable feto que siempre me habitará el
  aire que respiran mis hijos
mientras escribo?

8. déjame subir a ti, numen encogido,
ónfalo de risa,
liebre en la noche que me habita, sola
quiero estar sola

que nadie ocupe la cabeza de mi brisa.

una mujer está sola y al fin los trabajos duermen
el cuido, el marido huyendo
el rebaño duerme

ella (por alguna razón) no escapa

quiere estar allí donde están las cosas y su gravitación
donde las cosas la esclavizan a su tuerca que la despedaza y que
  la emplaza
que la vuelve a hacer otra cada dia.

ella espera, terca, el dolor, la interrumpción
terca que le saquen de su asiento para pedirle cosas

ella injuria, resiente, burla
pero no abandona mientras huye de su rebaño

se sienta y escribe.

¿será la culpa de a quien deja desatendido
será la desatención la vida misma desgajada
será que solo así y nunca entrega
sino de a gotas, sino pocamente
sino entera pero abierta, pero a dos gajos?

volvemos a la desgajadura

¿será que desgajarse es la escritura?

9. (sarah bartman/venus hottentote)

¿habrá que abrirse una
de nuevo al grupo de las labias

bicotiledona exagerada
en su serie de ataduras?

¿habrá que
esperar a que muera la materia
para que en el musée del homme descubran
el verdadero misterio de la carne?

¿dejarse abrir
cadáver, toda pausa

dejar de exhibirse como el monstruo
que habla siete lenguas
que nadie oye
porque el cuerpo, siempre el cuerpo es lo que asombra y bulle?

la venus hotentote
su espíritu ancestral visita

ella viajó
desde su tierra natal, cuna del mundo
hasta holanda, inglaterra, parís

allí se exhibió ante una muchedumbre
que miraba sus nalgas asombrado
y no su misterio

y luego, muerta
rescatada de los circos
los exploradores de la carne abrieron su entrepierna

encontraron
esa doble mariposa de carne
ese caos

ya sin palpitar
las siete lenguas que aprendió
(xhosa, zulu, holandés, africaans, inglés, francés, alemán)
ya silentes

aún así su cuerpo hablando

¿habrá que hablar siempre desde el cuerpo
para el cuerpo, para los cuerpos que una habita
mientras duda, pregunta, conoce
y seolo, algunos pocos, oyen?

¿será que la más sabia de las mujeres
la primeriza
tan solo puede hablar
dese su desgajadura?

10. habrá que abrirse una
a la palabra, a los mapos
a los hijos que duernen
al hombre una siempre ama a medias

habrá que abrirse
al poema que se evapora
entre los dedos
entre los sí querido
sin querer
porque ahí está
entre los ruidos
lo que una anda ansiando;

que la dejen sola
a una
con sus cosas
con sus dolores de sí y con la culpa
de no andar una abriéndse de más
ni estar allí cerrada cuando el numen ilumina

capaz de andarse sola en los tropiezos habrá
y una sangrando

no existe la soledad
y sin embargo
es la única compañera.

habrá que asirse una al bando
andarse sola
para poder copiar.

NICOLE SEALEY

INSTEAD OF EXECUTIONS, THINK DEATH ERECTIONS

I wish the day hadn't.
Dawn has claimed
another sky, its birds.

I watch from my burning
stake the broken necks.
Once, this lot

allowed wildflowers,
nothing worse than bruised
wildflowers. Darling

dawn, death mask
to which I've grown
accustomed, show me

one pretty thing
no heavier
than a hummingbird.

VIRGINIA IS FOR LOVERS

At LaToya's Pride picnic,
Leonard tells me he and his longtime
love, Pete, broke up.
He says Pete gave him the house
in *Virginia.* "Great," I say,

"that's the least his ass could do."
I daydream my friend and me
into his new house, sit us in the kitchen
of his three-bedroom, two-bath
brick colonial outside Hungry Mother Park,
where, legend has it, the Shawnee raided
settlements with the wherewithal
of wild children catching pigeons.
A woman and her androgynous child
escaped, wandering the wilderness,
stuffing their mouths with the bark
of chokecherry root.
Such was the circumstance
under which the woman collapsed.
The child, who could say nothing
except *hungry mother*, led help
to the mountain where the woman lay,
swelling as wood swells in humid air.
Leonard's mouth is moving.
Two boys hit a shuttlecock back and forth
across an invisible net.
A toddler struggles to pull her wagon
from a sandbox. "No," Leonard says,
"It's not a place where you live.
I got the H *In V. H I—*"
Before my friend could finish,
and as if he'd been newly ordained,
I took his hands and kissed them.

EVEN THE GODS

Even the gods misuse the unfolding blue. Even the gods misread
the windflower's nod toward sunlight as consent to consume.
Still, you envy the horse that draws their chariot. Bone of their
bone. The wilting mash of air alone keeps you from scaling
Olympus with gifts of dead or dying things dangling from your
mouth—your breath, like the sea, inching away. It is rumored
gods grow where the blood of a hanged man drips. You insist on
being this man. The gods abuse your grace. Still, you'd rather live
among the clear, cloudless white, enjoying what is left of their
ambrosia. *Who should* be happy this time? *Who brings* cake
to whom?
Pray the gods do not misquote your covetous pulse for
chaos, the black from which they were conceived. Even the eyes
of gods must adjust to light. Even gods have gods.

IN IGBOLAND

After plagues of red locusts
are unleashed by a jealous god
hell-bent on making a scene,
her way of saying hello or how dare you,
townspeople build her a mansion
of dirt, embedded with bone china,
decorated wall-to-wall with statues
made from clay farmed from anthills—
statues of tailors on their knees
hemming the pant legs of gods;
statues of diviners reading
sun-dried entrails cast onto cloths
made of cowhide; statues of babies

breaching, their mothers' legs spread
wide toward the sky, as if in praise.

Sacrifices of goats and roosters
signal headway behind the fence
that hides the construction. A day is set.
Next spirit workers disrobe and race
to the fence, which they level, heap
into piles and set ablaze, so the offering
is first seen by firelight, not unlike
a beloved's face over candlelight.
The West in me wants the mansion
to last. The African knows it cannot.
Everything aspires to one
degradation or another. I want
to learn how to make something
holy, then walk away.

LORENZO THOMAS

INAUGURATION

The land was there before us
was the land. Then things
began happening fast. Because
the bombs us have always work
sometimes it makes me think
God must be one of us. Because
us has saved the world. Us gave it
A particular set of regulations
based on 1) undisputable acumen.
2) carnivorous fortunes, delicately
referred to here as "bull market"
and (of course) other irrational factors
deadly smoke thick over the icecaps,
Our man in Saigon   Lima   Tokyo   etc   etc

MMDCCXIII ½

The cruelty of ages past affects us now
whoever it was who lived here lived a mean life
each door has locks designed for keys unknown

Our living room was once somebody's home
our bedroom, someone's only room
our kitchen had a hasp upon its door.

Door to a kitchen?

And our lives are hasped and boundaried
because of ancient locks and madnesses
of slumlord greed and desperate privacies

Which one is madness? Depends on who you are.
We find we cannot stay, the both of us, in the same room
dance, like electrons, out of each other's way.

The cruelties of ages past affect us now

THE LEOPARD

The eyeballs on her behind are like fire
leaping and annoying
the space they just passed
just like fire would do

The ground have no mouth to complain
and the girl is not braver herself

She is beautiful in her spotted
leopard ensemble. Heartless so

to keep her fashionable in New York
Leopards are dying

Crude comments flutter around her
at lunchtime. She sure look good
She remembers nine banishing speeches

More powerful than this is the seam
of the leotard under her clothing

Her tail in the leotard is never still
The seam!
She feels it too familiar on her leg
As some crumb says something suggestive

the leopard embracing around her
is too chic to leap and strike

Her thoughts fall back to last semester's karate

Underneath, the leotard crouches up on her thigh
It is waiting for its terrible moment!

DIRGE FOR AMADOU DIALLO

It is hard to have your son die
in a distant land

If they said he was a soldier
we would pray
the way we always pray
that his would be the final sacrifice
and we would understand

Questions will fill
that churning emptiness
shaped like a boy
grown beautifully into a man
There'll be no answers
still, we'll understand

If he was a true believer
or a missionary

apostle or a revolutionary
ardent altruist or visionary
     —in these mean times?
Maybe instead
a hard and nerveless man,
a mercenary
     then we would dread
his noble loss or petty glory
and we would understand

     It is hard to have your son die
in a distant land

     If accident
or heart attack
we could blame chance
or curse our earthbound ignorance
     Vow to concoct new mythologies
that wouldn't
forge us such raw cruelties
marching our hope
in coffles toward the grave

We'd understand
if someone said he was,
this son, a prodigal:

     The kind of man who desperately
needs the vise of suffering
and hurt and desolation
some eccentricity to hold him firm
to help him shape his heart
into an instrument of praise

The kind of man
who dares to summon whirlwinds
to winnow wisdom from sophistication,
   o we would wail
and hold our heads
astonished by the wastefulness of Fate
   This repetitious wastefulness of Fate
and understand

But now they tell me
of a peaceful man
a mother's son, a father's pride
   seeking to study
in the learned halls
of a distant, splendid,
powerful, affluent land

   A young man murdered murdered
and murdered at the hand
of men sworn to uphold the Law
not thugs or bandits
   And there's no justice?
There's no recompense?

   O no,
   in spite of all our history of terror
in the world
   Uncountable eons of sorrow
of the world
   O no, O no
we do not understand

It is hard to have your son die
in a distant land
    And harder still
when we can't understand

GOD SENDS LOVE DISGUISED AS ORDINARY PEOPLE

We never quite could tell
    strength from stupidity
pride in perseverance
the point where stubbornness
purchased a harvest of futility

If the body has forgotten how to sleep
    what chance has thought
to teach its subtleties
like tenderness or faith

All that could matter
    is the reciprocating warmth
of flesh—wordless and beyond translation
    to idea or category
Nothing numerical and yet
not boundless, either
nothing so grand or abstract

In other words
    we were not brutes for lack of feeling
nor sorrowful in spiteful isolation
Not lonely yet
but damaged by avoiding touch
Being only smart enough to trust

that there's some
  gifted outcast family

Somewhere a troop of *djalis*
that still performs the music we need
to reconnect our feet to dirt
to fling our arms like windmills
spinning in dusted twilights

The point being not that you beat
  yourself up appreciating
what so and so has done for you
but that you finally remember
you've been her gypsy too

JOAQUÍN ZIHUATANEJO

ARCHETYPES

3

I will tell you three things about my father and one will be a lie:
my father left the year I was born; my father's heart like mine
and yours is made up of four chambers, but only three work well;
my father's left atrium broke the day he walked away from me.

There were three of us. We all came from different fathers, but
the same mother. We all have different colored eyes but the
same smile.

We're all different but the same. We're all different but the
same. We're all different but the same.

4

I think I have only loved four women well in my life.

At some point you should take all the money in your wallet
and spend it on the women in your life that you have loved
well. At the moment, counting the change in my pocket I
currently have just under seven dollars on me. I would buy the
first woman a white peach because she once moaned
passionately after biting into one. I would buy the second one
a pack of sugarfree gum because she is diabetic. I would buy
the third one a disposable camera, which seems insignificant,
but oh, can you imagine the possibilities in those 24 exposures?
The fourth woman, I would give this poem, as I would likely be

out of money at this point. This section of this poem says as much about the fourth woman's love of poetry as it does about my ability to budget money well.

I'm writing this poem in an airport. My flight lands at 4:00 p.m., and there's a very good chance my phone will be dead by then. When I land, I don't want to call the four women I've loved well, I want to call all the women I did not love well and tell them just how sorry I am.

I'm sorry. I'm sorry. I'm sorry. I'm sorry.

7

My favorite movie growing up as a kid was The Magnificent Seven. A remake of a classic Japanese film, The Seven Samurai. In terms of film, my favorite childhood movie is an American bastard, but it's a good one. So am I. So are my brothers. You could teach a class on archetypal symbolism from just that film alone.

The star of that film, Yule Brenner, died of lung cancer. Just before he died he shot one of the most poignant and powerful public service announcements. That PSA ends with Yule Brenner staring into your soul from inside the black and white television repeating three words, just . . . don't . . . smoke. I swear it must have run seven times a day during the prime time of my youth. And though I can't be certain of it, I think those may have been Yule Brenner's last words.

When I was seven I learned that my father smoked non-filtered Camels, so did Yule Brenner. And though I can't be certain of it, I think in the end it will not be my father's metaphorical broken heart nor will it be his actual broken heart that gets the best of him, in the end it will be his lungs. And I, his first-born son, will not be there to hold his hand when he dies. I will not get to hear his last words. I will not get to ask for or accept his forgiveness. In the end there will only be silence.

I forgive you. I forgive you. I forgive you. I forgive you. I forgive you. I forgive you. I forgive you.

I just found out my flight is delayed. It will not land until 7:00 p.m. Will the women I have not loved well forgive me for my silence, or for the times I should have been silent but was not? Will they forgive my carelessness with money, or my carelessness with all four chambers of the human heart? Will they forgive me for loving words more than I loved them? Will they forgive me for all the poems I've written about them or all the poems I haven't written about them?

I want to write a collection of 28 poems. Seven poems for each of the four women I have loved well. And though I love them all, I will reserve the use of closed form for only one of them. I will write her seven Shakespearean sonnets. No, I will write her seven villanelles. No, I will write her seven epic poems written in rhyming couplets. No, I will write her seven powerful and poignant PSA's that will all end the same, with three words.

I love you. I love you. I love you. I love you. I love you. I love you. I love you.

WE ARE BECAUSE THEY WERE

We are Mexican
because our grandmothers were Mexican
We are American
because our grandmothers were American
Sometimes we are both at the same time
at Applebee's, Target and Six Flags Amusement Park we are both
(Two of the six flags that flew over Texas were
the United States of America and Mexico)
But other times we are not
At border crossings,
in small Texas towns,
in airport security lines
we are only one

We are poets
because our grandmothers were poets
We are warriors
because our grandmothers were warriors
In my dream
my grandmother picks cotton
with my grandfather
and their four sons
I cannot tell if it is Southern Oklahoma
or East Texas in the dream
though I know they picked cotton in both
because I was there when they did
trying my best to help
And though my fingers were small enough to do the job effectively
I lacked the dexterity and attention span
to be much help at all
I remember watching my grandmother pick cotton

surrounded on all sides by men
She was so much faster than the others
The ball of cotton
housed in a crown made of sharp prongs
one thoughtless move
meant unforgiving cuts
If you ask me today
what is the color most associated with sacrifice
I will tell you
blood red on a field of stark white

We are comedians
because our grandmothers were filled with laughter
We are magicians
because our grandmothers were filled with magic
My grandmother's wand was a rolling pin
My grandmother's cape was an apron
My grandmother had magic in her hands
Her tortillas tasted like revolution
Her salsa tasted like resistance
Her picadillo tasted like redemption
If the foreigners in the surrounding suburbs
had ever tasted her lengua
a war would have surely ensued
In those same suburbs today
you will find organic grocery stores
that look sterile and cold
like hospital floors
In the market deli in the back
they sell seven different kinds of wraps
If she were alive today
my grandmother would laugh loudly and say
"A wrap ain't nothing but a cold ass taco."

WHAT YOU HAVE TAKEN THIS POEM REDEEMS

Co-Written with Antwaun "Twain" Davis

What you have taken
this poem redeems
California,
Arizona,
Nuevo Méjico,
Tejas,
All of the . . .
North Mexico
This poem reclaims
In defense of children with skin the color of earth
Their skulls . . .
Crushed . . .
By the boots of U.S. Calvary
to save money for the cost of bullets
For them,
this poem seeks vengeance
This poem is a street kid with hair like black flame, eyes like
    warrior poet
His sword,
a permanent marker
red
and with it he writes the word *redemption* on every sideview
    mirror he can
Cuidado!
Objects in mirror are closer than they appear
This poem makes the use of slang clear
Sets free 'patnas doin' bids for thangs they never did
Breathes life into every son and daughter slain by racism
Its words . . .
spoken with precision to a beat

Break . . .
Dancing to lips and tongues
made to sound like stereos
until stereotypes backspace
and type . . .
"Who are you to judge me?" in its place
This poem is Teteo Innan, Aztec Mother of the Gods
tattooed on the back of an inmate who stands in the middle of a
   cell
covered in urine and feces flung at him by other Chicano
   prisoners
You see, sometimes sharing brown skin does not make two men
   brothers
Those who saw him as a coward
because he chose not to fight
But he stands there smiling, baptized by their filth
reborn,
made clean
because for the first time in his life he has found free thought
At dawn . . .
this poem blankets the rural roads of Jasper, TX
remembering James Byrd like Osiris
but completely like cycles unbroken
he stands . . . Byrd,
clean
erect
unbroken
in front of his killer's truck
with burnt chains that once tasted neckline
tucked under waistline
Every line in this poem like fire under his feet
He races back in time
Men inside truck behind to DC

8/28/63

And glues their ears to King's lips
as he drips dreams
I've been told by men of means
that hip-hop is not a revolution
Hip-hop is one half of a revolution,
180 degrees always bringing the movement back . . . to you
always bringing you . . . back to where you came from
they say . . . hip-hop is a closed fist raised high in the air
Hip-hop is an open palm falling on a small white coffin
and if that is the case
then Pancho Villa is hip-hop
Muhammad Ali is hip-hop
This poem is hip-hop
This poem unlocks the coffins of children
who caught confused hollow tip bullets with body parts
Children handed wings and halos by angels
introduced to death by parents
This poem unlocks the caskets of thousands
bound by ropes
hung from thousands of trees
dangling on thousands of limbs
like broken black Christmas ornaments
like bleeding tire swings
planting red rain into the soil to grow Negro spirituals
This poem sings those unheard songs
brings back their voices
returns everything to red
Return, the sacred verb
Red, the sacred color
The color of the blood of children
and the children will be reborn . . .
but as waves

a never-ending undulation
because Tonantzin, ancient goddess of the moon and waters
stands on the shore calling the children to return home to the
   arms of brown people
calling the children to return to what is rightfully theirs
You can make the check payable to our children
in the amount of 500 years worth of reparations
for all the brutality we've endured
for all the tears we've shed
Don't you see?
You will take from us no longer
You have taken our lands from us
You have taken our children from us
What you have taken I redeem
What you have taken the dream of King redeems
What you have taken the spirit of La Raza redeems
What you have taken
this poem redeems

ABOUT THE POETS

ELIZABETH ACEVEDO is the youngest child and only daughter of Dominican immigrants. She holds a BA in Performing Arts from George Washington University and an MFA in Creative Writing from the University of Maryland. With over fourteen years of performance experience, Acevedo has toured her poetry nationally and internationally. She is a National Poetry Slam Champion, Cave Canem Fellow, CantoMundo Fellow and participant of the Callaloo Writer's Workshop. She has two collections of poetry, *Beastgirl & Other Origin Myths* (YesYes Books, 2016) and *Medusa Reads La Negra's Palm*, winner of the 2016 Berkshire Prize (Tupelo Press, forthcoming). *The Poet X* (HarperCollins, 2018) is her debut novel. She lives with her partner in Washington, DC.

GUSTAVO ADOLFO AYBAR is a Dominican writer, raised in New York, Los Angeles and Miami Beach. He graduated from the University of Missouri-Kansas City, where he received his MA in Romance Languages & Literature. He is a Cave Canem and Artist Inc. fellow, plus member of the Latino Writer's Collective (501c3). His work can be found in their anthology, *Primera Página: Poetry from the Latino Heartland*. Aybar's chapbook, *Between Line Breaks* was released in 2016 (Spartan Press) and his first collection, *We Seek Asylum*, won the Willow Books Literature Award for Poetry in 2016 and will be released early 2017. Currently, Aybar is working on his second poetry manuscript and on translating the works of Mexican author/playwright Glafira Rocha from Spanish to English. Some of his translations of Rocha's stories can be found in the online journals *EZRA*, *Asymptote* and Brooklyn Rail's *InTranslation* journal, where Rocha's short story, "Interspersed Signs," was selected as a Pushcart nominee for fiction in 2014.

Born in Santurce, Puerto Rico in 1941, MIGUEL ALGARÍN moved with his family to New York City in the early 1950s. After obtaining advanced degrees in literature from the University of Wisconsin and Pennsylvania State University, Algarín spent more than thirty years as a professor at Rutgers University, where he taught Shakespeare, Creative Writing and U.S. Ethnic Literature. The founder of the Nuyorican Poets Café in New York City, Algarín is the author of more than ten published books of poetry, the editor of several anthologies and an accomplished writer for television and theater. He has received three American Book Awards and was presented with the Larry Leon Hamlin Producer's Award at the 2001 National Black Theater Festival. Algarín is also the translator of the Nobel Prize-winning poet Pablo Neruda's *Songs of Protest*. In his critically acclaimed book *Love Is Hard Work*, Algarín shares his own struggle with being HIV positive.

JANE ALBERDESTON CORALIN is a poet living and working in the land of her birth, Puerto Rico. She is a recipient of the Associated Writing Program's Intro Journals Award in poetry and co-author of *Sister Chicas*, a young adult novel published by Penguin Books. She graduated from Binghamton University in 2007 and is a member of Cave Canem, an organization for writers of African descent. A faculty member in the English Department at the University of Puerto Rico in Arecibo, Alberdeston Coralin recently completed a poetry collection entitled *Searching Solemn* and is working on a novel entitled *Invisible Choirs*.

PEGGY ROBLES-ALVARADO is a resilient tenured New York City educator, a CantoMundo, Academy for Teachers and Home School Fellow as well as a two-time International Latino Book Award winner and author of *Conversations With My Skin* and *Homenaje A Las Guerreras/Homage to the Warrior Women*. As an initiate in the Lukumi and Palo spiritual systems, Peggy uses her experiences and her incredible rhythmic energy to challenge social taboos, celebrate womanhood and honor cultural traditions. She is a 2014 BRIO performance poet award winner and in 2016 she was named one of the 25 Most Influential Women of the Bronx, a BCA Arts Fund and Spaceworks Bronx Community Artist grant recipient. Peggy has been published in 92Y's #wordswelivein, NACLA, The Center for Puerto Rican Studies and The Bronx Memoir Project. She has been featured on HBO's *Habla Women*, Lincoln Center Out of Doors, Poets & Writers Connecting Cultures Reading and The BADD!ASS Women Festival. Peggy is continuously creating and supporting literary events through Robleswrites Productions and is currently pursuing her MFA in Performance and Performance Studies at Pratt Institute. Her latest book *The Abuela Stories Project*, an anthology of women writers, debuted December 8, 2016 at The Bronx Museum of the Arts. For more information please visit Robleswrites.com.

JOSEFINA BÁEZ, born in La Romana, Dominican Republic lives in New York. She is a storyteller, performer, writer, theatre director, educator and devotee. Founder and director of Ay Ombe Theatre (1986), she is the alchemist of the creative life process she calls Performance Autology, based on the autobiography and wellness of the doer. Her works include *Dominicanish Comrade*, *Bliss Ain't Playing* (translated into Portuguese, Spanish, Hindi, Russian and Swedish), *Dramaturgia I & II*, *Levente no. Yolayorkdominicanyork*, *Como la una/Como uma*, *De levente. Cuatro textos para teatro performance*, *As Is E'* and *Why is my name Marysol?*, a children's book.

CARMEN BARDEGUEZ BROWN is a poet and educator from Puerto Rico. She migrated to the United States in 1984. She was part of the spoken word/poetry scene that took place in the early 1990s at the Nuyorican Poets Café and was a member of Steve Cannon and Bob Holman "Stoop" Writing workshop. Her work was showcased in the documentary *Latino Poets in the United States*. Her work has been published in such magazines as *Tribes, Long Shot, Fuse, School Voices*, as well as in the anthologies *Aloud: Voices from the Nuyorican Poets Café, La Pluma y La Tinta* and *Nuyorican Poets Writers Vol. 1*. She has produced a poetry cd titled *Straight From the Drum*, and the poetry book *Straight from the Drums: Al Ritmo del Tambor*.

ARIANA BROWN is an Afromexicana poet from San Antonio, Texas. She is the recipient of the Andrew Julius Gutow Academy of American Poets Prize and was recently awarded the title of Best Poet at the 2014 College Unions Poetry Slam Invitational, a national competition in which her team representing UT Austin, took first place. In 2015, her poem "Invocation" won the "Best Poem" award. Ariana is currently working on her first manuscript and pursuing a degree in African & African Diaspora Studies at UT Austin, where she co-founded Spitshine Poetry Slam in 2011. When she is not on stage, she is probably eating an avocado, listening to the Kumbia Kings or validating brown girl rage in all its miraculous forms. Her work is forthcoming in *Huizache*.

NATALIE N. CARO is a Quarter-Rican, Bronx-born poet and educator. Currently a PhD candidate at the Center for Inter-American Studies, Bielefeld University, she holds an MFA from City College/CUNY and BA in English Literature/Philosophy from Lehman College/CUNY. She was selected as one of the first recipients of CCNY's MFA Creative Writing Fellowships and was the winner of the 2013 Bronx Recognizes Its Own (BRIO) award in Artistic Excellence for Poetry. Her work has appeared in *Obscura Literary Magazine*, *Keep this Bag Away from Children*, *Frost Writing* and *NYSAI Literary Magazine*. She was nominated for The Pushcart Prize, one of the most honored literary projects in America, in 2015.

In 2013, NATASHA CARRIZOSA won the National Poetry Award for multi-cultural poet of the year. She is a poet, writer and spoken word artist. Her work is deeply rooted in her childhood and life experiences. Raised as the daughter of an African-American mother and Mexican father, her writing reflects the dichotomy of these two rich cultures. Natasha is able to speak about the appreciation and beauty of our diversity that lives within us all. She is a published author of several projects, including *heavy light*, *mejiafricana* and *of fire and rain* (co-authored with Joaquín Zihuatanejo). She has performed her work and conducted workshops for audiences in Madrid, Paris, St. Lucia, New York, Chicago, Houston and countless other cities. Since 2009 she has hosted one of the most dynamic poetry open mics in the country, natty roots & rhyme in Arlington, Texas.

ADRIÁN CASTRO is a poet, writer and interdisciplinary artist. Born in Miami, Castro's work searches for a cohesive Afro-Caribbean-American identity, honoring myth on one hand and history on the other. He addresses the migratory experience from Africa to the Caribbean to North America, and the eventual clash of cultures. He is the author of *Cantos: Blood & Honey*, *Wise Fish: Tales in 6/8 Time*, *Handling Destiny* and has been published in many literary anthologies. He is the recipient of a Cintas Fellowship (2008), the State of Florida Individual Artist Fellowship, New Forms Florida, the Eric Mathieu King award from the Academy of American Poets, NALAC Arts Fellowship and several commissions from Miami Light Project and the Miami Art Museum. He has performed with many dancers and actors, including Chuck Davis and African American Dance Ensemble, Heidi Duckler and Collage Dance, and Keith Antar Mason and the Hittite Empire. He has taught at the University of Miami, Miami Dade College and Florida International University as a visiting professor and/or guest lecturer. Adrián is also a Babalawo and herbalist.

RÍO CORTEZ is a Pushcart-nominated poet, who has received fellowships from Poet's House, Cave Canem and Canto Mundo foundations. She was a recipient of the Sarah Lawrence College Lucy Grealy Prize in Poetry, the 2012 Poets & Writers Amy Award and a 2015 Jerome Foundation Grantee. She is a graduate of the MFA program at NYU and co-founder of the Good Times Collective and BLKGRP. Her work has appeared or is forthcoming in a number of journals, including *The Miami Rail*, *The Offing*, *Cortland Review*, *Prairie Schooner*, *Huizache* and *The New Yorker*. Río has been selected by Ross Gay as the inaugural winner of the Toi Derricotte & Cornelius Eady Chapbook Prize for her manuscript, *I Have Learned to Define a Field as a Space Between Mountains*, available from Jai-Alai Books. Born and raised in Salt Lake City, she now lives, writes and works in book publishing in New York City.

ANTWAUN "TWAIN" DAVIS was raised in Dallas, Texas. He is a youth teaching artist, writer, actor and an award-winning performance poet. His work has appeared in various stage plays, publications, schools and an assortment of television and radio shows. His poetry slam titles include Dallas Grand Slam Champion, Arkansas Grand Slam Champion and Texas Grand Slam Champion. Most recently, Twain ranked as one of the top ten poets in the nation at the 2014 Individual World Poetry Slam. Performing with an indefinable style and intensity, Twain's passion is evident in every poem. He is an advocate of truth, inspiring his audience while shedding light on subjects that society tends to overlook or ignore.

Embracing both lyrical and experimental forms, he presents his audience with snapshots of life.

Poet and visual artist, SANDRA MARÍA ESTEVES, known as "The Godmother of Nuyorican Poetry," has published several collections of poetry, including the following self-publishied titles: *Tropical Rain: A Bilingual Downpour* (1984), *DivaNations* (2010), *Wildflowers* (2009), *Portal* (2007); *Poems in Concert* (2006), *Portfolio* (2003), *Finding Your Way, Poems for Young Folks* (1999), *Contrapunto in the Open Field* (1998), *Undelivered Love Poems* (1997). Her major books include *Bluestown Mockingbird Mambo* (Arte Público Press, 1990) and *Yerba Buena* (Greenfield Review Press, 1980; selected Best Small Press Book by the *Library Journal* in 1981). One of the first Dominican Boricua Nuyorican women to publish a recognized volume of poetry in the United States, she is the recipient of numerous awards and fellowships, including: a Pregones Theater/NEA Master Artist Award, 2010; the Con Tinta Award from the Acentos Poetry Collective, 2007; Poet Honoree from Universes Poetic Theater Ensemble Company, 2006; The Owen Vincent Dodson Memorial Award for Poetry from Blind Beggar Press, 2002; Arts Review Honoree from the Bronx Council on the Arts, 2001; The Edgar Allan Poe Literary Award from the Bronx Historical Society, 1992; and a Poetry Fellowship from the New York Foundation for the Arts in 1985, among others. Esteves was formerly the executive director/producer of the African Caribbean Poetry Theater, where she produced several seasons of full-length, staged, equity showcase, off-Broadway plays, touring productions, multimedia spoken-word performances, poetry series, theater workshops and literary publications.

Puerto Rican poet and performance artist MARIPOSA (MARÍA TERESA FERNÁNDEZ) was born and raised in the Bronx. The first in her family to graduate from college, she earned a BA and an MA at New York University. In her poems, which often combine Spanish and English lines, Mariposa explores themes of empowerment, family and identity. She is the author of *Born Bronxeña: Poems on Identity, Love & Survival* (2001). Her poetry has been included in *The Norton Anthology of Latino Literature* (2010), *The Afro-Latin@ Reader: History and Culture in the United States* (2010) and *Bum Rush the Page: A Def Poetry Jam* (2001). Her work has been featured on the HBO series *Habla Ya!* and in the HBO documentary *Americanos: Latino Life in the United States*, as well as in programming on the PBS, Lifetime TV and BET networks. Mariposa has performed her poetry at the United Nations World Conference against Racism, the Essence Music Festival and the Black Enterprise Women of Power Summit. Mariposa has taught poetry at Poets House, the Bronx Writers Center and the Caribbean Cultural Center and through Poets & Writers. A passionate educator, Mariposa teaches creative writing, public speaking and workshops in self healing. Mariposa curates open mics and literary readings to build community and create spaces for emerging and established writers to share their work.

SHAGGY FLORES is, in his own words, a "Nuyorican, Massarican, bilingual, Spanglish-speaking, Afro-Taíno, santero, Iota, warrior, urban jíbaro, mason, Borinquen Poeta" hailing from Spanish Harlem, Cupey y Guaynabo (Puerto Rico) and Springfield (MA). He graduated from the University of Massachusetts with a degree in the African Diaspora and from Virginia State University with an MA in History. Flores follows in the tradition of Arturo Schomburg and Louis Reyes Rivera believing the poet should always serve as cultural worker. His second collection of poetry, *Obatala's Bugalu: A Nuyorican Books of Sights and Sounds*, deals with issues of stereotypes, cultural preservation, racism and personal growth. His work can also be found in *Labor Heritage–George Meany Labor College Journal*, *Centro Journal of the Center for Puerto Rican Studies*, *Bum Rush the Page: A Def Poetry Jam Anthology*, *Role Call An*

African-American Intergenerational Literary Anthology, *The Bandana Republic*, *DiVerseCity: An Anthology Celebrating Ten Years of the Austin International Poetry Festival*, the 2003 National Poetry Slam Anthology and the *Hostos Review: New Rican Voices Journal*. He is one of the founders of the annual Voices for the Voiceless Poetry Concert, which occurs in the five-college Amherst area. He currently works in the DC Metro area as a C-Suite MarComm executive, advising national associations and non-profits.

ARACELIS GIRMAY is the author of the poetry collections *Teeth*, *Kingdom Animalia*, *The Black Maria* and the collage-based picture book, *changing, changing*. Girmay received the GLCA New Writers Award for *Teeth*. *Kingdom Animalia* was the winner of the Isabella Gardner Award (BOA Editions) and a finalist for the National Book Critics Circle Award. Most recently, Girmay's poetry and essays have been published in *Granta*, *Black Renaissance Noire* and *PEN America*, among other places. She has received grants and fellowships from the Jerome, Cave Canem and Watson foundations, as well as Civitella Ranieri and the National Endowment for the Arts. Current collaborations include work with the Critical Projections collective and a translation project with writer and visual artist Rosalba Campra.

MODESTO FLAKO JIMÉNEZ is a Dominican-born, Bushwick-raised theater director, writer, poet, actor, producer and educator. While still in high school, he co-founded Real People Theater, a company best known for reworking plays by combining some of the language of the original texts with street slang and Spanish. Since then, Flako has been profiled by *The New York Times* and *The Wall Street Journal* and in 2016 was awarded the Princess Grace Honoraria in theater for 2016. As the ATI & HOLA Award Winner for 2015 and 2016, Flako is best known for original productions and three signature festivals—Ghetto Hors D'Oeuvres,

One Catches Light and Oye! Avant Garde Night!—produced with his company Brooklyn Gypsies Collective. Flako has appeared on *TEDxBushwick*, *BK Live*, *NY1*, Comedy Central's *The Daily Show with Jon Stewart* and *The Charlie Rose Show*. In 2012 he published a poetry collection addressing gentrification, *Oye, Para Mi Querido Brooklyn*.

Born in 1950 in Santurce, Puerto Rico, TATO LAVIERA accompanied his mother to New York in 1960, settling in the Lower East Side. After graduating from high school, he attended Cornell University and Brooklyn College for a short while. He soon went to work, however, as director of the "University of the Streets," an educational alternative established in the Lower East Side that offered classes to adults at community centers and helped them get into college. In addition, he taught Creative Writing at Rutgers and other universities on the East Coast. His legacy—he was deceased in 2013—includes five books of poetry, all with Arte Público Press in Houston: *La Carreta Made a U-Turn* (1979), *Enclave* (1985), *Mainstream Éthics/Ética Corriente* (1988), *AmeRícan* (1999) and *Mixturao and Other Poems* (2008). Several of Laviera's plays have been presented in New York: *Piñones* (1979), *La Chefa* (1981), *Here We Come* (1983), *Becoming García* (1984), *AmeRícan* (1986) and *The Base of Soul in Heaven's Café* (1989). His poetry is widely anthologized in collections such as *Herejes y mitificadores: Muestra de poesía puertorriqueña en los Estados Unidos* (1980), *Papiros de Babel: Antología de la poesía puertorriqueña en los Estados Unidos* (1991) and *Aloud: Voices from the Nuyorican Poets Café* (1994).

RAINA J. LEÓN, PhD, Macondo fellow, CantoMundo graduate fellow (2016), Cave Canem graduate fellow (2006) and member of the Carolina African American Writers Collective, has been published in numerous journals as a writer of poetry, fiction and nonfiction. She is the author of three collections of poetry: *Canticle of Idols, Boogeyman Dawn and sombra: (dis)locate* (2016) and the chapbook, *profeta without refuge*. Her work has been nominated for The Pushcart Prize and been a finalist for the Cave Canem First Book Prize, the Andrés Montoya First Book Prize and the Naomi Long Madgett Priza. She has received numerous fellowships and residencies, including the Macdowell Colony, the Vermont Studio Center, the Tyrone Guthrie Center in Annamaghkerrig, Ireland and Ragdale. She is a founding editor of *The Acentos Review*, an online quarterly, international journal devoted to the promotion and publication of LatinX arts. She is an associate professor of education at Saint Mary's College of California.

ESPERANZA MALAVÉ CINTRÓN grew up on the Motown sound with a salsa backbeat, a sensibility that is reflected in her work. She has written three collections of poetry, *Chocolate City Latina* (2005); *What Keeps Me Sane* (2013), which won the 2013 Naomi Long Madgett Award; and *Visions of a Post-Apocalyptic Sunrise* (2014). She has been the recipient of a Michigan Council for the Arts Individual Artist Grant, The Metro Times Poetry Prize and Callaloo Creative Writing fellowships at Brown University in 2012 and Oxford University in 2015. Her poetry, fiction, essays and reviews appear in a number of anthologies, including *Double Stitch*, *Erotique Noire*, *Abandoned Automobile*, *13th Moon* and *The Little Magazine*. She also writes romantic fiction under the pseudonym Alegra Verde; some of her novellas have been translated into Italian, German and Japanese. While earning a doctorate in English Literature from The University of the State of New York at Albany, she co-founded The Sisters of Color Writers Collective and created and served as editor of its literary journal *Seeds*, which was published from 1989 to 2006.

REYNOLD MARTÍN is spoken-word artist from Dominica, by way of Brooklyn. Reynold studied Urban Studies at Fordham

University. Reynold's poems blend general history with family history to illustrate the complex realities Caribbean immigrants face. Reynold has led workshops at institutions such as NYU and Monroe College, where he showed the link between urban planning and the creation of Hip-Hop, using rap lyrics as an entry point to investigate urban policy and planning. Reynold's life goal is to design and build a just, sustainable city through participatory design and community engagement.

TONY MEDINA, two-time winner of The Paterson Prize, is the author of fifteen books for adults and young readers, including *DeShawn Days* (2001), *Love to Langston* (2002), *Committed to Breathing* (2003), *Follow-up Letters to Santa from Kids Who Never Got a Response* (2003) and *My Old Man Was Always on the Lam* (2010). Medina's poetry, fiction and essays appear in some ninety publications and two CD compilations. An advisory editor for *Hip Hop Speaks to Children*, edited by Nikki Giovanni, his most recent work is featured in the anthologies *Poets against the Killing Field*; *Family Pictures: Poems and Photographs Celebrating Our Loved Ones*; *Fingernails across a Chalkboard: A Literary and Artistic View of HIV/AIDS Affecting People of Color*; *Full Moon on K Street*; *Let Loose on the World: Celebrating Amiri Baraka at 75* and *Spaces Between Us: Poetry, Prose and Art on HIV/AIDS* (2010). Medina earned an MA and PhD in English from Binghamton University, SUNY. Currently, he is an associate professor of Creative Writing at Howard University in Washington, DC.

MARIANELA MEDRANO was born and raised in the Dominican Republic and has lived in Connecticut since 1990. A poet and a writer of nonfiction and fiction, she holds a PhD in Psychology. Her work has appeared in numerous anthologies and magazines in Latin America, Europe and the United States, including *The Black Scholar 45.2: Dominican Black Studies* (2015), *Phati'tude* (2012),

Letralia (2011), *Callaloo* (Summer 2000), *Sisters of Caliban: Contemporary Women Poets of the Caribbean* (1997), among others. Her books include *Oficio de vivir* (1986), *Los alegres ojos de la tristeza* (1987), *Regando esencias/The Scent of Waiting* (1998), *Curada de espantos* (2002), *Diosas de la yuca* (2011) and *Prietica* (2013).

One of the original founders of the Nuyorican poets' movement, JESÚS PAPOLETO MELÉNDEZ is a recipient of a 2001 New York Foundation for the Arts Fellowship in Poetry. Originally from East Harlem, Papoleto Meléndez is a recipient of an Artist for Community Enrichment (ACE) Award from the Bronx Council on the Arts, New York (1995) and a COMBO (Combined Arts of San Diego)-NEA Fellowship in Literature, in recognition of "his innovative multi-disciplinary works in poetry, playwriting, and performance art which speak with eloquence and compassion for society's victims of indifference, racism, and intolerance" (October, 1988). His career as a poetry facilitator working in the public schools spans more than thirty years, during which time he has coordinated many successful poetry and creative writing workshops impacting the lives of tens of thousands of young people. He has developed a unique workshop curriculum, which offers creative writing experiences for the youth, emphasizing poetic form and expression, while merging computer desktop publishing technology and techniques in the classroom. *Hey Yo! Yo Soy! 40 Years of Nuyorican Street Poetry, A Bilingual Edition* is a 386-page collection, comprised of three previously published books, *Casting Long Shadows* (1970), *Have You Seen Liberation* (1971) and *Street Poetry & Other Poems* (1972), that consist of stories about growing up Puerto Rican in New York City's El Barrio.

E. ETHELBERT MILLER is a writer and literary activist. His father Egberto Miller was born in Panama and came to the United States as a young boy. Much of Ethelbert Miller's work grapples with themes of identity, social justice and cultural exclusion. He is the author of several collections of poems and two memoirs and serves as a board member for The Community Foundation for the National Capital Region. Miller is an inductee of the 2015 Washington, DC Hall of Fame. In 2016, he was the recipient of the AWP 2016 George Garrett Award for Outstanding Community Service in Literature and the 2016 DC Mayor's Arts Award for Distinguished Honor. Miller's poetry has been translated into Spanish, Portuguese, German, Hungarian, Chinese, Farsi, Norwegian, Tamil and Arabic. His most recent book is *The Collected Poems of E. Ethelbert Miller*, edited by Kirsten Porter and published by Willow Books.

"The true definition of an artist" is how the iconic Harry Belafonte describes AJA MONET who is a Cuban-Jamaican poet, educator and activist from Brooklyn. A graduate of Sarah Lawrence College (2009), Monet received her BA in Liberal Arts and was awarded the The Andrea Klein Willison Prize for Poetry. She received an MFA in Creative Writing from the School of the Art Institute of Chicago. At age nineteen, she was the youngest poet ever to win the Nuyorican Poet's Café Grand Slam title. As a teaching artist for Urban Word NYC as well as Urban Arts Partnership in the city, she uses poetry as a therapeutic tool with at-risk inner city youths, showing how words can empower and encourage holistic healing in youth education. She is author of two books of poetry: *The Black Unicorn Sings* (2010) and *Inner-City Chants & Cyborg Cyphers* (2015).

ANTHONY MORALES is a poet/writer/educator/activist from the Bronx who has appeared on HBO's *Def Poetry* and toured the United States and Puerto Rico. He is a VONA alum and facilitator of La SOPA workshops in NYC. He has been an English teacher in public schools for over 15 years. He has published *Story Avenue* (2005), *Chevere Cafre* (2007), *dice queso* (2010), *Hood Night* (2011), *So*

Far (2015), *Ponerme Yo* (2016) and *Half Empty* (2017). He graduated from Columbia University and Teachers College with degrees in English Education and Latino Studies. He still writes by the chessboard benches in Clason Point Gardens. He can be found at various cyphers, open mics, conferences and corners spitting his Nuyorican Gospels for the blocks, hoods, titerres and illiterati alike.

JOHN MURILLO'S first poetry collection, *Up Jump the Boogie* (2010), was a finalist for both the 2011 Kate Tufts Discovery Award and the PEN Open Book Award, and was named by *The Huffington Post* as one of "Ten Recent Books of Poetry You Should Read Right Now." His honors include a Pushcart Prize, two Larry Neal Writers Awards and fellowships from the National Endowment for the Arts, Bread Loaf Writers Conference, Cave Canem Foundation, the Fine Arts Work Center in Provincetown and the Wisconsin Institute of Creative Writing. His work has appeared in such publications as *Callaloo*, *Court Green*, *Ninth Letter*, *Ploughshares* and *Angles of Ascent: A Norton Anthology of African-American Poetry*. Currently, he teaches in the creative writing program at New York University and at Hampshire College, where he serves as assistant professor of Creative Writing and African-American Literary Arts.

RAQUEL I. PENZO is a Brooklyn native of Dominican descent who has carved a career for herself as a writer, editor and literary event curator. In 2007, she earned an MFA in Creative Writing from Fairleigh Dickinson University. She hosts the New Voices Reading Series each quarter in New York City and works as a copywriter at Brooklyn Public Library. Raquel authored the self-published *My Ego Likes the Compliments . . . And Other Musings on Writing*, and the short stories, "Grey Matter" (*Blue Lake Review*), "Perspective on a Murder" (*Mason's Road*), "On a Blue Day" (*You Should Be Here*) and "Enfermos" (*Rose Red Review*). An anthology of works from participants of her reading series was released on April 2014.

WILLIE PERDOMO is the author of *The Essential Hits of Shorty Bon Bon*, a finalist for the National Book Critics Circle Award in Poetry; *Smoking Lovely*, winner of the PEN Beyond Margins Award; and *Where a Nickel Costs a Dime*, a finalist for the Poetry Society of America Norma Farber First Book Award. He has been a recipient of a Woolrich Fellowship in Creative Writing at Columbia University and a two-time New York Foundation for the Arts Poetry Fellow. His work has appeared in *The New York Times Magazine*, BOMB, *Mandorla* and *African Voices*. He is currently a member of the VONA/Voices faculty and is an Instructor in English at Phillips Exeter Academy.

MIGUEL GÓMEZ PIÑERO was born in 1946 in Gurabo, Puerto Rico. He was self-educated and raised on the Lower East Side of New York City. He was a prize-winning playwright, the receiver of the New York Drama Critics Circle Award and the Obie (Off-Broadway) and was an Antoinette Perry (Tony) Award nominee, 1974-1975. He began to write for the theater while serving time at the Ossining Correctional Facility (Sing Sing) for armed robbery. The result was "Short Eyes," a searing portrayal of violent prison life, which started at the Theater of the Riverside Church, was transferred to the Public Theater by Joseph Papp and then ran at the Vivian Beaumont Theater in Lincoln Center. "Short Eyes," which won an Obie Award and the New York Drama Critics Circle Award as best American play in 1974, was later made into a film with a screenplay. His other works for the theater included "Straight From the Ghetto," "Eulogy for a Small-Time Thief," "The Sun Always Shines for the Cool" and "A Midnight Moon at the Greasy Spoon." A published poet, Piñero was one of the founders of the Nuyorican movement and the Nuyorican Poets Café; with Miguel Algarín, he edited the anthology *Nuyorican Poetry* (1975). After his death in 1988, Arte Público Press published *Outlaw: The Collected works of Miguel Piñero* (2010).

NOEL QUIÑONES is an AfroBoricua writer, performer and educator born and raised in the Bronx. He has received fellowships from Poets House, CantoMundo, the Watering Hole and Brooklyn Poets. He has been published in Pilgrimage Press, Kweli Journal, Winter Tangerine Review, Asymptote and elsewhere. He was most recently a member of the 2016 Bowery Poetry Club slam team, placing among the top twenty teams in the nation. Visit him at www.elninoquinones.com or @NQNino322.

MAYRA SANTOS-FEBRES (born 1966, Carolina) is a Puerto Rican author, poet, novelist, professor of literature and literary critic who has obtained fame at home and abroad. In 1991, Santos-Febres garnered attention and critical acclaim for her first two collections of poetry, *Anamu y manigua* and *El orden escapade*. In 1996, Santos-Febres won the Juan Rulfo Award for her short story, "Oso blanco," which was published in her collection of short stories called *Pez de Vidrio*. *Pez de Vidrio* (published in English as *Urban Oracles*) contains 15 short stories about the complicated relationships between sexual desire, race, identity and social and political status in modern Caribbean society. Her first novel and one of her most famous books is *Sirena Selena vestida de pena* (published in English as *Sirena Selena*), in which she describes the life of a teenaged homosexual male drag queen who works in the streets and has a talent for singing boleros. Santos-Febres completed her undergraduate work at the University of Puerto Rico and holds an M.A. and Ph.D. (1991) from Cornell University. She currently teaches at the University of Puerto Rico, Río Piedras Campus. Her more recent publications include the collection of essays *Sobre piel y papel* and a novel about Isabel la Negra, *Nuestra Señora de la Noche* (*Our Lady of the Night*).

GABRIEL RAMÍREZ is a writer, actor, poet, playwright and teaching artist. In 2012 he won the Knicks Poetry Slam Championship and in 2013 the National Youth Poetry Slam Championship in Boston. He is a member of the 2012 Urban Word NYC slam team, which placed 6th in the international Brave New Voices Festival. Later that year, an off-broadway production titled "Black Ink," staged "Sankofa," a one-man show he wrote and acted in himself. Ramírez has performed on Broadway at the New Amsterdam Theatre, the United Nations, New York Live Arts, Lincoln Center, Apollo Theatre and other venues and universities around the nation.

LUIVETTE RESTO was born in Aguas Buenas, Puerto Rico, but was raised in the Bronx. Her first book of poetry, *Unfinished Portrait*, was published in 2008 and named a finalist for the 2009 Paterson Poetry Prize. She has served as a contributing poetry editor for *Kweli Journal*, a CantoMundo fellow and a member of the advisory board of Con Tinta. Her latest book, *Ascension* (2003),was selected for the 2014 Paterson Award for Literary Excellence. Some of her latest work appears in *Luna Luna Magazine*, *Toe Good Poetry* and the *Altadena Anthology 2015*.

Known as the "Janitor of History," poet/essayist LOUIS REYES RIVERA has more than twenty awards, including a Lifetime Achievement Award (1995), a Special Congressional Recognition Award (1988) and the CCNY 125th Anniversary Medal (1973). Rivera, born in 1945 and deceased in 1988, assisted in the publication of some two hundred books by other writers. Considered by many as a necessary bridge between the African and Latino American communities, he was a professor of Pan-African, African American, Caribbean and Puerto Rican literature and history; his essays and poems have appeared in numerous publications, including *Areyto*, *Boletín*, *The City Sun*, *African Voices*,

In Defense of Mumia, ALOUD: Live from the Nuyorican Poets Café, Of Sons and Lovers, Bum Rush The Page and his own Scattered Scripture.

BONAFIDE ROJAS is the author of Renovatio, When the City Sleeps and Pelo Bueno: A Day in the Life of a Nuyorican Poet. He was featured on Def Poetry Jam, Spitting Ink and has been published in the journals and anthologies: Chorus: A Literary Mixtape, Bum Rush The Page, Role Call, Learn Then Burn, Me No Habla Con Acento, The Centro Journal, Letras, The Hostos Review, The Acentos Review and Palabras. He is the bandleader for the band The Mona Passage & founder of Grand Concourse Press.

Born in St. Thomas, U.S.V.I. and raised in Apopka, Florida, NICOLE SEALEY is the author of Ordinary Beast, forthcoming from Ecco in fall 2017, and The Animal after Whom Other Animals Are Named, winner of the 2015 Drinking Gourd Chapbook Poetry Prize. Her other honors include an Elizabeth George Foundation Grant, the Stanley Kunitz Memorial Prize from The American Poetry Review, a Daniel Varoujan Award and the Poetry International Prize, as well as fellowships from CantoMundo, Cave Canem, MacDowell Colony and The Poetry Project. Her work has appeared in The New Yorker and elsewhere. Nicole holds an MLA in Africana Studies from the University of South Florida and an MFA in creative writing from New York University. She is the executive director at Cave Canem Foundation.

LORENZO THOMAS was born in 1944 in Panama and moved with his family to New York in 1948. He attended Queens College and joined the Navy in 1968. After serving in Vietnam, Thomas moved to Houston, Texas, as a writer-in-residence at Texas Southern University in 1973. A writer whose work was both political and personal, he was the author of five poetry collections before his death in 2005: A Visible Island (1967), Dracula (1973),

Chances Are Few (1979, 2003), *The Bathers* (1981) and *Dancing on Main Street* (2004). Thomas was the recipient of a National Endowment for the Arts grant and the Houston Festival Foundation Award. Thomas was part of the Black Arts Movement in New York City and a member of the Umbra workshop. Often addressing the civil rights movement and Vietnam, his poetry reveals his familiarity with black music, surrealism, contemporary American popular culture and cinema, as well as empathy for the underprivileged. He taught writing workshops at the Black Arts Center, through the artists-in-the-schools program and as an English professor at the University of Houston's downtown campus. He organized the Juneteenth Blues Festival in Houston and other cities in Texas.

JOAQUÍN ZIHUATANEJO is a poet, spoken word artist and award-winning teacher. Born and raised in the barrio of East Dallas, he was a National Poetry Slam Finalist, Grand Slam Spoken Word Champion and HBO's *Def Poet*. In 2005, he was featured on season five of *Russell Simmons Presents Def Poetry* for HBO. For seven years, he was an award-winning English and creative writing public high school teacher for ninth- and eleventh-grade students, and published their work in the *Stand Up and Be Heard* anthology. In 2008, he won the Individual World Poetry Slam Championship, besting 77 poets representing cities all over North America, France and Australia; he was also the poet chosen to represent the United States at the 2009 World Cup of Poetry Slam in Paris, France, a competition that he won.

PERMISSIONS

Elizabeth Acevedo: "February 10th, 2015," "Regularization Plan for Foreigners, 1937" and "Juan Dolio Beach," with permission of the author.

Gustavo Adolfo Aybar: "Wallflower Mambo" and "An Absolute Necessity," *Poets and Arts*. 3.1 (January 2010): 40; "Baseball's Travelin' Men," *Somos en escrito* (online literary journal) in August 2014; "Breaking Strength;" "Morir Soñando," *Many Windows: Magnapoets Anthology* Series 4 (Aurora Antonovic 2011). Reprinted with permission of the author.

Miguel Algarín: "Survival," "A Mongo Affair," "A Salsa Ballet: Angelitos Negros," "Relish / Sabrosura," "Ray Barreto: December 4, 1976," "Proem II," "HIV," "Nuyorican Angel Voice" and "Nuyorican Angel Papo," *Survival Sobrevivencia* (Arte Público Press 2009), with permission of the press.

Jane Alberdeston Coralin: "Taína Dreams," *Bum Rush the Page: A Def Poetry Jam* (Broadway Books, 2001) and *Poetry Quarterly*, 2.3 (Summer 2001); "Rosa's Beauty," *Bum Rush the Page: A Def Poetry Jam* (Broadway Books, 2001) and *Poetry Quarterly*, 2.3 (Summer 2001); "For Black Girls Who Don't Know," *Poetry Quarterly*, 10.2 (Spring 2009); "Portorican Anthem," *The Bilingual Review* (1998) and *Poetry Quarterly*, 10.2 (Spring 2009); "Pull" and "Make-Believe," *Homenaje a Las Guerreras / Homage to the Warrior Women* (Robles-Alvarado 2012). Reprinted with permission of the author.

Peggy Robles-Alvarado: "Boca Grande," "Negrito Lindo," "¡Bomba!," "When They Call My Name" and "If Only They Knew," with permission of the author.

Josefina Báez: "Nosotros no somos como ustedes," "Pedacito de mi alma" and "Com'on everybody clap your hands, ooooh you're looking good," *As Is E. Textos reunidos de Josefina Báez* (i.om.be press 2015); "My name is pure history," *Levente no. Yolayorkdominicanyork* (i.om.be press 2011), with permission of the author.

Carmen Bardeguez Brown: "Remembrance," "Señora," "Oye Miguel," "El Bronx" and "Rican Issues," with permission of the author.

Ariana Brown: "Recover," "Ahuacatl," "Coatl: An Old Myth & A Few New Ones, In Three Parts" and "A Quick Story," with permission of the author.

Natalie N. Caro: "Cruz" and "Dear White People," with permission of the author.

Natasha Carrizosa: "Pennies in my blood," "Mejiafricana" and "Catch A Fire," with permission of the author.

Adrian Castro: "Mokongo Y To' Esa Gente," *Conjunctions*, 27 (Fall 1996); "Incantation For The Word" and "Misa Caribeña," *Wise Fish* (Coffee House Press 2008), with permission of the author.

Río Cortez: "I'm Forced to Imagine There Are Two of Me Here" and "Havana Ghazal," *Huizache*, 4 (Fall 2014); "Trip for a While, After Curtis Mayfield," *Clementine Magazine* #4, with permission of the author.

Sandra María Esteves: "To These Poets, for Tato Laviera" *Crossroads Residence* (Air Loom Publications 2015); "Where I'm From," *Portal* (Limited Editions Press 2007); "Philosophy of

Cool," *Contrapunto in the Open Field* (No Frills Publications 1998); "In the Beginning," "amor negro" and "Puerto Rican Discovery Number Three, Not Neither," *Tropical Rain: A Bilingual Downpour* (African Caribbean Poetry Theater 1984); "For Tito," *Nuyorican Poetry: An Anthology of Puerto Rican Words and Feelings* edited by Miguel Algarín and Miguel Piñero (William Morrow and Company, Inc. 1975); "From Fanon" and "Here," *Yerba Buena* (Greenfeld Review Press 1980), with permission of the author.

Mariposa (María Teresa Fernández): "Love Poem for Ntozake & Me," "Homage to my Hair," "1980," "Ode to the Diasporican" and "Poem for My Grifa-Rican Sistah Or Broken Ends Broken Promises," with permission of the author.

Shaggy Flores: "Negritude," *Obatala's Bugalu: A Nuyorican Book Of Sights and Sounds* (South of Harlem Libros 2013); "Lucumí" and "We, the Children of Juan Epstein," with permission of the author.

Aracelis Girmay: "Arroz Poética," "Santa Ana of the Grocery Carts" and "Teeth," *Teeth* (Curbstone Press 2007), with permission of the press; "Ode to the Little 'r'," "Night, for Henry Dumas" and "Running Home, I Saw the Plants," *Kingdom Animalia* (BOA Editions, Ltd 2011), with permission of the press.

Modesdo Flako Jiménez: "Gracias, Margarita Agramonte," "The Curse of the Goat" and "El Taxista," with permission of the author.

Tato Laviera: "Tito Madera Smith," and "Jorge Brandon," *Enclave* (Arte Público Press 1985); "angelitos eulogy in anger" and "the salsa of bethesda fountain," *La Carreta Made a U-Turn* (Arte Público Press 1979); "commonwealth" and "negrito," *AmeRícan* (Arte Público Press 1985); "Lady Liberty," *Mainstream Ethics-Ética*

Corriente (Arte Público Press 1988);" "Mixturao" and "nideaquinideallá," *Mixturao and Other Poems* (Arte Público Press 2008), with permission of the press.

Raina J. León: "Two pounds, night sky notes" and "Southwest Philadelphia, 1988"; "Maldición de Borikén a los León: la ciega en paraíso" and "Tango criollo," *Black Gold: An Anthology of Black Poetry* (Turner Mayfield Publishing, 2014); "bull | machete | bullet | laurel |time," *sombra : dis(locate)* (Salmon Poetry 2016), with permission of the author.

Esperanza Malavé Cintrón: "Chocolate City Latina," "This poem is about God," "mis hermanos," "Home" and "Song for My Father," *Chocolate City Latina* (Swank Press 2005), with permission of the author.

Reynold Martín: "Wade," "Amie-Rica Sees a Therapist" and "Mama's Legend," with permission of the author.

Tony Medina: "Dame Un Tragito," *North American Review* (Winter 2015) and *African Voices* (Summer-Fall 2014); "Broke Baroque," *Broke Baroque* (2Leaf Press 2013); "Poem for Victor Hernández Cruz," *Emerge & See* (Whirlwind Press 1991); "My Father Is a Brown Scar" and "Arrival," *My Old Man Was Always on the Lam* (NYQ Books 2010); "Broke Celebrity (Culture)," *Broke on Ice* (Willow Books 2011), with permission of the author.

Marianela Medrano: "Jamón y Queso" and "Cara Sucia," *Calabash: A Journal of Caribbean Arts and Letters*, 5.1 (Summer-Fall 2008); "El Corte," *Black Scholar*, 54.2 (Summer 2015); "Crossing El Masacre," with permission of the author.

Jesús Papoleto Meléndez: "A San Diego Southern / African Night," "sister, para nuestras hermanas," "Message To Urban Sightseers" and "¡HEY YO / YO SOY!," *Hey Yo / Yo Soy—40 years of Nuyorican Street Poetry* (2Leaf Press 2012), with permission of the author.

E. Ethelbert Miller: "Panama," "Tomorrow," "Juanita," "Spanish Conversation," "Solidarity" and "The Sea," *First Light: New and Selected Poems* (Black Classic Press 1994), with permission of the author.

Aja Monet: "Una Ofrenda," "Granma" and "Left Behind," with permission of the author.

Anthony Morales: "Clason Point Angel of the BackPark / Clason Point Angel of Holy Mercy," "Anti Gentrification Spell," "Abuelita Abuelita" and "Afro Latinidad," with permission of the author.

John Murillo: "Practicing Fade-Aways," "How to split a cold one," "Renegades of Funk," "Sherman Ave. Love Poem," "The Corner" and "Trouble Man," *Up Jump The Boogie* (Cypher Books 2010), with permission of the press.

Raquel I. Penzo: "My Brooklyn (In Response to Gentrification)" and "The Talk," with permission of the author.

Willie Perdomo: "Ten-Pound Draw," "The New Boogalo," "Look What I found" and "Should Old Shit Be Forgot," *Smoking Lovely* (Rattapallax Press 2004); "Side A (3:2)," *The Essential Hits of Shorty Bon Bon* (Penguin 2014), previously appeared in *The Acentos Review* (August 2014). Reprinted with permission of the author.

Miguel Piñero: "A Lower East Side Poem," "The Book of Genesis According to San Miguelito," "The Menudo of A Cuchifrito Love Affair," "New York City Hard Time Blues," *Outlaw: The Collected Works of Miguel Pinero* (Arte Público Press 2010), with permission of the press.

Noel Quiñones: "Afro/Rikan," *FreezeRay* (Issue #8), with permission of the press; "Wepa: Babel Tongue," *The Acentos Review* (August 2015), with permission of the journal; "The Puerto Rican Maid Responds to Kendrick Lamar's Yell," *Winter Tangerine* (Spotlight Series: Reshaping the Bell Jar), with permission of the journal.

Gabriel Ramírez: "resilience," "what i learned in u.s. history class" and "alive=blk," with permission of the author.

Luivette Resto: "The Legendary Legs of the Rodriguez Women," "Painted Walls" and "Solitary Encounters," *Journal of Mujeres Activas en Letras y Cambio Social* (Loyola Marymount University 2015), "Garcia Folklore #27," with permission of the author.

Louis Reyes Rivera: "no hole in punctured poem," *who pays the cost* (Shamal Books 1977); "the adverb" and "like Toussaint, so Marti," *Scattered Scripture* (Shamal Books 1996); "Excerpt from cu / bop," *The Afro-Latin@ Reader: History and Culture in the United States* (Duke UP 2010); "The Disdirected," *Bum Rush the Page: A Def Poetry Jam* (Broadway Books 2001); "Witness: Imagination," with permission of Barbara Killens Rivera.

Bonafide Rojas: "Notes On The Return To The Island," "Thirty Ways To Look At A Nuyorican," "Mother" and "The Old New Story;" "Remember Their Names," *when the city sleeps* (Grand Concourse Press 2012); "The Creed of A Graffiti Writer," *Pelo Bueno: A Day In The Life Of A Nuyorican Poet* (dark souls press, 2004), with permission of the author.

Mayra Santos-Febres: "a Woman that Writes," with permission of the author.

Nicole Sealey: "Instead of Executions, Think Death Erections," "Virginia is for Lovers," "Even the Gods" and "In Igboland," with permission of the author.

Lorenzo Thomas: "Inauguration," "MMDCCXIII ½" and "The Leopard," *Chances are Few* (Blue Wind Press 1979), with permission of the press; "Dirge for Amadou Diallo" and "God Sends Love Disguised as Ordinary People," *Dancing on Main Street* (Coffee House Press 2004), with permission of the press.

Joaquín Zihuatanejo: "Archetypes" and "We Are Because They Were" by Joaquín Zihuatanejo, with permission of the author; "What You Have Taken This Poem Redeems," by Joaquín Zihuatanejo and Antwaun "Twain" Davis, with permission of the authors.